A "FORGOTTEN WAR"...

of almost fifty years ago provides the background for this story of a few good friends, bootcamp buddies, who experienced their first year in the United States Marine Corps—bootcamp followed by the Korean War. The period from bootcamp graduation until the shock of their first night in a Korean fox hole was a tremendous transition: physically, mentally and culturally. Indeed, as they became a part of this Korean War environment, they also became aware of all surrounding them—the mystic Orient and the inscrutable Asian—friend and foe alike. Who was friend? Who was foe? Suddenly, they were really Marines! And, this was combat and their baptism of fire.

"I've been shot. Right through butt. Both cheeks. Some damn sniper shot me." Santiago was embarrassed.... "Just take me to Battalion Aid." He was hurt and didn't want to talk.

I said, "But , I've got to find "Fox" Company. We're gettin' the hell beat out of us up there!" My company was in imminent danger of being overrun by the North Koreans on Hill 749. I had to get help. I had to find "Fox," our reserve company.

Santiago didn't care, "Andy, just get me to Battalian Aid."

I shouldered his arm around my neck and we began to run across the ridgeline of no man's land. Then, the 76s started to come in. I heard the roar a split second before the blinding flash....

I spent a couple of months on [Hill] 749 or near it and never failed to be amazed and to admire what you guys did in taking it. All the best, as ever....

—James Brady,
Platoon leader, Dog Co., 7th Marines, Korea
Author, *The Coldest War,* Orion Books, 1990
Contributing Editor, PARADE, The Sunday Newspaper Magazine
Editor-At-Large, ADVERTISING AGE

Semper Fidelis

Butler J. Arnold

WE CLAIM THE
TITLE

By

Burton F. Anderson

Tracy Publishing
Aptos, CA

WE CLAIM THE TITLE

Printing History
First Printing: November 1994
Second Printing: July 1995

While information in this book has been carefully researched, neither
the author or the publisher assume any liability for errors or omissions
in the actual content of the book. Stories of persons which the author
has reported in this memoir were obtained from oral or written commu-
nication, audio taping or mutual experiences in the Marines. It was the
author's intention, utilizing all of this information, to make this memoir as accurate as possible, recognizing, however, the fallibility of
forty-four year old memories.

For historical accuracy, the following official U.S. Marine Corps document was referenced extensively: Montrose, Lynn, Hubard D. Kuokka,
and Norman Hicks. *U.S. Marine Operations in Korea.* Vol. IV, *The
East-Central Front.* Washington, D.C.: Historical Division, U.S.
Marine Corps, 1962., also cited, condensed, as *U.S. Marine Operations
in Korea,* Vol. IV.

Library of Congress Catalogue Card Number: 94-61241

ISBN 0-9643110-0-3

DEDICATION

TO

Ross, Gene, Jim, John C. and John O.
and the rest of
MCRD Training Platoon I-65, September 1950

ALSO

Dog Company, 2nd Battalion, 1st Marines
1st Marine Division, FMF
Korea

AND IN MEMORY OF

Raymond Turner
Killed In Action, October 31, 1951
Korea

THE MARINES' HYMN

From the halls of Montezuma,
To the shores of Tripoli;
We fight our country's battles
In the air, on land, and sea;
First to fight for right and freedom
And to keep our honor clean;
WE ARE PROUD TO CLAIM THE TITLE OF
UNITED STATES MARINE

ACKNOWLEDGMENTS

A special thanks to those who contributed their recollections of Marine Corps Bootcamp Platoon I-65, 1950, as well as to those who recalled their experiences of the Korean conflict, 1950-1953. My deep appreciation goes to Gene Burnett, who not only has an awesome memory but also the compassion to be my mentor in this endeavor. I must commend Jim (Swartzwelder) Forrest, John Camacho, John Ontiveros and all the others who added their voices and are acknowledged in my last chapter. My appreciation goes to George McGarity for his volatile story of Dog Company on Hill 749. Indeed, a special accolade goes to Weldon (Ross) Rosser, my hometown buddy, who joined the Marine Corps and shipped out to Korea with me almost half a century ago.

An additional thanks to Bill Hyatt, who read and suggested changes to some early revisions. But, most of all, I must thank my indefatigable editor and counselor, Sharon Gray, for all her valuable time.

Finally, credit and acknowledgment is directed to the official history, *U.S. Marine Operations in Korea.* Vol. IV, *The East-Central Front.* Washington, D.C.: Historical Division, U.S. Marine Corps, 1962., which I utilized extensively.

CONTENTS

ILLUSTRATIONS

Figures

MAPS

Maps

Introduction

B urt Anderson landed in Korea on the fifth of March 1951 and immediately reported to D Company, 2nd Battalion, 1st Marines, 1st Marine Division. The heroic defense of the Pusan Perimeter by the Marine Brigade was past as well as the 1st Marine Division's brilliant landing at Inchon and its epic fighting withdrawal from the Frozen Chosin mountain fastness.

Ahead for replacement Burt Anderson was General Ridgeway's Operations Killer and Ripper to drive back the Chinese Communist hordes from Central Korea, the campaign to seize the heights around the Punchbowl in North Korea, and the vicious fighting to take Hill 749, part of North Korea's Main Line of Resistance. The elite 1st Marine Division took the point on all of these operations.

Burt left Hill 749 and Korea on 13th of September 1951 in a helicopter, wounded-in-action (evacuated).

The book's title, "We Claim The Title," comes from the last line, first verse of the Marine Corps Hymn; "We are proud to claim the title of United States Marines." Marine units on parade pass in review to its strains. Whenever it is played Marines and their families come to attention. This was the 175-year-old service Oklahoma Sooner Anderson joined the day after Labor Day in September 1950. His experiences in training and six and one half months of combat are a mirror of the Marine Corps in peace and war, in and out of combat.

Burt's experience in combat and in the lulls between action are told in equally authentic terms. He employs a device many historians and writers have not mastered. The overall context of the war and the Marine Division are set forth by excerpts from official histories and other sources. Interspersed are Anderson's personal account of each action as well as the versions of friends. The felicitous result is an integrated story of six and one-half months of warfare of every type — attack, defense, retrograde movements, mountain warfare, attack of a fortified position — a gamut of infantry tactics reading like the table of contents of a tactical manual.

There are many memoirs of our wars by cutting edge participants but few are so honest, accurate, and authentic as Burton Anderson's.

—Col. F. Brooke Nihart, USMC (Ret.)
Former Commanding Officer 2nd Bn 1st Marines

A Prologue Of
Old War Stories

"Andy! Andy!"

I heard him call before I actually saw him through the trees, lying on the trail down by the bunker. I heard his yell between the North Korean artillery bursts, exploding on the perpendicular ridge line that ran to the west. The explosions were not close; but a shell from their 76's sounded like a freight train passing overhead. That gave me some small consolation. I had been told that you don't hear the shell that has your name on it. And, at least, I could hear these pass over.

Down the trail, however, something was wrong. Andrew Santiago from my bootcamp platoon was alone and in "no man's land." My troops, D or "Dog" Company, 1st Marines, 1st Marine Division, Fleet Marine Force, had already passed along this trail the night before. We had relieved some 7th Marines; that was his regiment. In fact, I had even spent a few sleepless hours in this bunker before we moved out in the attack up the intersecting ridgeline this morning. Santiago had not been here then. Why was he here now?

As the trail dropped down to the bunker, I slipped and slid down the sandy loam to his side.

"I've been shot. Right through the butt. Both cheeks."

He was embarrassed and was almost apologetic.

I was not comprehending. "But, Santiago, what the hell-happened?"

"Well, yesterday evening, some damn sniper shot me." He hurt and didn't want to talk. "You got to take me to Battalion Aid."

"Shit, Santiago, I'm supposed to find 'Fox' Company. Man, we're gettin' the hell beat out of us up there. Lieutenant says we could get overrun if we don't get help. 'Fox' was supposed to relieve us this afternoon. Where are they?"

My company was trying to relieve an isolated company of the 7th Marines somewhere near Hill 749 on that fateful 12 September 1951, east of the "Punchbowl." Although "Dog" company took many casualties in a fierce attempt, we were unsuccessful and I was ordered to go find help. If only Santiago had seen "Fox," I wouldn't have to go across that ridgeline where the gooks were dropping in the 76's.

The lieutenant's command had been quite simple, "Go find Fox." They were our back-up. My God, it must have been over a half mile of ridgeline back down to the 2nd Battalion CP. But, that half mile rumbled under heavy bombardment in the middle, had snipers to the rear and assaulting bands of gooks to the front. "Fox"Company, 1st Marines could be any place along that deadly ridgeline.

I repeated, "I got to find Fox."

Santiago didn't care. He hurt. "Andy, just get me to Battalion Aid."

The immediate problem was that ridgeline to the west. Seventy-five to a hundred yards it ran before a large rocky promontory jutted up some fifty feet and hid the trail that turned south and down to Battalion. The North Korean artillery had not lifted their bombardment, apparently believing that our troops still occupied this ridge.

"Santiago, you're going to have to run like hell." I might make it if I ran as fast as I could; but how could we make it across together, when he was shot in the butt? I said again, now scared, "You're going to run like hell."

I took his wrist and shouldered his arm around my neck and reached down, grabbing his belt in the back. With a struggle, he was on his feet. We began to run.

We ran amazingly fast, as I yelled again and again as loud as I could, "Run! Run! Run!"

We were almost across. We were going to make it.

I heard the roar a split second before the blinding explosion.

***

Less than a half mile to the northeast, Hill 749 was protected by a deadly NKPA crossfire of bunkered machineguns and mortars from transverse ridgelines with fields of interlocking fire—an infantryman's nightmare. Marines called this the North Korean T-Formation. From such entrenchments, the North Koreans from the top of the "T" could bring volumes of firepower to bear on the marines attempting to assault the stem.

For "Fox" Company, 7th Marines, 1st Marine Division, it was a hot, desperate afternoon on 12 September as they attempted to press the assault while waiting for the 1st Marines to extricate them. Hill 749 was a steep climb and after almost two weeks in the attack, first securing YOKE Ridge and then crossing the valley and fighting up Hills 680 and 673, the 7th Marines were exhausted. Yet, here loomed the last objective—Hill 749. But where were the 1st Marines?

Not in the lead platoon, PFC Jim Swartzwelder, squad leader, was tired and he moved slowly up the path following the column ahead.

These old seemingly never-ending Korean trails and paths over the mountains and across the valleys were centuries old and reflected the millions of footfalls of solitary wayfarers. These single sandy threads provided a path for men in column only. PFC Swartzwelder plodded wearily up the trail behind the last man in his platoon's machinegun outfit.

After seven months in combat PFC Swartzwelder was an old hand. According to Marine Corps T/O's, he should have been a Sergeant in order to be in charge of a squad. But casualties depleted old hands until only the lucky and the brave were left. After all, he was taught in bootcamp that a Marine PFC could take command of a platoon—and some had. He didn't ponder this; he had other things on his mind and he was so tired.

Jamie Marsh, the machinegun ammo carrier, in front of Swartzwelder was tired also and dangerously inattentive to his surroundings—and the mines. The word had been passed to stay on the trail because both sides had been mined. That was a difficult order to follow since the stop-and-go, stop-and-go of the column provided a short spell to rest beside the trail.

Finally, the column stopped and Jamie turned around and sat down on a mine. It blew him asunder.

Squad leader Swartzwelder, behind him, sailed through the air off the trail and into a gully, down into a small stream.

It was here that he, stunned, hazily noted his many shrapnel wounds, and as if in a movie, watched the stretcher bearers coming down the trail bringing back a marine with a leg wound. The wounded marine yelled, "I've got a million dollar wound. I'm going home."

It was here, at that instant, that Squad leader PFC Swartzwelder watched as one of this group stepped off the trail and onto a land mine to eternity.

It was here, at that time, that a volley of North Korean

mortars from the ridgeline above zeroed in on the trail exploding in a deadly cloud of dust and fire.

***

By 15 September, Lieutenant Colonel Franklin B. Nihart's 2nd Battalion, 1st Marines, had extracted the remnants of the 7th Marines from the slopes of Hill 749. On that black September night his 2nd Battalion again assaulted that ravaged ridgeline. The North Koreans unleashed a holocaust of fire against his marines which, according to division reports, "reached an intensity that was estimated to surpass that of any barrage yet encountered by the First Marine Division in Korea."

These were "die-hard" NKPA troops who were charged to stand or die. The summer truce talks had allowed their army to build its depleted strength. Now, as the war began anew, each army, both Korean and Marines, tried to take ground so that at future negotiations their side could negotiate from strength. With a torrent of fire, these fanatic North Koreans were ready to die to repulse the Marines.

The 2nd Battalion took a torrent of fire from 76-mm., 105-mm., 122-mm., 82-mm., and 120-mm. artillery and mortars. Then began a frenzied counterattack. In wave after human wave, with bugles and whistles screaming signals, the North Koreans threw themselves against the marine line. The marines bent but did not break.

PFC Richard Blasongame upheld the highest traditions of the United States Naval Service during that night as the acting platoon sergeant of the heavy machinegun platoon serving with COL Nihart's Weapons Company, 2nd Battalion, 1st Marines. PFC Blasongame's extraordinary heroism was one reason why the line did not break.

He was acting platoon sergeant in charge of the machinegun emplacements at the point of the battalion perimeter most exposed to attack. Again and again, the North Koreans assaulted his emplacements through the night. When gunners were wounded, he manned the guns. He hurled grenades. He evacuated wounded. He rallied his men. When ammunition and grenades became critically short, he left his foxhole and exposed himself to a hail of hostile fire in order to inform his commander and to supervise resupply.

When a grenade exploded under his last remaining machinegun, inflicting wounds to his face and hands, and jamming the traversing mechanism, PFC Blasongame continued to fire through the night by moving the tripod from side to side.

As morning dawned, only four survivors remained out of his sixteen-man section. Two hundred and eighty-seven enemy dead lay in front of his point position. An unknown number of enemy dead and wounded had been carted away by their cohorts.

Acting platoon sergeant PFC Richard Blasongame was recommended for the Medal Of Honor.

***

These are the stories of a few good men, members of training Platoon I-65, MCRD, who became troops of the 1st Marine Division in Korea, a division with a distinguished history displayed by courage and valor: Guadalcanal, New Guinea, New Britain, Peleliu, Okinawa; and the Pusan Perimeter, Inchon-Seoul, Chosin Reservoir, East-Central Front, Western Front; and Chu Lai, Da Nang, Dong Ha, Qui Nhon, Hue, Phu Bai, Quang Tri; and Desert Shield/Storm.

The 1st Marine Division organization in Korea for 1951-1952 appears in Appendix 2.

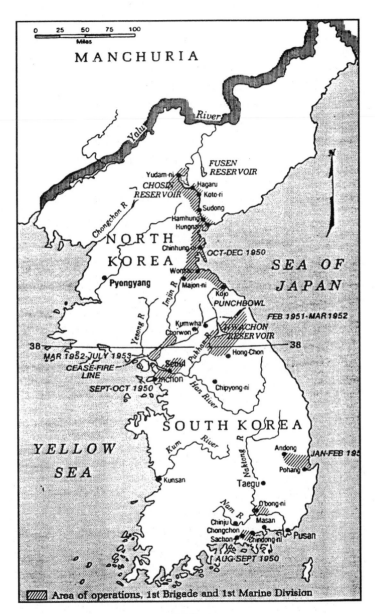

MAP 1

CHAPTER ONE

THE ONCE
AND ALWAYS MARINE

An ancient Marine Corps axiom maintains: Once a Marine, always a Marine. The sentiment has something to do with pride, and honor and a mystical brotherhood. But, more than this it is spirit...the spirit of the Corps...to fight and die because we are Marines. This story is about that.

This is a boy-to-manhood story; a story about masculine rite-of-passage; the growth of scared replacement kids into seasoned infantrymen; a baptism of fire.

This is a story of a year in my life as well as in the lives of a few good friends. Not a calendar year, really, but rather a span from September 1950 through September 1951 in which "a few good men" experienced their first year in the United States Marine Corps—bootcamp followed by combat in the Korean War. This period could not be assimilated essentially without some explanation of our late adolescence, our "growing up," in the 1940's, as well as the history of both the era and the war.

When the North Koreans invaded the South in the summer of 1950, the US government, although reluctant to participate in coming to the aid of that distant land, finally did. Unfortunately, the majority of citizens maintained some opposition throughout the war.

After all, the big war, World War II, was over. Everyone

had jobs. Our land was prospering and we were on a roll. So why bother with this small country that few could find on a map?

This consensus had a direct bearing on the way this unpopular war for communist containment was conducted by the president, Congress and the military, on its termination without victory, and on the suddenness in which it was forgotten.

Yet a few young men heard a call of distant drums and trumpets. Through the 1940's, they had matured into their teens, raised on news of the world at war. They missed the soldiers' pride of glorious victories of World War II and the triumphant adventures of heroes in exotic far away lands. They too wanted the adventure.

Consequently these bold young men of the Korean War era joined the most elite fighting force in world, the United States Marine Corps. The tradition continues today.

The Corps changes a young man or woman by tearing away childish ways and replacing chaos with tradition, discipline and training. The Drill Instructor banishes the old, then teaches the new, forging the recruit into a modern warrior.

General Alfred M. Gray, Jr., Commandant of the U. S. Marine Corps from 1987 to 1991, introduced this term "warrior" to be synonymous with "Marine." He felt that marines don't spend much of their career in fighting wars, but when they do, they better be ready to do it. Therefore only the Marines are a profession. The other outfits are occupations. His belief that the Marines are our national warriors, always superbly ready and able, is the basic philosophy behind recruit training today.

The Marine Corps' bootcamp has always provided the best and most comprehensive military training. But more than that is the training in the Corps tradition—the history and glory of the Corps. And in this fact may be found the difference between this elite Corps and other military forces.

Forged into the recruit is the Corps' code of comradeship and esprit de corps, both of which were the forces behind all the special marines that have gone on before to glory in battle, to kill or be killed, to vanquish our country's enemies. This is burned into the soul of the marine.

As the heroes of the past have brought glory to the Corps, so also does each marine want to leave his brush stroke of splendor on the Corps' bright banner. And they have. Among countless medals for courage and bravery received by marines since 1863, 293 marines have received 300 Medals of Honor. Two Marines received the Medal of Honor twice for separate acts: Daniel J. Daly, 1900 and 1915, and Smedley D. Butler, 1914 and 1915. During World War I, when separate medals existed, five marines received both an Army and a Navy Medal of Honor for the same act.

Each new recruit receives the opportunity to be among those honored by the Marine Corps War Memorial at Arlington National Cemetery, the giant green-bronze statue of the Iwo Jima flag-raising, with its golden inscription, "Uncommon valor was a common virtue." Indeed, on November 10, 1975, President Ford called the U. S. Marine Corps' 200th birthday, "the bicentennial of its uncommon valor."

In his birthday message to the Marines printed in *Leatherneck* magazine, November 1992, General C. E. Mundy, Jr., Commandant of the Marine Corps, asks, "What is it that makes Marines?"

> It's not something you can touch or measure, or even explain. It's a mystique...a spirit...the spirit of

the Corps.

We're Marines because we choose to be something more than just ourselves. We seek a challenge—we spend hard times away from home and family, we hope never to be second into line, and we fight and die simply because we're Marines—and our Nation calls us.

...That's the spirit of the Corps.

We serve with pride in those who've gone before us, those who serve beside us, and those who will follow us. We're part of an unbreakable, 217 year bond of courage, honor, comradeship, valor and pride. These are intangible things "such as regiments hand down forever."

...That's the spirit of the Corps.

As we celebrate the 217th year of this extraordinary band of which we are privileged to be a part, let me say simply, as I have before

...Stand tall, you're United States Marines!

So long as you do, the spirit of the Corps will go on forever.

In the Korean War some may not have known what they were fighting for. But we marines knew. It was what marines always have fought for in Tripoli or France or the Pacific or any other "clime or place!"   FOR THE GLORY OF THE CORPS!

CHAPTER TWO

OUR MEMORIAL

Almost everyone has a best buddy: a friend with whom they went to school; a buddy with whom they grew up; a confidant with whom they weathered the awful 'teens. Weldon Gale Rosser was my best buddy in our home town of Enid, Oklahoma. I think we met when we were around 13 years old in 1942 or 1943 when we became neighbors; he was 9 months older than I.

I think I always called him Ross, short for Rosser, and never called him Weldon, although others, such as girls and adults, did. But one of the great mysteries of my life is why Ross calls me, Al. I don't remember that he ever called me Burton or Burt, like almost everyone else did. For some unapparent reason dimmed by time, he still calls me this strange nickname. No matter, one thing about Ross is that he has always been fun. He always has a trace of a smile as if he had just heard a joke and was about to repeat it.

In the summer of 1944, Ross was 15 and I was 14. We had been buddies for some time and were about to become sophomores in the fall. World War II continued, the Normandy invasion became a reality and the Marines attacked Saipan. That summer we wondered how long the war would last. We wondered if it would continue until we graduated. We wondered which service we would join after graduation.

This was a time when we were nurtured by war. We were a product of war news and the propaganda of war. But we did not ponder these questions at any length. Girls were more important subjects.

Those were not promiscuous times. Sex was something discussed in hushed tones and the majority of boys were virgins. But praise be to the one who accomplished the act and told his buddies, because he became an instant hero. Ross was a hero.

In the summer of 1944, Ross had a Cushman motor scooter. The Cushman had one drive wheel in back and two wheels which steered the vehicle in front on each side of a large metal box. The motor scooter made a paper route easy, even fun, for Ross and me, particularly because the box was large enough to carry a passenger or two and the evening newspapers. We always folded the papers first; then he drove the Cushman and I threw.

One summer evening, we stopped to talk to a good-looking girl, Frances, about whom Ross had been daydreaming. Finally he convinced her to ride with us for the rest of our route, which naturally ended at his house. His parents were on vacation and no one was home.

The beautiful Frances said she really should go home but Ross insisted that she stay for a soft drink while I excused myself and went to his room to listen to the radio. I knew the scenario.

Later at dusk I tired of the radio and wondered how Ross' pursuit had progressed. I slipped into the dining room where I could personally overhear and verify his conquest. With stealth, I perceived them kissing on the sofa. Between the kisses, she attempted feeble pleas.

Almost convinced that she should succumb to his seduction, her last faint arguments centered on her Catholic upbringing and the fear that someone might find out.

"No one will find out. I won't tell." Ross assured.

"I know," she replied, "but, God will know."

There was a long silence.

Finally, Ross said, "Yea, but He won't tell either."

That's my point. My buddy, Ross, always had a sense of humor. Incidentally, his remark threw me into fits of laughter and ruined his day. No conquest for Ross.

Unlike Ross' home, mine always seemed to be filled with friends or relatives—acquaintances from off the farm rooming as they went to business school; aunts and uncles rooming until times got better; and Grandmother who lived with us until she was 92.

On the corner in front of my house was the bus stop and bench. A sidewalk separated the grassy and tree covered parking from our front yard. But my house, a white two-story, five-bedroom cube built in 1907, dominated the corner. The peaked roof formed a green pyramid over all and the green roofed porch stretched completely across the front, a touch of the ante-bellum South. Above the porch stared the double windows of my room like eyes looking out on the world.

Supporting the porch roof, four tall round, white pillars stood like Doric columns. To the right rested a blue porch swing and, at the end, a lattice work supporting vines growing up to the porch roof. On the left side of the porch stood a steel glider with multi-colored pads. On that side, too, a lattice work with vines at the end of the porch provided shadow against a western sun.

The living room was just that. The family came together there, lingered there, related and lived there. My view of life in the 1940's came from my favorite place—prone on the rug in front of the RCA Victor console radio in the living

room. Framed above the radio hung a classical picture of
splendid groves of green towering, bending, and converging
to a point slightly left of center. There, the artist's zeal drew
perspective to a small vibrantly lit forest glen, where danced
three tiny nymphs.

The green forest picture wove a sinister tale as I listened
to my radio heroes after school. In my youthful dream world
I fantasized the adventures of "The Green Hornet," "Captain
Midnight," as well as "Jack Armstrong, the All American
Boy," as they peeked out of the forest at the nymphs.

Beside me, prone on the rug in front of the radio, snoozed
my small black and white Boston bull terrier. Pepper was a
pug-nosed, screw-tailed bull dog; her tail twisted up tight
to her backside. She was an obedient dog. She might chase
a cat; but if Mother clapped her hands sharply, Pepper would
stop so fast she would skid on her back sides—and so would
I. There was no doubt, Mother was a dominant force in our
family, a stern and strict disciplinarian.

Sunday was a day of rest. After our Sunday dinner, our
noon meal, the family relaxed in the living room reading
the Sunday papers. I might ponder the "Funnies" from the
divan by the bay windows. Along the back wall of our gathering place, Grandmother, sitting in a massive old chair,
might read a section of the local paper or her Bible. Mother
might glance at the Society pages from her occasional chair.
But Daddy always sat in his big over-stuffed chair between
the front window and the front door, reading news.

On Sunday, Daddy was always relaxed. Mother,
Grandmother and I always went to Sunday school and church
on Sunday morning. Daddy never did. He searched for his
bliss away from the teetotaling women folk, out in the garage
with a cigar and a nip from a half-pint.

After school, the smell of cookies baking told me that

Grandmother was making goodies. On the stool in the pantry she sat and rolled out dough for the oven. She made all the pastries at our house—cookies, pies and cakes. Sometimes Grandmother let me taste the raw dough for the goodies she made. She let me taste hot cookies right out of the oven. She gave me tidbits of warm cake. Grandmother was always very special to me.

In 1945, World War II ended and so did my childhood. Shortly after, we were driving cars to high school and, on weekend dates, even to Hennessey or Oklahoma City. I still remember the thrill of that "Friday afternoon" feeling, the anticipation of the weekend adventure.

We were in our late 'teens and life was full of excitement. We thought the whole world went dancing on Saturday night, particularly after the war was over. We had formal dances in the ballroom of the Youngblood Hotel. The girls donned long dresses and the boys sported suits. Above our heads was a ball of great girth, studded with tiny mirrored squares. As the ball revolved, red, blue, white and green spot lights beamed upon it and the ballroom became a many splendored thing.

Most Saturday nights we danced at "The Rat," although out front, the neon sign called the place, the "Mickey Mouse Club." No matter, this large one story concrete block building, with a rounded metal roof resembling an oversized quonset hut was always "The Rat" to us. Of course, it had a spectacular revolving mirrored ball.

Before the dance we visited our favorite bootlegger. In this dry state there were no liquor stores. It would not have mattered; we were too young to buy liquor if there had been. But bootleggers were rampant, bringing in the labeled whiskey from Kansas and Missouri. With a knock to their door, we were ushered to a bedroom closet filled with bottles, where we selected our choice at $5, a pint, and $10, a fifth.

The management of the "The Rat" sold a 7-Up and a bowl of ice for 50 cents, each; glasses were free. Hiding our bottle under the booth, we brought it forth to mix our drinks—bourbon and 7-Up.

Fortunately, "The Rat's" location in an open field outside of town provided ample space to get sick. Ross and I agree that there was hardly a square inch surrounding the building that we had not baptized. To this day I cannot stomach the taste of bourbon and 7 Up.

Slow dancing was the vogue; the dancers held each other. The songs were romantic and melodious. We danced to the big band greats: Woody Herman, Harry James, Stan Kenton, Les Brown, and all the big names. Our songs were sung by Frank Sinatra, Nat "King" Cole, June Christie, Doris Day, Peggy Lee. But each dance ended with Artie Shaw's version of "Stardust." We thought the song would last forever.

No matter if a dance band were playing, no matter if the dance music came from records, no matter if the dance were formal or informal, the last song played was Artie Shaw's dreamy recording of "Stardust." Indeed, for twenty years, the signal that the dance was over was the playing of this song.

At the end of August 1947, Ross and I entered Oklahoma A&M, now Oklahoma State University. He was 17 and I was 16.

By the end of our sophomore year, June 1949, we were placed on academic probation and could not return for a year. Obviously we were playing bridge too often at the Frat Shop.

This ouster from college meant that it was time to go to work.

Through 1949 and the first half of 1950, I sold paint in the Paint Department of Long-Bell Lumber Co. in Enid.

Through 1949 and the first half of 1950, from the Liggett and Meyers black Chevrolet panel truck, Ross sold Chesterfield cigarettes throughout most of Northwest Oklahoma. In early 1950, he bought a very long, sleek, almost gargantuan automobile, a 1949 Oldsmobile 98 convertible. He parked it in his parents' garage.

Ross would tour Northwest Oklahoma during the week and find the girls. And on the weekend I drove his convertible to where ever he had found the prospects. At other times he kept the car in Oklahoma City and I would charter a plane at Enid's small airport and fly there. One of the greatest thrills in my life was to see Ross with two girls in the convertible waiting for me at the Oklahoma City airport.

We liked to think of ourselves as playboys, but seriously, we were really from the establishment generation. Since our lives began in the Great Depression we were security oriented and devoted to family.

Our early 'teens meant Sunday afternoon after church, surrounded by aunts, uncles and grandma, reading the funny papers and listening to "One Man's Family" on the radio. Maybe some game was played by the family members.

Men were the bread winners. Women were essentially wives, mothers and keepers of the home fires. The sense of commitment ran deep.

When World War II began, we as a nation were outraged. Quickly we converted all our resources to winning this new global war. Our manufacturing plants turned to making war material and our men went away to fight. This generated a period of extreme patriotism that became one of the basic tenants in our generation's value system.

We would never burn the flag nor could we condone draft dodgers, nor the complaining of those called to serve. We were and are devoutly patriotic.

We are what we were when we grew up.

This was the personal and yet generic background of the young men about to be thrown onto the historical scene that began on 25 June 1950, when the North Korean army invaded South Korea. This is the background for the military action that would soon dominate our lives.

***

With patriotic pride, Ross and I joined the U.S. Marine Corps in the summer of 1950. Prodded not only by the opportunity to see some action in Korea, but also by our draft notices, we forged a pact to join the Corps. Being very cooperative, the Marines scheduled us and three other enlistees for a September 5th morning induction in Oklahoma City. By that Tuesday afternoon, we were on the train headed west.

But what the Marines did not know was that Ross was married. The Corps' policy was to induct only single enlistees. However, Ross had married Maurine, one of the Oklahoma City girls in the convertible who met my plane during our bright spring of 1950. Naturally, I stood up for them along with Maurine's best friend when they were married by a Justice of the Peace. Perceiving that her parents would not approve of the marriage, both of them remained living with their parents and only revealed the marriage just before our enlistment.

The Atchison, Topeka and the Santa Fe train that took Paul Bailey, Phillip Meek, Milo Yellowhead, Weldon Rosser and me from Oklahoma City to San Diego rolled west for four days. It was an indirect route via Los Angeles and down the Pacific coast to our training. Maurine was on the train as far as Los Angeles, where she met her aunt and uncle. That fall she lived with them. On Sundays when visitors were permitted at picnic areas at the recruit depot, she came along with her relatives, carrying a large picnic basket to cheer us. She, of course, posed as Ross' cousin.

According to the United States Marines Corps, we five young men from Oklahoma were headed for a spectacular adventure. After embarking from the train with a number of other new recruits and transferring to a Marine Corps bus, we were taken to the U.S. Marine Corps Recruit Depot, San Diego, for our first indoctrination. This came quickly when one poor boot snickered as the other boots attempted to stand at "Attention." The DI stepped up to the boot and slugged the recalcitrant in the stomach for his outrageous disregard for bootcamp protocol. He fell to the deck (floor), unconscious.

Thus we joined the 67 members of Training Platoon I-65 (Item Company, Platoon 65), who completed the metamorphosis of tearing the civilian away, physically and mentally, then building a marine.

Our platoon received the best military training in the world and much more—we graduated as the "Honor Platoon."

Not all the new Privates First Class would be sent to the Fleet Marine Force in Korea. Some, perhaps 20 percent, were ordered to guard duty and "Sea Going," (ship duty) as well as various Marine Corps schools. But in December, most of the platoon received orders for Advanced Infantry Training, Camp Pendleton at Oceanside, some thirty miles up the coast from San Diego.

The Camp Pendleton training not only covered combat situations but also became a familiarization course for all the Marine Corps weaponry. It was here that we new marines became as professional as possible except for the training of actual combat.

The Marine Corps had been sending replacements to Korea since late August 1950, each group called a

Replacement Draft. Although using the same name, these replacement drafts had nothing to do with the nations conscription of men for the armed forces. The normal stay or tour of duty would be for 13 months. The Fourth and Fifth Drafts were flown to Korea in January 1951 to replace the heavy casualties suffered by the Marines in December as they fought their way out of the frozen mountains from the Chosin Reservoir.

The Sixth Replacement Draft of which Rosser, Bailey, Yellowhead, Meek and I were members boarded the troop carrier USNS Randall on 13 February 1951 and sailed the next day for Korea. After stopping at Kobe, Japan, to store our seabags containing all our non-combat gear, we arrived at Pusan, Korea on 5 March 1951. This is the date that we began our personal entry into the Korean War. The war, of course, had an earlier beginning.

***

To follow the chronology of events, see Map 1 and Appendix 3.

On 25 June 1950, when the communist North Koreans crossed the 38th Parallel, President Truman did not immediately take action. But as the North Korean army sliced through the thin defenses of South Korea, Truman changed his mind. Working through the United Nations, the US was fortunate to instigate the United Nations Security Council to officially condemn the North Korean aggression, particularly since the Soviet representative was off in an official snit that week and could not veto the action.

Led by the American military response, most of the United Nations participants would eventually send troops to what was termed the UN "police action," a simple disciplinary step to bring the North Koreans in line.

Unfortunately five years after World War II, the US military was composed of raw and green troops. The national conscience was no longer on a wartime basis. And these badly commanded, undertrained, underarmed troops were no match for the well disciplined, well trained and armed North Korean army. The Americans were pushed back to the Pusan perimeter at the southeastern extremity of the Korean peninsula.

Enormously shocked, we Americans were appalled that the troops of the most powerful nation on earth could be knocked around by a bunch of "gooks."

At his headquarters in Japan our national champion and hero from World War II, General Douglas MacArthur, was also shocked. He threw in his occupation troops from Japan to stem the communist tide and pushed out from the Pusan Perimeter. Daringly from the Yellow Sea, he launched a Marine counterinvasion by amphibious landing at Inchon, the port of the South Korean capital, Seoul, half way up the peninsula. And with grandeur, he said, "I will crush them." He did that. By the end of September 1950, he had turned the war around.

The UN forces under his command, now consolidated across the peninsula, pursued the "gooks." Fleeing north, the battered North Korean army left behind a guerrilla contingent to harass the UN supply lines and communications—a knife perpetually held at the back of the advancing troops.

The autumn of 1950 displayed the General at his tactical best, or so he believed. He would send his army up the peninsula and he would send his Marines north to a landing at Wonsan. But his tactics were flawed.

From the Sea of Japan to Wonsan on the east coast, the Marines made their second amphibious landing. Then up the coast to Hungnam, they thrust to the Chosin Reservoir. Their ultimate objective was the Yalu River.

Like extended fingers on a hand, MacArthur's army quickly penetrated the now cold and increasingly frigid north. North to the Yalu River that separated North Korea from China they sped. Troops and supplies, like stretching tentacles with nothing in between, formed long logistic nightmares with as much as forty miles between contingents.

Although cautioned many times, MacArthur refused to heed warnings that the Chinese might come to the aid of the North Koreans. More than once, our allies had rumored that the Chinese would stomach a reasonable occupation of part of North Korea but would not tolerate UN troops along the Yalu River across from their Manchuria. Although aware that the Chinese had massed troops in Manchuria, MacArthur gave no credence to their possible entrance into the conflict. He thought it a ploy.

The general was doomed for his blunder. The Chinese, under cover of darkness, had been sending small cadres across the river since early fall. These small contingents were re-assembling in the hidden ravines and depressions of the mountainous area south of the Yalu. They hid in the remote areas between the "fingers" of the UN forces. They kept well out of sight during the daytime in fear of spotter planes. In fact, the first engagement of troops was 25 October 1950 by a ROK unit (Republic of Korea, the South Korean army) with a few Chinese captives taken.

On 1 November the Chinese counterattack began. Striking out from their hidden positions, they cut off the UN "fingers." Although attempting defenses and counterattacks to stop the Chinese surge south, MacArthur was not successful and by December the UN forces were in disarray.

Major General Oliver P. Smith, Commander of the 1st Marine Division, as well as Colonel Homer L. Litzenberg,

Commander of the 7th Marine Regiment, had no faith in the analysis of the situation by MacArthur and his proteges. They were more apprehensive when a Marine spotter plane had detected Chinese troops close at hand after they had made their landing at Wonsan and began their attack from Hamhung, some 50 air miles up the coast. Their objective, Yudam-ni, was in the mountains past the Chosin Reservoir, up the cut of a narrow gauge railway some seventy-six miles.

Although the road began in flat land and rolling hills, it abruptly changed to passes through formidable mountain peaks. Colonel Litzenberg and the 7th Marines led the attack through the 2,500 foot Funchilian Pass to Koto-ri with cliffs on one side and a drop off on the other. Then to Hagaru by the "Frozen Chosin" and up through 4000 foot mountain passes to Yudam-ni. But before they reached Koto-ri, they were fighting the Chinese in those frigid, snow-covered mountains on 2 November at Sudong.

After finally reaching their objective, the Marines had been so badly mauled by the greater Chinese forces that their position at Yudam-ni was no longer tenable and they began a breakout of their surrounded positions on 30 November. Initially anticipating a Chinese attack, General Smith had secured his supply route with the 1st and 5th Marine regiments. By leap frogging back down the snowy passes, the Marines fought their way back to Hamhung and safety, a few miles from the seaport of Hungnam. They did not retreat; they fought in a different direction. As one unit covered the other, the covered unit passed through.

By 16 December, the last of the Marines had made it to the Hungnam area and were evacuated by the Navy. They had brought their equipment, packs, parkas, sleeping bags, and weapons down frozen roads and mountains. And, at the same time, they defended themselves with such zeal that half a dozen Chinese divisions were left at the point of exhaustion. But, more importantly, they brought their dead and wounded with them. This march of the Marines from Yudam-ni past the Chosin Reservoir to the sea would go down in military history as one of the greatest successful withdrawals.

General MacArthur had lost face at home. He had promised a quick victory, but had blundered and apparently been defeated. He panicked and asked for huge reinforcements or he would have to evacuate Korea. The UN requested a cease fire from the Chinese. Being aware of the despair in Washington and the UN, the Chinese would only recognize a complete withdrawal of the UN military force from Korea. On 15 December, President Truman declared a state of emergency, the next thing to a state of war. The National Guard was called up. The portent was perilous. This could begin World War III.

But, as so often happens, situations are overcome by events and the future took an unanticipated turn.

The Chinese were exhausted after the nearly two months of heavy fighting with predictably heavy casualties. Their supply lines were perilously extended and supported transportation only when weather or night hid their activity from US aircraft. Not surprisingly, they curtailed their attack. The last half of December 1950, was quiet, which allowed the UN troops to regroup.

Although MacArthur had controlled the UN armies from Japan, a subordinate commander in Korea, Commander of the Eighth Army, General Walton Walker was killed in a jeep accident while touring his front lines on 23 December. General Matthew B. Ridgway was appointed to take his place on Christmas Day. With his new commander in place, MacArthur ceased his direct leadership role.

When the Chinese resumed their offensive on New Year's Eve, the UN strategy had changed with the changing of command. Ridgway's was a positive strategy without the previous flamboyance. He delayed the Chinese advance by moving back to successive positions and by inflicting maximum punishment on the Chinese by air and artillery. Eventually he slowed the Chinese advance and then slowly pushed them back up the peninsula.

Early 1951 began with the Eighth Army consolidating positions. The Marines, who had returned from the Chosin Reservoir to Pusan at the tip of the Korean peninsula, were assigned the task of rooting out and destroying those remaining North Korean guerrillas that had been left behind by the North Korean army in its August retreat. In February they returned to the line to counterattack north of Wonju in central Korea.

Unfortunately during the volatile spring of 1951, MacArthur could not just fade away. He loudly voiced his opinions on winning the war against communism in Asia. (He wanted to drop THE BOMB on China, for example.) He openly opposed and subverted official Washington policy. President Truman could not tolerate this and summarily fired General Douglas MacArthur on 10 April 1951.

General Matthew B. Ridgway was ordered then to take command of the American forces in the Far East.

Heavy fighting would continue until late September 1951. At that time the UN forces had fought northward to approximately the 38th Parallel. The lines had been formed and were relatively stationary and both sides were tired from the mauling each had taken. Certainly skirmishes continued, but decisive battles and movement in force were over. Negotiations began at Kaesong and continued at Panmunjom, progressing to an armistice on 27 July 1953.

The long protracted war in Vietnam of some twelve years has captured the attention of the American public in the last two decades of the twentieth century and completely overshadowed the first confrontation of the "big" powers in the early 1950s. Korea established a conventional warfare tableau in an atomic age. Despite its technological pre-eminence, the United States was forced by public opinion and by its allies' abhorrence of general and atomic war, to fight a conventional war with World War II arms under restrictions that prevented a winning victory. Additionally this Korean War established the Russian technique, which lasted until their Afghanistan debacle, of involving their satellites in military operations while the USSR remained aloof. This scenario was replayed even more forcefully in 1960 and early 1970 in Vietnam.

Yet over four decades later, the Korean War remains as hazy in America's memory as the mist-shrouded mountains that were the killing fields of the "Land of the Morning Calm." It is truly the forgotten war. Was anything accomplished? Definitely.

a) the southern half of the Korean peninsula was saved from communism and sent on the road to prosperity.

b) Japan was transformed into a superpower.

c) a rift, developing into a chasm, was created between China and Russia.

d) the Truman policy of containment was enhanced—to hold off the communists and hope democracy could develop.

But the Korean War never gained the gripping attention of the nation. After the great victories over Germany and Japan the people weren't interested in battling to a stalemate with China and North Korea. It was like the San Francisco

49ers tying Stanford a week after winning the Super Bowl.

Making a comparison to Vietnam, Ohio's Senator John Glenn, who was a Marine combat pilot in Korea and astronaut, explains, "Korea didn't come into every American life the way Vietnam did because you didn't have blood flowing out of your TV set every night."

Vietnam was set against a background of American domestic violence, whereas, the generation who fought in Korea grew up amid a crusade against foreign evils. They were not rebels fighting against perceived evils at home.

We and our allies may have paid a heavy price to stop Communist aggression in Korea, but history will probably agree the price was worth paying.

And, after forty-five years, a memorial to the Korean War veterans is a long time overdue.

***

In June 1989, the design of the Korean War Veterans Memorial was selected from the entries of Penn State student architects who had no concept of Korean War combat.

Predictably, bureaucracy flourished and this design was revised. Although the American Battle Monuments Commission is charged by law with overseeing the establishment of the memorial, the Korean War Veterans Memorial Design Jury made the original design choice which the Battle Monuments Commission passed to the Washington, D.C. Commission of Fine Arts.

Pondering this choice until the summer of 1991, the Commission of Fine Arts found the design was too complicated to build, although it was even scaled down once in an attempt to satisfy Commission concerns.

Although the decision on building languished for years, the need for a Korean War Memorial had been established much earlier.

COL William B. (Bill) Ryan, Director of Operations and Finance, American Battle Monuments Commission, had been promoting a Korean War Memorial since 1968.

Unfortunately, Congress made COL Ryan wait until the Vietnam War was over before they would consider his request. But after that war those Vietnam veterans raised such a lachrymose demand for a memorial that the Korean War Memorial was side-tracked. Fortunately by 1989 a competition was held. However, the controversial Penn State architectural students' design was adopted. It has moved with snail-like speed through seven agencies, been modified several times, and experienced a law suit regarding design change by Penn State which was settled by the Supreme Court--in Battle Monuments Commission favor. Finally, in July 1993 the Army Corps of Engineers applied for building permits. By September the subcontracts had been let. And by October 1993 site preparation was completed and construction was begun.

When President Bush broke ground in June 1992, the monument was scheduled for completion in July 1994; not only law suits but also budget constraints prolonged the completion date to the summer of 1995.

This final design, exceeding $15 million, features sculptures of 19 seven foot poncho-shrouded ground troops advancing toward an American flag. A reflecting pool, to image another 19 troops, brings the number to a symbolic 38. A grove of linden trees completes the tableau. A low granite wall along one edge of the triangular field is etched with images of those who supported the troops in combat. The site is on the opposite side of the Mall Reflecting Pool from the Vietnam Veterans Memorial.

For our memorial, then, we got 19 poncho-shrouded statues, straggling along; but, by reflection, 38 troops representing the Army platoon of the era, the 38 months of war and the 38th parallel that divided North and South Korea.

***

The Korean War as well as the Vietnam War fought communism. In the outcome, the policy of containment was valid. Communism was vanquished. The veterans of both these wars should stand with pride because they stopped the steady encroachment of communism and they possibly prevented World War III.

In the Mall, close to the long reflecting pool, down Constitution Avenue from the Washington Monument, near the Lincoln Memorial is "The Wall," the Vietnam Veterans Memorial. Across from it, across the reflecting pool, on the other side of the Lincoln Memorial is the site of the Korean War Veterans Memorial, OUR MONUMENT.

Here, the two adjacent memorials reflect testimony to those who fought and died in these controversial, seemingly non-victorious wars and, yet, by the end of the century, these wars have emerged as decisive contributors which led to the containment and downfall of communism.

We have triumphed at last! These are OUR MEMORIALS!

CHAPTER THREE

BOOTCAMP INCREDIBLE

The American people, who backed the war, as well as government and military leaders were appalled at the "kicking around" that our troops had taken from the North Koreans during that summer of 1950 and were not consoled by the marine amphibious landing at Inchon in September. The military geared up. More men were drafted. More men enlisted. Basically the country needed to build up the armed forces as soon as possible.

We responded to the need, Ross and I, by raising our hands to be inducted into the Marine Corps the day after Labor Day. With Ross in possession of our reporting orders, we boarded the west-bound Atchison, Topeka and Santa Fe that very day.

In Los Angeles, a number of other recruits joined us bound for the U. S. Marine Corps Recruit Depot, San Diego. After our arrival at the railroad station, our expanded group of ten or twelve boarded the Marine Corps bus for MCRD. It was our group who experienced sudden shock when the DI struck the new boot, "shitbird,"in the stomach and he fell, comatose.

After this gut-wrenching horror, we learned we were all "shitbirds." For the duration of our training, most of the time, this was our new name, both singly and as a group.

Actually, however, our appellations were only limited to the imagination and vocabulary of our DI. Generally these centered around bodily functions, our mothers, impossible sexual acts, and animals. Oh, occasionally, we were called, "Girls." This initiation into Marine Corps bootcamp got our attention, although at that moment, I'm sure we all wondered what had ever possessed us to join an outfit like this.

It may seem a bit strange, but Ross remembers his first day as probably his best day in bootcamp. While aboard the train on our four day journey to San Diego, he recalls that a real marine aboard had explained about bootcamp. The marine was emphatic, "Don't take anything in with you because it can cause trouble. Besides they will take it away from you. So take nothing." Ross believed him. He left all his possessions with his wife, Maurine, and took no personal gear.

But two guys from Colorado did. And when the DI's asked everyone to empty their pockets, one of them had a cute little fingernail manicure set. This gave the DI's an opportunity to call other DI's into the room to see the effeminate devices and ridicule the guys from Colorado.*

Like us, a lanky kid from the Los Angeles area, Floyd "Gene" Burnett rode the train down to San Diego with a group of enlistees, one of whom carried the orders for the whole group. Unfortunately, Gene got on a different bus to MCRD than the person with his papers.

Being separated from some kind of leadership, he was taken in tow by a marine, who directed him to the main gate. Meandering casually up the street, they were accosted by

---

* Although somewhat out-dated in modern jargon, the slang expression, guy, meaning a boy or man, fellow or chap found extensive use during the World War II era.

the MP in charge of the main gate and severely cussed out for causing a traffic hazard. Gene explained that he was supposed to report to MCRD but had gotten separated from the guy with the orders.

At 11:30 at night and with three more recruits showing up, a DI was called to handle the situation. Gene recalls:

He takes us back to the barracks and throws some sheets and blankets at us and tells another guy that was already there to show us how to make up our bunks in a military way. When the DI leaves, this guy says that he just got here a half hour ago and doesn't know how to make a bunk in a military way. So we attempted it, anyway.

At that time of night, the barracks were empty. The next morning, there were 40 or 50 guys. I mean they brought guys in all night.

Another Gene had a more difficult time getting into boot-camp. At twenty-one, William "Gene" Burleson was older than most of us and taller. A raw-boned man that was well over six feet tall, he tended to plot his own course and few stood in his way.

After enlisting in Washington state, he traveled by train south to San Diego along with Robert Bulletset from Oregon. They drank liquor most of the way. By the time they got off the bus with a number of other recruits in front of the main gate of MCRD, they were feeling pretty good, at best, or drunk, at worst.

A DI had them fall in (got them into some order) and then insisted that all the recruits in his party empty their pockets to get rid of personal gear. The DI also asked that anyone who had liquor to deposit it in a box. At that point Gene Burleson decided that these guys were after his liquor and they weren't going to get it. He proceeded to take the bottle out of his pocket, unscrew the cap and dump the contents on the ground. This caused an instant chain reaction: the DI rushed over and grabbed Gene's arm, Gene swung a hay-maker and hit the DI, several DI's in the vicinity pounced on Gene and wrestled him to the ground.

He wasn't taken immediately to the receiving barracks. Actually, Gene spent three days in the brig subsisting on bread and water before joining the rest of us.

Of course, no Marine training platoon could exist with-out a few Texans.

From the Waco-Ft. Worth area, Otis Goldsmith and Donald Skains had been friends a long time before joining the Marines. They got to talking one night and convinced each other that joining up was the thing to do.

Unfortunately, by the time Otis had told his parents and then went to pick up Donald, he was fast asleep. Donald maintains that he had changed his mind and had forgotten about it. It took Otis another half an hour to again convince Donald to join. Incidentally, in bootcamp, they still appeared to be friends.

Raymond Turner, Roy Holland, Ross Norris and Steve Kerr enlisted on 3 September 1950, at Beaumont, Texas. Kerr and Turner had been friends for years. These boys boarded a bus and went to Houston for their medical exam-inations. Then they were sworn in and boarded the train, Argonaut, for California. Another group from Houston, Jose Garza, John Ontiveros and Joseph Tim enlisted on 5 September and entrained with them for a trip that took three nights and two days. Their train picked up recruits all along the way.

Their arrival at MCRD at 2:00 in the morning did not endear them to the DI, who was very unhappy to be awakened in the middle of the night. After much screaming and yelling, he commanded the recruits to empty their pockets and place everything neatly at their feet. After confiscating dice, knives and other contraband, he ordered that they remove all clothing and take cold showers.

Steve Kerr remembers, "Raymond Turner and I had been buddies all our lives. We grew up together, attended the same church, and joined the Marines together. We had, in the years past, done some dumb and idiotic things, but I believe we had outdone ourselves this time. I can still remember after the cold shower, I looked at Raymond and he looked at me, and I said,`What in the hell have we gotten ourselves into this time?' He just shook his head. I can tell you this: It didn't get any better."

For the next few days we experienced anticipation and boredom as we "lounged" on the deck in "Receiving Barracks." In fact, I "celebrated" my 20th birthday, September 11, on the deck, waiting to start bootcamp. But this was not to be quite yet.

We had joined on September 5, but others, who joined later came into the barracks and daily our number grew. Apparently, time for a proper number of recruits to fill our training platoon meant that we would not go "on schedule" for several weeks.

Initially, we received hair cuts, a "bucket" issue of clothes and bedding, and mailed our civilian clothes and unnecessary items home. Sporting bald heads, we received our clothing issue, an amount that could be carried in our bucket—just enough to provide a change of utilities. At this point not much else was needed.

We had been shown how to make our bunks the Marine Corps way. So our day began with reveille, a shave and face wash. Then we made up our bunks and went to chow.

When we returned we swabbed the deck and cleaned the heads (restroom facilities). Always a DI supervised our every task and made sure our squad bay was immaculate for daily inspection. About the only thing the DI did not supervise was our language. In fact, he taught us a new vocabulary—replete with words no one could use with their mothers.

In that era almost everyone smoked, but not at a person's discretion in bootcamp. Only with permission, when the DI spoke the mystic words, "The smoking lamp is lit," could a person smoke. This was a mystery to me and still is. What was a "smoking lamp?" I never saw one, nor ever really knew the history or reason behind that phrase.

An "old salt's" tale, true or not, relates that a "smoking lamp" was hung in the rigging of 19th century sailing ships, indicating permission to smoke. The lamp was extinguished if the danger existed of an enemy seeing light across a dark expanse of water.

In the Marine Corps, however, if smoking was restricted, only the phrase, "The smoking lamp is lit," would allow the smoking to begin. In our squad bay the smoking lamp was rarely lit.

Very little occupied the day except playing cards, writing letters or reading. Bunks, however, were off limits except for sleep. So we lounged on the decks. Showers were left for the evening and, of course, we looked forward to marching outside to the mess hall for the other meals. We needed the DI's permission to leave the squad bay to go to the head.

Our "casual company" only lasted into the next week when we were herded into buses and dispatched to Camp Matthews, up the coast in the vicinity of La Jolla. At that time, the facility was used as the rifle range, where the recruits qualified on the Garand M-1 rifle. Most of us served in the mess hall, waiting on the recruits who were qualifying. Some lucky few had other jobs.

During the mid-weeks of September we mess hall drudges began our day at 3 a.m. with the DI's horrible, booming voice tearing us from our dreams, yelling, "Reveille!! Drop your cocks and grab your socks. Reveille!"

On the run we made up our bunks, showered and shaved, got dressed, and reported to the mess hall, where we prepared to serve breakfast under the supervision of the cooks.

During breakfast I served in the mess hall by refilling milk containers and plates of food. This was not a buffet. The food was served on the table and when a dish was emptied, it was held aloft or "surveyed." The dish was taken by those like me and refilled, then returned to the person who had held the emptied dish aloft.

After serving the meal we ate breakfast. Then we swabbed the decks. Around 10:30 a.m., we got a break and lay on the grass, adjacent to the hall. But at 11:00, as again at 4:00 p.m., it was all to do over. In the evening a complete, detailed swab down was ritually performed. We got to hit the sack at 10:30 or 11:00 p.m. We worked 18 hours a day with two 30 minute breaks, morning and afternoon, and another 30 minutes to get ready in the morning and a few minutes to get to bed.

Not everyone worked this hard. Some had it easy like Gene Burnett, who was assigned to some supply PFC along with others of our cadre. Each day his group was marched to the supply outfits' big warehouses where they would unpack utensils. Other than that, all they did all day was sit around, then march back to the mess hall for chow.

Luck was with Otis Goldsmith when he was chosen for a special work detail on a garbage truck. Each day his detail would go to La Jolla and dump trash. He says he remembers reading the newspapers and keeping up with the ball scores.

Likewise Californian, Cecil Gardiner, says, "For two weeks, we were kept busy picking up cigarette butts and policing the area while waiting for assignment to a training platoon back at San Diego."

But for me and the other mess drudges this was a very long two weeks.

At last, during September's final week, we went "on schedule." Formed up as Training Platoon I-65 (standing for Item Company, Platoon 65) by our permanent DI's, Private First Class Ernest E. McFarland and Staff Sergeant P. H. Smith, we totaled almost 70 recruits. We graduated with 67. Our final unofficial roster listed 28 recruits from California, 18 from Texas, 5 each from Oklahoma and Minnesota, 4 from Colorado, 2 from Washington, 1 each from Arkansas, Iowa, Oregon and Utah and one from an unknown location.

From time to time we had a third DI, but none was permanent. Our "live-in" DI, our "mother hen," and our tormentor, PFC McFarland tore us down both mentally and physically, then built us back as marines. In the minds of the members of Platoon I-65, he was and always will be our personal Drill Instructor—our creator. The one we loved to hate in bootcamp.

McFarland began bootcamp with a familiarization party; he wanted to get to know us. When he went from recruit to recruit, he seemed such a concerned fellow as he bellowed, "Where're you from, boy?" Of course, he placed his nose one inch from the nose of the recruit when he ask the question. When it came my turn, quaking, I immediately answered, "Oklahoma, sir."

It was mandatory that we call all DI's, "Sir," and jump to attention when addressed or when the DI entered the premises.

In bootcamp the DI received the treatment of an officer.

Meeting a few Texans, McFarland asked if they were cowboys and could ride a horse. "Sir, yes, sir," was the answer in unison—for simple answers, for emphasis, or to make the DI hear, two "Sirs" were necessary. McFarland didn't have any horses in the barracks, but he had brooms, which he gave to the unlucky Texans.

"Now," he said, "Ride." The Texans galloped about the room.

Understandably, as the Texans chased about the barracks, the entire platoon roared with laughter. But laughter was forbidden; recruits could scarcely grin—at least not in front of McFarland. He lunged at Gene Burnett and asked, "What are you laughing at, boy?" Gene was speechless.

"Do you think I'm funny?"

Summoning up all his courage, Gene yelled, "Sir, no, Sir." (We had to yell our replies.)

He was so scared that he bit his mouth until it was raw.

As our DI continued around the barracks, attacking everyone and leaving few unscathed, those few left ahead of his rampage prayed not to be pilloried.

Then strangely McFarland became philosophical, "Do you, shitbirds, realize that the second biggest mistake your mother made was when she let you join the Marines?" I guess the first was conceiving us. In reassurance, however, he added, "But, now, give your soul to God because we've got your ass."

Proceeding on around the room, he came to a guy from Minnesota, Jack Collins, and asked him what he did before he joined the Marine Corps. Jack answered that he had been a professional singer.

McFarland ordered, "Well, sing me a song."

By that time, however, McFarland had the Texans riding

around the room on their brooms with buckets over their
heads, bumping into walls and bunks. Pandemonium was
rampant.

In the din, Jack began to sing "Oh, Danny Boy, the pipes,
the pipes are calling....." His voice was spectacularly beautiful. All noise stopped. Pandemonium stopped. Only the
pure notes of the song swept the room. In that instant our DI
was rendered speechless.

***

Quickly McFarland formed the platoon. Basically he
aligned us from the tallest member to the shortest. Four
columns called squads were formed of one individual behind
the other. A squad leader was chosen for each squad and were
Richard Paddock (California), Johnny Pitts (Texas), Weldon
Rosser (Oklahoma) and William McCartney (Washington).
Among those in Ross' squad were Gene Burnett, John
Camacho, Phillip Meek and I. For me to land in my buddy
Ross' squad was a stroke of luck.

Behind each of the squad leaders, in column, were either
15 or 16 of us. Two squads had 16 members and two had 17
members, including the squad leaders, for a total of 66. Our
67th man, the Right Guide, set the point where we formed up.
In explanation, the Right Guide positioned himself, and the
rest of the platoon aligned themselves to his left. He also led
us when we marched. He was out front, positioned on the
right side, ahead of the first rank of our platoon.
(See Figure 1)

Since the DI had composed each of the four squads with
the tallest recruits at the front and the rest of the squad suc-
cessively shorter, the last ranks were formed by the short
guys, called, "feather merchants." Of course, it was hard to
keep up with the big guys, and these small recruits had a

doubly hard time. They were singled out; nothing fair in bootcamp. But the underlying philosophy was that the battlefield would be rougher for the smaller guy, so he had to be doubly tough. John Camacho, Phillip Meek and Bill Diffee were in the rear.

John Camacho's youth and innocence had no bearing on the way John was treated as a feather merchant in bootcamp. The DI's gave him no leeway. He was in Ross' squad, the same as I, and I remember that we tried to help him out when we could, not because we felt sorry for him but because he really was young and inexperienced. We felt some kindness in our hearts and wanted to help. Always, Ross called John, "Ka-me-ko," not Ca-ma-cho.

Gene Burleson remembers being Right Guide for a while until he had a strong enough disagreement with McFarland that it ended in a fight. Our DI always offered the challenge to take anyone out in back behind the bushes to duke it out— if the recruit were man enough. I believe Gene was the only challenger. Apparently, the fight was private because few of us witnessed it. However, Gene did have to march three paces behind the "feather merchants" after that; and Harold Heidt from Los Angeles became our permanent Right Guide.

Beginning bootcamp for real, we received a seabag full of clothes and gear: bedding, buckets, and other necessities. In the barracks we were assigned to bunks, placed neatly down each side as well as down the center. Each man had a wooden foot locker in which to store his recently acquired possessions. In front of the barracks were racks for our rifles.

Among all the important things for us to remember and memorize, two were the most important: our serial number (each of us had a specific Marine Corps serial number; today replaced by the social security number) and the serial number of our rifle.

Next in importance were the General Orders. Unlike special orders required for particular situations and places, General Orders do not change. There are 11 general orders and we were required to memorize them and be able to recite them whenever we were called upon to do so. Likewise, this required recitation included our personal and rifle serial numbers as well. Specifically the General Orders began:

1. To take charge of this post and all Government property in view.

2. To walk my post in a military manner, keeping always on the alert, and observing everything that takes place within sight and hearing.

... By rote, we memorized nine more.

For the next four or five weeks we spent the majority of our time on the grinder (parade field) learning to march and to perform the manual of arms.

We learned to stand at attention. We learned facing movements: right face, left face. We learned to salute. We learned to march and drill. We learned the means by which we were to move our rifle in an orderly and precise manner from one position to another—the manual of arms.

While learning we were encouraged by this pleasantry, "Girls, you're as graceful as a pregnant water buffalo."

The following scenario from our military education is etched in my memory:

It involved marching with our Garand M-1 rifle at "Right Shoulder, Arms." The weapon's butt was held in the palm of the hand, the lower arm of which extended straight out from the body at the elbow. In this position the rifle becomes the hypotenuse of the right triangle formed by the right angle of the right arm.

With the rifle in this position, it is important to know

there exists a small lever, an operating rod handle less than an inch long, that sticks out of the side of the rifle. As the recruit marches with his rifle at "Right Shoulder, Arms," this operating rod handle is in a position which points directly at the mastoid immediately behind the right ear.

If a recruit did not have his rifle in an exact upright position, if he held the rifle canted or he held the rifle at the wrong angle of the hypotenuse, McFarland would slam his hand into the rifle driving the operating rod handle into the recruit's head. I have seen many recruits bleeding from behind their right ear.

I was fortunate. He only hit me once.

Later, our curriculum included classes in Marine Corps history, military organization, weapons familiarization, mapping and compass.

From 5:30 in the morning until Taps at 10:00 p.m., activity crammed our days. Our DI's molded their raw recruits into men.

McFarland occupied a room next to our squad bay; he was not married. S/SGT Smith lived off base and was married. Both used McFarland's room/office as their Headquarters. If it became necessary to leave our squad bay to make a request of our DI's, the following ritual unfolded:

Recruit: (Knocks on door as hard as he can) Bang. Bang. Bang.

DI: "I can't hear you."

Recruit: (knocking, again, louder) Bang. Bang. Bang.

DI: "I still can't hear you."

This continues until the DI tires of playing. By this time, the recruit's knuckles are raw. (However, some recruits quickly learn that they are recognized sooner when they simultaneously knock and kick the door. The endurance of the doors is amazing.)

DI: "Get in here, boy."

Recruit: (coming to attention in front of DI's desk) "Private Smith reporting, Sir."

DI: "What do you want, gooney bird?"

Recruit: "Sir, may I get my laundry I dropped on the ladder (stairway)?"

DI: "I'll play your silly game, shitbird. May you?"

Recruit: "Sir, can I get my laundry I dropped on the landing?"

DI: "I give up. Are you able?"

Finally the DI tires of the game. Then, as if he has just discovered what has happened....

DI: (yelling, furiously) "Boy, get out of here and pick up the laundry you dropped."

Thus, the bootcamp scenario played out in many ways.

We had other fun things to do like breaking in our boon-dockers (our rough leather boots). A 25 mile hike form-fitted wet boondockers to our feet.

We soaked our boondockers in water filled buckets all night, at reveille poured the water out, put them on and marched to morning chow. With a happy stride after a filling breakfast, we marched to La Jolla and back. We spent the rest of the day on the grinder until our boots dried out. Squish! Squish! The boots were finally form-fitted.

On other occasions S/SGT Smith would get carried away. Particularly if he had been to the slop chute (beer bar on base) before going home to bed. One such night after Taps, he came in drunk, flipped the lights on and yelled, "Attention!"

Our bunks lining both walls and down the center of our squad bay were double decked, one over the other. At each head or foot of the double decked bunks sat wooden, khaki-colored locker boxes for each man, containing all his clothes and personal possessions and weighing more than 50 pounds.

When we were at attention, the wall bunk mates stood facing the center of the room. The center bunk mates stood singly at the head and foot facing the wall bunk mates. We were in this position when S/SGT Smith ordered Locker Box Drill.

This Drill meant performing the manual of arms, not with a rifle, but with the locker box. We precisely maneuvered our locker boxes to "Right Shoulder, Locker Box," next "Port, Locker Box," then to S/SGT Smith's favorite position, "Present, Locker Box." This final maneuver required the right hand and extended arm to support the bottom of the locker box at the side handle and the left hand on top at the handle on the other side. Thus the locker box was vertical, extended in front of the body by the arms. Then S/SGT Smith would forget to give another command.

The "Present, Locker Box" command continued until a recruit could no longer stand the pain and dropped his box. To most of us locker box drill may have been our most excruciating trial.

This made bayonet and rifle punishment appear easy. For bayonet punishment, the DI placed the bayonet between the fingers of the recruit. In a rigid stance, the recruit grasped the tip of the bayonet with his fingers and held it at arms length until relieved by the DI. For the rifle punishment the M-1 rifle weighing almost 10 pounds was placed on the outstretched hands of the recruit, arms extended straight out from the shoulders. In that stance he waited to be relieved by the DI.

Many times we marched in the sand at the beach. Specifically, we drilled in the sand just as we would on the grinder. When most of the platoon were coughing and bleary eyed from the sand dust our DI's would take pity and we would return to the grinder. Incidentally, the DI's drilled us in the sand on our knees!

There were other petty punishments. If any of us were caught smoking without permission, as many cigarettes as would fit were placed in the recruit's mouth and lighted. Then a bucket was placed over his head. Most of us got very sick.

Little annoyances challenged our day. In the dark of early mornings, we did calisthenics and then went to chow. After marching to the mess hall, we were dismissed and had to run into the hall. We ate as fast as we could and hurriedly finished and the tray had better be clean. Quickly each of us ran outside into formation because the last man out of the mess hall had to do push ups. Poor slow-moving James "Punchy" O'Connor from San Jose, California was usually the last man out.

Once, however, Punchy, the recipient of most mess hall punishment, received an unwanted mess hall kindness. During mail call, Punchy's mail included a box of gum from his mother. S/SGT Smith discovered this present and ordered Punchy to chew every piece, all at once, just before chow time.

While running from formation to the mess hall, Punchy slipped the wad out of his mouth and ate chow. Finishing chow he slipped the wad back in his mouth and returned to formation.

When we ran to chow, S/SGT Smith relaxed outside the mess hall, smoking and talking to other DI's. He was unaware of what Punchy had done.

As the platoon re-formed, S/SGT Smith checked Punchy's mouth and found the wad still there. In a show of great compassion, not thinking that poor Punchy had eaten, S/SGT Smith took him into the mess hall and had the cooks feed Punchy again!

But bootcamp was not all fun and games like this.

There was no previous life style that might have prepared any of us young men for this period of our lives. Some recruits were unable to handle the physical and mental hardships to become marines.

Those who could not cope were discharged.

At times, coping and conforming might become the same. For, if one recruit's "screw-ups" affected the platoon, the platoon might retaliate. In this way, the platoon maintained its internal discipline. It demanded duty to the squad and the platoon; lack of it meant retribution.

Should one of us be obviously singled out for unjust punishment, causing the entire platoon to run the grinder, the platoon would forgive. This appeared to be the case with the added burden forced on the "feather merchants." Conversely, should a recruit's dirty rifle cause the DI to run the platoon around the grinder, the platoon could forgive once, but not several times.

One punishment we gave repetitive offenders was the silent treatment. No one spoke to the offender for several days. Of course, some punishment was more severe. Our bootcamp-issued gear included a bucket and scrub brush—their basic purpose being utilized in washing our dungarees and skivvies each week. (utility uniforms and underwear) These items, however, had other uses; the buckets could adorn a smokers head, for example, and, the brushes could become something more sinister.

One very young member of our platoon had an aversion to bathing. Showers were not only a healthy endeavor but also a social necessity after a day on the grinder.

After one of his particularly long showerless periods, three or four of his squad determined to change his likes and dislikes. They overpowered the young man, dragged him to the shower, and proceeded to give him a GI bath. The scrubbers scrubbed him down with their stiff bristled brushes.

That is very sobering business, but looking back over almost half a century some events in this formative period were hilarious. Some events were not funny at the time, but are hilarious, now.

In the intense first half of our training we found the purpose of the Corps was to tear us down, mentally and physically, then rebuild. They absolutely broke the boot or he did not continue. At the start, everyone is an individual, but their individualism was wiped out. Then the rebuilding began. These former individuals were molded into a unit.

Something else, quite unique to the Corps, was molded into us—that Privates First Class could assume command of a platoon, if needed. We sincerely believed that.

Basically, this concept seemed to have been proved during World War II. With the Japanese, all responsibility lay with the Officer Corps and non-commissioned officers. When this leadership was removed in combat, the troops had no direction. No one assumed command. On the other hand, marines are taught not only combat tactics and weapons but also leadership. If necessary, the marine private can take command of a squad or platoon.

***

Believing ourselves to be almost marines after these intensive training weeks of phase one, we boarded buses and headed for phase two of bootcamp at Camp Matthews rifle range to qualify with our Garand M-1 rifles. This scheduled two weeks dictated that week one, we pull butts (targets) and week two, we actually fire the rifle to qualify.

On the range was a deep trench, the butts, perhaps eight

feet deep, in which a man could stand erect. Behind this trench was a high hill which caught the enfilading fire of the shooters. In front of the trench on a slight incline were diagonal leveled areas at intervals of 200, 300 and 500 yards. At these levels, the firing positions were marked for each shooter. Along this firing line and behind each recruit stood the rifle range coaches who were in charge for this phase of training. DI's now not in charge roamed the area offering advice and encouragement.

Although the deep trench was called the "butts," targets were the most important function here. In the butts on the back wall was a mechanism which allowed a front frame or rear frame to be pulled up over the parapet of the trench. They counter balanced each other. For example, the front frame was square and contained a large target. On the frame under the target was a cross bar which enabled the recruit "pulling butts" to push the target up or pull it down. On this mechanism likewise a rear target, identically fabricated, counter balanced the front target.

During the first week we made targets. We worked the butts. We "snapped in" and dry fired our rifles.

It took work to make the targets for the shooters. The target consisted of the center solid ball bull's eye surrounded by three concentric circular rings. Rapid fire targets, however, had a "bust" or "head and shoulders" configuration. These had been imprinted on a paper target which was pasted on cheese cloth stretched over a five or six foot square wooden frame. One day on the firing range might consume hundreds of these targets.

Before the firing began, two of these targets on wooden frames were placed into the front and back "slotted" frames of the mechanism in the butts. Then one or the other was raised completely when ready for firing.

When "pulling butts" we grabbed the bar and pushed up the target. Over loud speakers we all heard the order to commence firing and when to cease firing. After cease fire we brought the target down and located the holes where the bullets had penetrated. With adhesive patches, we called "pasters," we covered the holes. White pasters were stuck on the black bull's eye; black pasters on the rest of the white target. Firing was done in patterns, so that we butt pullers knew how many holes we should find in the target. For bullets that completely missed the target or fell outside the circles, we raised a red flag called "Maggie's drawers." Through binoculars, the range coaches noted the results and logged the score.

Pulling butts did not occupy a full day. When not in the butts, on non-firing ranges, we "dry fired." These ranges had stationary targets on which we practiced sighting-in and pulling the trigger. We practiced the correct firing positions as well as the correct rules for firing such as holding ones breath and squeezing the trigger. This "snapping in" prepared us for the next week.

On the rifle range qualification was absolutely the most important thing. Our DI's told us that no one could continue who could not qualify. We believed them and we feared flunking out at this late date.

The qualification requirement was simple, the achieving of it quite difficult. We would have 50 rounds to shoot. Each bull's eye was worth 5 points, the circle outside the bull's eye worth 4 points, next circle 3 points, and the very outside circle 2 points.

A perfect score was 250 or 50 rounds times 5 points for each bull's eye. Qualification was a score of 190. A Marksman's badge was achieved with a score of 190 to 209, a Sharpshooter badge took a score of 210 to 219 and the highest, Expert, 220 to 250.

This is the process that Training Platoon I-65 experienced to qualify. It took two days: firing for practice, 1 November 1950, and firing for score, 2 November 1950.

While qualifying at Camp Matthews, we lived in pyramidal tents, which were canvas on wooden frames. Our new "homes" had wooden planking floors with cracks between the planks. At least we were in our own community with our platoon tents facing each other down a platoon "street." Both of our DI's were at top form, making sure our platoon performed.

Loren Dickerson (California) remembers that his buddy Cecil Gardiner was cleaning his rifle when the firing pin dropped to the floor and bounced down a crack. It was impossible to get it out, so he improvised with a twig to take its place. Although the pin was crucial in holding the assembly together, Cecil foolishly thought he could get away with the substitution until S/SGT Smith inspected the rifle, pulling back the receiver which caused parts to fly in all directions. End of story; almost the end of Cecil.

Rumors about S/SGT Smith's temper tantrums were rampant. The most popular regarded sexual deprivation as the cause of his continual bad humor. At Camp Matthews, S/SGT Smith had to bunk with the DI's in one of the pyramidal tents and did not get to go home at night to his wife. That was understandable, having to spend two weeks babysitting us as opposed to being home every night. However, a rumor not so sublime suggested he had a bad case of hemorrhoids.

Whatever the reason, S/SGT Smith was a tyrant at the rifle range. One evening after chow, he ordered us into platoon formation at dusk. As he marched us to the boondocks, some detected a slur in his command and suspected he had been to the base slop chute.

The camp was built on slightly hilly terrain with occasional cliffs here and there—the better to throw rifles over. But this evening he had devised a more devious plan.

S/SGT Smith marched the platoon straight for a cliff that hung over a gully some six or seven feet below. The scene few of us will ever forget regards a platoon of men marching over the cliff. Each rank in turn dropped out of sight. In my squad of 16 or 17, I was probably 6th or 7th and will never forget the shock of the sight of the squad members in front of me as they disappeared. There was utter pandemonium in the gully at the bottom as each rank fell on the ones who had gone before. Had we had rifles someone could have been seriously injured.

Fortune finally smiled, however, on the "feather merchants." Being positioned at the rear of the formation, Goldsmith, Meek, Camacho and the rest were the last to fall.

There was no end to S/SGT Smith's ability to get our attention.

Although some congressman had been able to get candy machines installed on base, access was strictly "off limits" at Camp Matthews. DI's called candy, "pogey bait" and the machines became "pogey bait machines." S/SGT Smith marched us to the location of each "pogey bait machine," made sure we knew exactly where the machines were, and threatened any man who might procure a candy bar. "God help you" was his warning.

One poor boot tried his luck and got caught eating "pogey bait." Robert Gilmer (Colorado) always seemed to be among the 10% who didn't get the word and stumbled through bootcamp. S/SGT Smith demanded that we all chip in to buy him more, marched our platoon to a machine, placed the miscreant standing before us, and, made him eat. When

Gilmer said he could eat no more, S/SGT Smith insisted he could. He ate 26 candy bars and became very, very sick.

But these instances were scarce. Our close mentor, McFarland, was always the master and made us jump. He was so cocky and wise. Apparently his demeanor made a somewhat lasting impression on me because once I played the DI's part:

Gene Burnett and I were in the same tent with four other guys at the rifle range. One day, startled, they jumped to the stance when I walked into the tent, yelling, "Attention."

The first boot to notice the DI yells, "Attention." Everyone jumps at this command and stands stiff. We even might flinch if we heard the word from a half mile away, the reflex was so drilled into us.

At my order, my tent mates assumed the DI's entrance was imminent. As they stood there, to their surprise, I became McFarland. And they went along with the charade. I begin to berate these boots.

"Boy, you better straighten up." Pacing around the tent, I addressed each one in turn.

Warming to my roll, I proceeded, "I am sick and tired of you gooney birds screwing up all the time."

Then I began to lecture them about their faults and continued to move until I faced them with my back to the entrance of the tent.

Launching into an inspired mimic of McFarland, I did not see him approach and quietly enter behind me. As he listened to my spiel, the group looked on in horror. They were at attention, for real, now. They couldn't even move their eyeballs as a warning.

But, if they had I would not have noticed because I was too caught up in the act.

McFarland moved slowly around me until I glimpsed him out of the corner of my eye. At that point, I became absolutely speechless, my bones turned to jelly and an immediate departure from this life seemed the only appropriate response.

In a low guttural voice, he asked, "Anderson, which one is your bunk?"

"Right over there, Sir," came my high pitched breathy stammer.

McFarland moved to my bunk and lifted the mattress and, behold, there was a candy wrapper. He ripped back the blankets and sheets, proceeding to dump the mattress on the deck. He dumped all the other five mattresses on the deck. Without a word, he walked out.

Gene Burnett says, "Thanks to Burt, everybody in the platoon got to go marching."

But, I still don't believe I was foolish enough to hide a wrapper under my mattress. I think McFarland planted it, there.

Many of us remember run-ins with McFarland.

Henry (Ham) Hamilton (California) was one recipient. His doctors had signed a waiver, allowing Ham to enlist at 230 pounds. One doctor thought that he was soft so he would lose a lot of weight. McFarland believed this, too. He even bet the DI of another platoon that Ham would lose a specified number of pounds during bootcamp. McFarland thought he had the bet cinched when Ham did appear to loose weight. He lost 6 inches around the waist and could not keep his dungaree trousers up.

McFarland was all smiles. He thought he had it made. He was going to win the bet for sure.

At the rifle range he took Ham to sick bay where Ham could be weighed. He had lost 6 inches around his waist, that was true. But he had gained 2 pounds!

Ham continues his story:

> He liked to killed me. We'd go to the mess hall and McFarland started watching my tray making sure I wasn't getting too much to eat. So when we finished eating, we had to run out to the formation and stand at "Parade, Rest" until all the platoon was out there.
>
> Since I didn't get too much to eat with him watching, I was in the first bunch out there. So McFarland decided I should run around and around the mess hall until the rest of the platoon got out there. So I thought I was smarter than he was and watched out the window, looked the mess hall over, waited until most of the platoon got out there, then I would go out. So I didn't have to run around and around the mess hall. And McFarland thought this over.
>
> He decided he would make everyone mad at me. So instead of "Parade, Rest," he had the platoon stand at "Attention" while I ran around the mess hall. He'd bring me back and stand me out there and he would say, "Platoon, you're standing at 'Attention' because Hamilton is too damn slow. He's eaten too much, again."

But we didn't get mad at Ham. He was one of the special members of Platoon I-65.

Dick Blasongame (California) recalls yet another highlight of the Camp Matthews experience. (See Prologue) Our rifle qualifications were over and Dick had done well on the range. He felt so good about it, he didn't bother to clean his rifle that night.

But the next morning, S/SGT Smith bawled out the order for inspection. Not having touched his rifle after firing it the previous day, Dick was not surprised when the DI became somewhat deranged upon inspecting it. Dick remembers:

> S/SGT Smith says, "Put your hands out." I extended my arms full-length, palms up and the DI placed my rifle on my hands. He ordered, "You hold that, there." Then S/SGT Smith continued his inspection.
>
> You know how you get where you're just kind of leaning back bringing your arms up a little where you can hold it. And I think I had been holding that thing for about a half an hour because he was slow inspecting everybody's rifle. I think he had to go through the whole platoon. And about the time he got down to the end, here comes a runner. And it was a runner for me. Just when I wondered how long I could hold on.
>
> My grandmother and grandpa were here to see me. And S/SGT Smith had to let me go. Oh man! Did I feel good. I thought, "Lord, you're up there."

However, the prize for the best Camp Matthews rifle range story goes to Jim Swartzwelder who later Anglecized his name to Jim Forrest. (See Prologue) He tells it this way:

> I am not a movie person. I don't like to go to the movies. And they said to us out there one evening, "Go to the movies." Almost everybody said they

wanted to go to the movies. So, I thought, "I'm going to stay behind and I'm going to sack out in my tent." Remember the tents with the 2x4 railing around them that the tent was tied to. And there's a red bucket on the railing that says, "Fire," filled with water.

I was two tents down from the DI's tent, from McFarland's tent. So I heard him yell, "One man, get up here." I thought, "Why, who's going to go up there? There's no one here but me." I didn't move.

He hollered again, "One man, get up here." with a little more urgency in his voice. So I thought, "I better move up there or he's going to come looking and he's going to find me and I am going to be in a whole world of trouble." So I ran up there.

At the flap of the tent, there was a rock on the 2x4 for knocking and I took the rock and slammed it against the 2x4 and yelled, "Private Swartzwelder reporting, Sir."

He said, "Get in here." And I went in.

McFarland had two buddies with him, two DI's from other platoons. And he asked one of those lovely questions that DI's ask of all Privates, "Why did you join the Marine Corps, boy?"

What do you answer? Being somewhat of a smart ass, I said, "I thought I'd like it, Sir." That wasn't the right answer.

He said, "Do you think it's made a man out of you?" Again, one of those questions.

And I said, "Yes, Sir."

And he said, "See that locker box, there? Can you put that locker box over your head?"

Well, I remembered how old S/SGT Smith

would come into the barracks in San Diego, drunk, and wake us up and we would do "Right Shoulder, Locker Box"; "Left Shoulder, Locker Box"; "Port, Locker Box." And we would have to hold it straight out. So I KNEW I could put that locker box above my head. I'd like to throw that sucker through the overhead. (ceiling)

"Can you put that above your head?"

And I said, "Yes, Sir."

"Then, do it."

I grabbed it by both ends and flipped it up. But, McFarland had forgotten to latch it and when I flipped it up, the lid flew open and hit me on the head. At the same time, a big bottle of insect repellent flies out, lands at my feet and breaks open. There is a big puddle of repellant forming at my feet. He's got all his pressed khakis in there and out comes his pressed khakis, falling down in this big puddle at my feet.

He's got all his Marine Corps emblems in there, you know, with the screw backs and he has them all separated and those little round screw keepers for the emblems come raining down. They're rolling across the floor and they plop through the cracks in the wooden floor.

I'm standing there with the locker box over my head and I'm thinking, "My God, he's going to kill me."

Now these two DI's he has called in there to show how well trained his men are, they are just cracking up and he is getting mad.

So he says, "Boy, what are you going to do about this?"

I looked at his khakis and I sorta squeaked, "I'm going to wash them, Sir."

He says, "You bet your ass you're going to wash them. Go get your bucket filled with water."

I put his locker box down and I got out of there. I turned and right there on the 2x4 was a bucket. I thought, "Oh Hey, there's a bucket, and it's filled with water. It's hanging right there."

So I grabbed that red bucket that said, "Fire," on it and went back inside.

He looked at me and said, "Boy, do you see any fire around here?"

I said, "No, Sir."

And he took the bucket of water and turned it over right down on the top of my head.

Well, I went back and got my bucket and brush and I took those khakis down to where we washed. I scrubbed and I scrubbed on them. Why, it was way early in the morning before he came and got me and let me go.

***

After experiencing such an exciting, eventful stay at the rifle range, we reluctantly boarded buses to return to MCRD. For some of us it would be a return to mess duty for a week. For others, simpler tasks.

Nevertheless, my buddy and squad leader, Ross, assigned me to be in charge of the scullery.

During and after chow our squad would bring dirty trays from the mess hall into my scullery. After removing any excess food, I would put them in slots on a moving belt which entered a wash machine, a giant commercial dish washer. The machine dowsed the trays with scalding water, soaped them, rinsed them and dried them with hot air. I had a helper who removed the trays as they exited the washer and racked them on wheeled carts to be returned to the mess hall. In all, relatively easy duty.

Not so for Phillip Meek. He was back to swabbing the deck, just like he did at Camp Matthews before we went "on schedule." After every meal and particularly on November 10th, he and others of our platoon were swabbing the deck until it was spotless because this was the week of the 175th Marine Corps birthday. Dignitaries would be present for the celebration; everything must be ship shape.

It may be difficult for someone who has not been a marine to realize or understand the significance of the Marine Corps birthday or its celebration. As a holiday, combine Thanksgiving, Christmas and mix in a little 4th of July. There are festivities and extravagant menus for the troops. Seriously, it's like having a third holiday before Thanksgiving and Christmas. When possible, the celebration on November 10th is grand even in combat zones.

What is being celebrated is the birth of the Corps on November 10, 1775, when the Second Continental Congress, in session in Philadelphia, resolved that two battalions of marines be enlisted and commissioned to serve in the war between the colonies and Great Britain. Traditionally, 28 year old John Trevett was one of the first volunteers to sign up in Philadelphia's Tun Tavern.

Although most of us were on mess duty, a relative happiness pervaded the troops. Bootcamp was almost over and we had survived the rigors. We enjoyed the feasting; we worked next to the food. And a payday had filled our pockets.

Well, almost all of us got paid. Al Weideman's pockets

were nearly empty. He still remembers what happened:

> I always thought my name was Allen Henry
> Weideman. But, my father, my grandfather and I
> don't know how many more back along the line
> were named Henry. At my birth, in the hospital
> office, my father decided that I had to be Henry, too.
> To keep all that stuff going. But, he didn't tell any-
> body.
>
> So I enlisted as Allen Henry but my birth records
> said Henry Allen.
>
> Payroll in those days required the pay officer to
> sit at a table covered with a blanket. And, he had
> stacks of $20s, $10s, $5s, and $1s on the table along
> with a loaded Colt .45 pistol. You had to come to
> attention and salute, stating your name and serial
> number. Then you put out your hand and he count-
> ed out so much money and you signed the book
> where your name was listed and your amount of
> pay.
>
> So I did this and put out my hand. And he says,
> "There's trouble with your papers. You don't get
> paid."
>
> Well, I didn't get paid. I didn't get paid for all of
> bootcamp, because I thought I was Allen and the
> Corps thought I was Henry.

During the last week, the DI's honed us to a razor sharp-
ness and prepared us for the Friday parade when we would
officially become U.S. Marines. They worked us doubly
hard, not letting up like we had hoped, because we had mis-
behaved on the previous Friday. Our DI's had granted us
on-base liberty to the slop chute for our first beer since joining the Corps. In the short time we were allowed that

evening, most of the platoon seemed challenged to meet their personal best. The beer consumed was legendary.

In the aftermath of this drinking bout, naturally, there was pandemonium at "lights-out." The talking, snickering, running to the head prevented all but a few from sleeping.

This continued until McFarland had enough and stormed into the barracks, flipping on the lights and yelling, "Attention!"

Falling us out into the courtyard in front of our barracks on this rainy foggy night, he marched us around in the Quadrangle in our skivvies.

For many of us this remembrance will live as long as we do. As we marched McFarland led the platoon. Behind him from the troops long streams of water shot out to the sides. Some of the guys could not hold their beer any longer; they were urinating out of the formation. McFarland was none the wiser. But he retaliated for our drunken giggling.

We were ordered to run to our bunks, get our buckets, fill them with water from the showers and return to the formation. We had done this. McFarland then ordered us to throw water on the man in front if he did not march correctly and quietly.

At first some were reluctant; eventually the water throwing began. But this still did not sober up a number of us. So back to the showers for more water and more water throwing until every man was soaked and chilled to the bone.

When at last we were allowed to return to the barracks, the troops were sufficiently sobered to hit the sack quietly.

However, we all survived this sobering event. We even survived the final week and on the final Friday of bootcamp took our place on the grinder for our parade as the "Honor Platoon" of all those graduating.

Apparently the deciding factor of our winning this coveted

award was a mistake by S/SGT Smith. As our platoon was to begin the marching competition, S/SGT Smith had commanded, "Right, Face." This we did. He then commanded, "Forward, March."

This was in error because our rifles were at our sides. He should have commanded, "Right Shoulder, Arms." Then, "Forward, March." Being at the head of the column, he did not notice that everyone, without hesitation, went to "Trail, Arms." and began marching to cover the error. We marched with the rifle trailing along our right leg. After 20 or 30 paces, S/SGT Smith noticed, brought us to a halt and corrected the error. This did not go unnoticed by the judging team and we were rewarded with the title, Training Platoon I-65, Honor Platoon.

We became United States Marines that November day in 1950. Most of us would take bootcamp leave and go home. But all us left bootcamp knowing that we were boys no longer. We had become men of the Corps.

***

PFC E. E. McFarland and S/SGT P. H. Smith forged these boys into men:

ROSTER
TRAINING PLATOON I-65
MARINE CORPS RECRUIT DEPOT
SAN DIEGO
FORMED SEPTEMBER 1950

NAME	LOCATION ENLISTED FROM	1994
Bolton, William	Northern California	Unknown

NAME	LOCATION ENLISTED FROM	1994
Brown, Richard	Northern California	Deceased 1966
Camacho, John	Northern California	California
Dickerson, Loren	Northern California	California
Eliades, Louis	Northern California	Illinois
Gardiner, Cecil	Northern California	California
Johnson, Robert (Bob)	Northern California	California
King, Clarence	Northern California	Unknown
MacKenzie, Lincoln	Northern California	Deceased 1970's
O'Connor, James (Punchy)	Northern California	Unknown
Phillips, Richard (twin)	Northern California	Deceased 1983
Phillips, Robert (twin)	Northern California	Deceased 1988
Santiago, Andrew	Northern California	Unknown
Shryock, Donald	Northern California	California
Burnett, Floyd (Gene)	Southern California	California
Diffee, William (Bill)	Southern California	California
Forrest, James (Jim Swartzwelder, 1950)	Southern California	California
Duitsman, Dennis	Southern California	California
Gutterrez, Philip	Southern California	Deceased 1979
Hamilton, Henry (Ham)	Southern California	Alabama
Heidt, Harold (Right Guide)	Southern California	California
Hogue, William (Bill)	Southern California	California
Highest Score at Rifle Range		
Lewis, Albert	Southern California	Unknown
Moore, Richard	Southern California	Unknown
Morris, John	Southern California	Unknown
Paddock, Richard (Squad Leader) "	California	Deceased 1979
Simioni, Louie	Southern California	California
Weideman, Henry (Al)	Southern California	California
Andrews, Robert	Southern Texas	Texas
Field, George	Southern Texas	Texas

NAME	LOCATION ENLISTED FROM	1994
Garza, Jose	Southern Texas	Unknown
Irwin, Charles (Honorman)	Southern Texas	Texas
Kerr, Steve	Southern Texas	Texas
McGowan, Arnold	Southern Texas	Unknown
Norris, Ross	Southern Texas	Texas
Ontiveros, John	Southern Texas	Texas
Oxford, William (Bill)	Southern Texas	Texas
Sullivan, Nolen	Southern Texas	Deceased 1993
Tim, Joseph	Southern Texas	California
TURNER, RAYMOND	Killed in Action Oct.30, 1951	
Fagala, Raymond	N. Central Texas	Deceased 1979
Goldsmith, Otis	N. Central Texas	California
Martin, Max	N. Central Texas	Unknown
Pitts, Johnny (Squad Leader)	N. Central Texas	Deceased 1970
Skains, Donald	N. Central Texas	Texas
Warner, Virgle	N. Central Texas	Unknown
Anderson, Burton	Oklahoma	California
Bailey, Paul	Oklahoma	Deceased 1994
Meek, Phillip	Oklahoma	California
Rosser, Weldon (Ross) (Squad Leader)	Oklahoma	Mexico/Oklahoma
Yellowhead, Milo	Oklahoma	New Mexico
Collins, John (Jack)	Minnesota	Unknown
Dudeck, Thomas	Minnesota	Deceased 1981
Leon, Francis	Minnesota	Minnesota
Moldenhauer, Paul	Minnesota	Minnesota
Smith, Gilbert	Minnesota	Deceased 1987
Burleson, William (Gene)	Washington	Washington
McCartney, William (Bill) (Squad Leader)	Washington	Unknown

NAME	LOCATION ENLISTED FROM	1994
Blasongame, Richard (Dick)	Colorado	California
Gilmer, Robert	Colorado	Unknown
Hawkins, William	Colorado	Deceased 1951
Satterfield, Harry (Wayne?)	Colorado	Unknown
Schleiff, Dennis	Arkansas	Deceased 1989
Bulletset, Robert	Oregon	Deceased 1990
Allen, William (Bill)	Iowa	Unknown
Dalton, William	Utah	Deceased 1973
Clark, Don	Unknown	Deceased 1991

Figure 1 on opposite Page ☛

ROSTER OF PLATOON I–65
U.S MARINE CORPS, MCRD, 1950

Back Row Schleiff, Blasongame, Brown, Oxford, Burleson, Warner, Shryock, Sq. Ldr. Paddock, Smith, Norris, King, Martin, O'Connor, Field, Dickerson

2nd Row Bailey, Honorman Irwin, Turner (KIA, Korea), Andrews, Duitsman, Hamilton, Ontiveros, Bolton, Sqd, Ldr. McCartney, Sq. Ldr. Pitts, Bulletset, Sq. Ldr. Rosser, MacKenzie, High Score Dalton

3rd Row Leon, Yellowhead, Allen, Anderson, Sullivan, Moore, Gilmer, High Score Hogue, Clark, Skains, Weideman, McGowan, Gutterrez, Morris

4th Row Rt. Guide Heidt, Swartzwelder, Dudeck, Simioni, Johnson, PFC E.E. McFarland, S/SGT P.H. Smith, PFC R.F. Whittaker, Kerr, Hawkins, Burnett, Fagala, Satterfield

Front Row Camacho, Tim, Garza, Moldenhauer, Phillips, Phillips, Gardner, Lewis, Collins, Goldsmith, Eliades, Diffee, Santiago, Meek

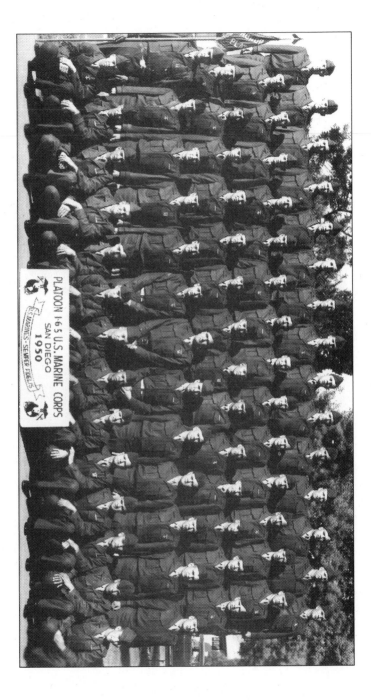

PLATOON 165 U.S. MARINE CORPS
SAN DIEGO
1950
U.S. MARINES · SEMPER FIDELIS

Figure 2 The Grinder–MCRD–Then
Marine Corps Recruit Depot,
San Diego, 1950.

Figure 3 The Grinder–MCRD–Now
Marine Corps Recruit Depot, San Diego, 1992

CHAPTER FOUR

IN TRANSITION

North along the southern Californian coast perhaps 33 miles from the Marine Corps Recruit Depot at San Diego is the Marine Corps Base, Camp Pendleton, at Oceanside, California. More than half a century has passed since President Franklin D. Roosevelt dedicated the base on 25 September 1942 in honor of Marine Corps Major General Joseph H. Pendleton.

Once a part of the huge Spanish land grant Rancho Santa Margarita y Las Flores which at one time included 130,000 acres, the base is located along the original route of the Spanish El Camino Real—the King's Highway now designated U. S. Highway 101.

Transferred here for advanced training after bootcamp, we heard rumors that the base encompassed an area of some 400 square miles, 20 by 20. The camp is not square, however. In fact, the perimeter bordering the Pacific extends 17 miles and extends inland even more than 20 miles at some points. Mountains, hills, canyons adjoining the coastline provided an ideal topography for our continued training.

Although some of our bootcamp platoon trained at Tent Camp One and at Tent Camp Three, Talega, (today Camp Las Pulgas and Camp San Mateo) many of the bootcamp platoon were stationed at Tent Camp Two (Camp San Onofre).

Our new barracks were quonset huts, structures dating back
to World War II, which obscured an earlier time referenced
by the tent camp designation. Here, no longer boots, we
began a more normal existence as marines, training during
regular hours, relative freedom after our daily routine and
week-end liberty.

During December, January and part of February, our
training concentrated on tactics and weapons. We learned the
fundamentals of living in the field and surviving on the battlefield; we learned land navigation with the compass; we
learned chemical defense, first aid and camouflage. We
became familiar with Marine Corps weaponry.

Our fire teams were composed of a fire team leader, an
automatic rifleman or BARman (Browning Automatic Rifle),
assistant automatic rifleman, and a rifleman. A fire team
was the essential element of the Marine Corps rifle platoon.
We practiced basic combat formations as well as hand-and-
arm signals for executing the maneuvers. The steep hills
near Tent Camp Two provided the location for charging up
hill as we practiced. To learn close quarter fighting, we traveled to the Main area to attack "combat town," a replica of
streets and buildings. Not only lectures on individual weapons
but also the actual operation of the weapon familiarized us
with the Colt .45 caliber pistol, the M1 carbine, grenades,
grenade launchers, the Browning Automatic Rifle, the .30 caliber Browning light machine gun and the Thompson sub-
machine gun.

The Thompson, which I fired, did not feed the .45 caliber
rounds from a "gangster" type drum, but rather from a long
magazine extending down from the chamber. Because the
"Tommy" gun tended to arc up when fired, my instruction
was to hold the sub-machine gun sideways or parallel to the
ground. If the Thompson were aimed to the left of the target,

its "kick" would sweep it across the target to the right. Consequently, this method of firing was necessary because its recoil could not be controlled by most men.

In addition, our familiarization continued with the .30 caliber Browning heavy machine gun, the 60-mm mortar, the rocket launcher, the flamethrower, explosives and demolitions. Our instructors provided us with the ability to operate almost any weapon in the Marine Corps arsenal except artillery.

Many of the old platoon were grouped together in fire teams. We all, however, were in close quarters during training; we trained together daily.

A sense of pride pervaded my being, particularly each time I completed the obstacle course and a sense of utmost well-being shot through my soul. Jumping the ditches of water, swinging on high ropes across chasms, traversing the monkey bars and scaling high vertical walls—faster than a speeding bullet, leaping tall buildings in a single bound, I was a superman and nothing could stop me. With pardonable pride I looked back on those who struggled.

Nevertheless, there were chinks in my armor of invincibility.

Located at the Main area of Camp Pendleton, a large swimming pool provided training to simulate abandoning ship. Across the deep end of the pool, a platform at the height of 25 feet yielded space for a rank of six to eight men, four deep. The intent was to jump from the platform fully clothed in dungarees, then swim to the opposite end of the pool, thus imitating an abandoning ship experience of jumping over the side and swimming to a life boat.

The instructors insisted upon discipline. Failing to jump, being inattentive, or horsing around resulted in orders to jump from the 40 foot tower. Caught "grab-assing," Ross had to jump from the 40 foot tower. I did not. But before I jumped from the 25 foot platform, I remembered the S/SGT Smith "cliff" debacle at Camp Matthews. Fearfully I took a step in space, and as I fell, I tried to step back on the platform. My legs never quit churning all the way to the water.

Finally, I will never forget winter maneuvers in January at Idyllwild in the mountains above Palm Springs. This was a five day exercise of hiking through snow each day and setting up a bivouac each night. To give us the feel of Korea in these snow covered mountains, Korean veterans were the "enemy" and would harass us. They ambushed us on the trails during the day; then stole food and equipment from us at night. They would yell, scream, blow bugles and fire blank cartridges to scare us. And they succeeded.

Although the advanced training at Camp Pendleton lasted as long as bootcamp, this ordeal was quite different. Bootcamp was crammed with action and allowed little time for contemplation. Conversely now our activities allowed ample time to assess the future. These months were the more poignant, because we knew we were about to ship out to Korea—we were headed for combat. And the ominous presence of combat hovered over us. On the one hand, we tried to experience all life's cup had to offer in the short time left to us, but on the other, we needed family solace as well as a grasp for immortality.

Before the transfer to Camp Pendleton, most of us had received bootcamp leave. We were allowed two weeks to go home, a reward for becoming marines.

As soon after graduation as possible, I boarded a bus in San Diego and I headed for Enid, Oklahoma and home.

This was not an uneventful trip. Sometime after midnight in Arizona, my bus lurched wildly, jarring everyone awake. The driver stopped the bus, saying that cows were crossing the highway and he had barely missed them. He wanted help to drive them off the road. The many new marines aboard obligingly joined outside the bus and headed for some dark objects back down the highway.

At some great distance down the road, we became aware of the far-off whine of a speeding engine and a glow on the black horizon. We saw lights of a car coming at terrific speed and a curve in the highway. Between us and the curve, meandered several cows. As if watching a movie, we knew what was to happen. We could not reach the cows in time. And because of the curve, the driver would not see the cows until too late.

On this desolate stretch, the speeding car rounded the turn. The impact propelled the car in a spectacular trajectory, end over end, straight up before it crashed to earth. At the same time, the cow receiving the major impact became a projectile, flying down the highway and striking one of us marines.

Over a period of time other cars stopped to help; the highway patrol happened upon the scene; we sent out search parties. But we never found the driver.

To the general public this disaster would have been an excruciating experience, a matter to sky-rocket their blood pressure. Yet, although exceedingly helpful, we marines remained inexpressive—doing what had to be done with robot efficiency—so ever present was the anticipation of war and its numbing single mindedness.

I continued home, enjoying an uneventful leave with my parents.

Ross did not go home. He and Maurine found a bungalow in Leucadia, a few miles from Oceanside. And he reported his marriage to the Marine Corps, who were obliged to tender spousal and dependent benefits. He had excitement enough; Maurine was pregnant. Also he bought a Ford club coupe for his Camp Pendleton commute.

Unlike Ross, the rest of us continued *sans souci*, seemingly without care in our rush to down life's cup. With chauvinistic pride some of us boasted glaring tattoos, the result of alcoholic binges in Oceanside. Among the more defying mottoes was "Death Before Dishonor" displayed over a dagger, dripping blood.

One of our exceptionally handsome quonset hut bunkmates insisted that on every weekend liberty he had spent in Hollywood he was with the actress, Pat Neal. True or not, did it matter? To him and to us, his near future loomed with much greater importance. This was a time to grab everything life had to offer.

I was not so prideful to indulge in tattoos nor handsome enough to play with movie stars. Since Gene Burnett had transportation, I spent many weekends at his home in Highland Park near Los Angeles. Sometimes we searched for our fantasies at the "Palladium" in Hollywood to see what girls we might "pick-up." Other times, he found dates for us among the local girls he knew. All were futile attempts to mask our apprehension—the mind-set of impending combat.

At Christmas, we received a final leave.

With three fellow Oklahomans, I rented Ross' Ford to drive back home. Our destinations were all close to Enid and the four of us alternated driving straight through on Highway 60.

At Christmas, I renewed many old friendships. Of course, this was the time of year that everyone seeks to be home. I was no different; I needed the consolation of home. It was both a happy time and a sad time. A happy time seeing my friends and family; a sad time feeling their sadness at my departure for Korea. A special time feeling the closeness of my parents; and a spiritual time receiving blessings from my grandmother. Never had I been so aware of my deep innermost feelings—even of my mortality.

For several years, I had had a crush on "Mona." I was going to war; I needed a love to bring me courage. Now more than ever I needed her special person. But there loomed a formidable obstacle. She was a freshman at Oklahoma University. Here was a wonderful campus. Here was a great football team. Here were outstanding sororities to pledge. And here was an enviable place to find the right husband! To my disappointment she had little serious time for a Korea bound marine. Her disinterest in a more personal relationship became evident, but being patriotic, she promised to write.

So I left home feeling sorrow for my parents watching their only son leave for war; feeling a strange spirituality, a divine touch from my grandmother; but also feeling the let down coming from unfulfilled love.

While I had been in Enid, Ross' parents had visited him and Maurine in Leucadia. Around the first of February, his in-laws came and accompanied Maurine back to Oklahoma.

So Ross and I took our last liberty, together, catching a ride to North Hollywood, where his relatives lived. In February 1951, his cousins, Ken and Dayton Osmond, had completed parts in the musical movie, "Seven Brides For Seven Brothers." A framed promotional picture, placed on their living room mantel, showed these two young boys sitting on a barn roof watching the dancers. Pearl, their mother, was an actor's agent and their father, Thurman, built movie sets. Not surprisingly, Pearl asked me if I wanted a date with a young starlet. But I declined. I had no transportation. What would I do with Ross? Besides, who had ever heard of Debbie Reynolds?! (Interestingly, several years later, Ken Osmond became the mean kid, Eddie Haskell, on the TV program, "Leave It To Beaver.")

Inevitably, the day arrived to pack our seabags and board buses for San Diego to embark for the Orient. We packed up and boarded the USNS General G.M. Randall, a Navy transport or troop ship, on 13 February 1951. We sailed from San Diego on the 14th. Anticipation had become reality—we were headed for combat.

***

Designated the Sixth Replacement Draft, we were a group of Marine replacements sent to Korea by ship for arrival in March. Unknown to us at the time, the required stay would be 13 months, each draft's tour of duty.

Because of the Marines' heavy casualties at the Chosin Reservoir in December, a combined air-sea lift of replacements went into action in January. Three replacement drafts were ready; but the 3rd Draft was in Japan and the 4th and 5th at Camp Pendleton. With fast coordination by the Navy, Army, Air Force, and the Marine Corps, the troop lift was virtually completed by 21 January. As a result, the shortage of personnel in the 1st Marine Division was overcome. With our Sixth Draft, a scheduled monthly replacement began.

Our ship the Randall was crammed with troops. From deck to overhead, from fore to aft, somewhere between 2000 and 2500 marines found bunks for the voyage. About 800 officers found their quarters in cabins. The size of a very small modern cruise ship, the Randall was small and slow. Its top speed was 12 knots. (See Figure 4)

It had several decks below the Promenade or Main deck— the open deck which permitted walking around the ship. Below decks were bays—fore, mid-ships, and aft, or large compartments containing rows of bunks. The bunks consisted of a rectangular pipe frame to which was lashed a rectangular piece of canvas which filled the frame. Attached at each corner of the inside frame, the bunk was flexibly affixed to two metal poles, upright from deck to the overhead. To the outside corners of the bunk was attached a chain, also attached to the pole. This permitted lowering the bunk solidly for sleeping or raising the bunk perpendicular to the deck when not in use.

Consequently, every morning over the intercom loudspeaker, we were awakened by the boatswains whistle and the announcement, "Reveille! Reveille! Trice up your bunks. Clean sweep down fore and aft."

The bunk on the right of the pole shared the space with a like bunk on the left. The two, together, formed a lazy V because the bunks did not lie in a flat position for sleeping; the outside of each bunk was slightly higher than the inside. This was particularly fortunate in a storm because the outside frame could be grabbed with both hands while one's back was placed firmly against the inside frame.

Although the above describes two adjacent bunks affixed to the poles, in actuality, each bank of bunks between the poles contained eight bunks. From deck to overhead rose four tiers on each side of the poles; when the bunks were lowered, the space between them was essentially the same as the width of the bunk, obviously engineered for effective tricing.

Our days fell into a routine: reveille, morning chow, clean sweep down and swab down of quarters and heads, out on deck to await inspection of quarters, noon chow, evening chow. Additionally, we received assignments of guard duty, mess duty or clean-up. Gene Burnett became a cook for the voyage. I was assigned guard duty.

Jim Swartzwelder (Forrest) appears to have slipped through the crack and avoided assignments. Seemingly, he boarded the ship with the same equipment as the rest of us.

But not really. Belted to three sides of our pack was our bed roll in which we carried, among other things, the pegs for our shelter half. Not Jim. He carried a bottle of booze. As we embarked, he started drinking. And he remembers to this day:

> I don't know what I got sick from first—whether it was the roll of the ship or the booze. But five days later I finally came up for air. I was really sick.
>
> You know that piercing whistle that the boatswain makes before he makes an announcement. Well, he makes that whistle and it was for "Lifeboat" drill. And I'm lying in my bunk, really sick, and I thought, "Hell, this sucker isn't going to sink, and if it does, well, it will be a relief." So I just stayed in my bunk.
>
> And so this Navy Lieutenant and his entourage, his whole long line of flunkies, came down there to the third level. And they came in there, and they saw me lying in my bunk.'
>
> He says, "What in the hell are you doing?"
>
> And I say, "I'm being sick, sir."
>
> And he says, "Get up that ladder, now."
>
> I got up and started up the ladder. I got as far as the bulkhead door and opened it to the deck when I could feel it coming up again.
>
> There was a whole mass of guys out there, but when I opened the door and gurgled, "Make a hole," it was just like you hit those guys with an ax. They just shot apart right to the rail. And I headed for the rail and was so sick. Five days, boy, that was terrible!

My own deck experience was less gut wrenching. After cleaning our large compartment where perhaps 100 or more troops slept, we were required to fall out on deck until the Navy inspecting officer inspected the entire ship. Sometimes it took hours.

One blustery rainy morning, awaiting inspection of quarters and permission to go below, we huddled against the superstructure, trying to keep out of the rain. This was an exceedingly long inspection and I knew my bladder couldn't wait.

Across the deck from us adjacent to the rail was an isolated large funnel which provided air below decks. It could adequately shield a man. I saw an opportunity.

I ran to its hidden, railing side and urinated on the deck.

That morning, I started a trend many others took advantage of. We gave literal meaning to those words, often thought but seldom spoken: "Piss on the Navy!"

But not all experiences were as memorable as the preceding. My first letter home, written aboard ship and posted in Kobe, Japan, reveals a more typical picture of two weeks at sea. I promised my parents that I would write about the war, honestly and truthfully, no matter how disturbing. Indeed, I was to be their war correspondent as well as the correspondent for their neighborhood and the First Methodist Church of Enid. For her part, my mother promised to save my letters. And she did.

February 28, 1951

Dear Folks,

This has certainly been a long voyage, but not a bad one. Right now, we are just about 150 miles off the coast of Japan. Today, we found out we were just going to let off some air, tank and weapons detachments at Kobe and go on to Pusan, Korea. We are not even going ashore in Japan. Supposedly,

the Communists are massing on the border and we
are being shipped into the front lines as fast as possible. I wish they would give us a little training in
Korea before we go to the lines. We are stale from
just lying around for almost two weeks.

The second and third day out, more than half of
the troops were seasick. But, apparently, it was not
lasting because very few are sick now after two
storms. Today, however, another storm began and the
ship is rolling more than usual and the problems
may start again.

The storms always bring about odd happenings,
especially for the boys with weak stomachs.
Sometimes they just can't make it to the rail. But
rains come and wash the decks clean for the next
person. At times, it is impossible to get "above"
decks to the rail, so the "heads" are full of groaning
sufferers.

Eating chow is the biggest problem in a storm.
Lines are formed to the galley at six in the morning,
11:30 at noon, and 4:30 in the afternoon for chow.
After waiting about 15 minutes, hanging on the rail
with all our might, we finally get in the mess. After
only a few days at sea, we learned there was an art to
grabbing the food as we went through the galley,
cafeteria style.

With each roll of the ship, we grab the railing
attached to the bulkhead with one hand to balance
ourselves; and, with the other hand, hold the food we
already have on our tray. Then we tight-rope walk to
a table, which has a rim that will hold the tray on the
table. After putting the tray down, the confusion
begins, however.

As a bite is undertaken, your tray may slide to the other end of the table or some other's tray slides down to your end. Food goes flying in all directions. Should someone get sick, another situation is added to the confusion because it causes a chain reaction which leaves the galley with only a few stalwart "chow hounds" still eating. And, there is a problem walking when the "chow hounds" have finished eating because, by this time, the deck is rather slick with digested and undigested food. They go as skiers to their hatchways.

We have had duties since we boarded the ship in San Diego. I am on guard duty. I have a 24 hour duty period, every third day. This consists of four hours on and eight off, four on and eight off for the 24 hours. The posts vary but mine has usually been above-decks, over the Captain's bridge, the top most deck.

At night, we seem to bear right into the moon's beam. Most of the time, the wind is cold and the salt spray coming over the bow is really invigorating. It is on this post at night that I enjoy my voyage most. Thinking about the past and wondering about the future take the monotony away from standing the post. It seems my surroundings help me think. I get a great uplift standing there facing into the wind and spray, at night, all alone.

This ocean is magnificent. Near land the water is green; but, far out from land, it is royal blue. It is thick and syrupy, like grape soda pop, as it boils and foams around the ship. All the colors are in vivid contrast. The sky, clouds, ocean, foam and ship make up the picture.

When I see nothing but water surrounding us—
the deepest royal blue with the whitest foam that
you can imagine, it leaves me full of awe and wonder. At Camp Pendleton, I dreaded getting aboard the
ship. I feared the ocean; but, now, I greatly revere it.

We have crossed the 180th Meridian, the inter-
national date line. For example, today is Wednesday,
but it is Tuesday back home. There was an initiation
on deck where we were doused with fire hoses. But,
I managed to stay out of the main streams and did not
get very wet. Afterward, we got certificates to prove
it. It says that the "Imperial Domain of the Golden
Dragon" certifies that I was duly inducted into the
"Mysteries of the Far East."

I hope this goes off the ship when we dock
tonight in Kobe. So, write when ever you can.

Love,

Burton

What I heard aboard ship and I repeated in my letter
were rumors. They were not always accurate. We did dock
at Kobe and we did go ashore. In fact, we stayed there several days. We arrived on the night of Thursday, March 1st.
During the next two days, we went ashore and stowed our
seabags, containing all our uniforms and personal gear except
that necessary for combat. We kept our packs and dungarees.
On the first night, our half of the ship went on liberty in
Kobe. The next day, we stowed our gear in waterfront warehouses while the other half went ashore.

In our minds and hearts lurked a covert hatred, a deep
enmity for the Japanese. We had been taught well. We
knew of the outrageous atrocities committed by the Japanese
during World War II.

We knew the Japanese had an utter disregard for human life, even their own. Very few Japanese were ever captured during the war, and the war ended with Kamakaze pilots committing suicide by diving their planes onto Allied ships. Our loathing was focused by Japanese savagery toward our brother marines. We had been told of many incidents.

When Wake Island marines were captured and enroute to Shanghai, the Japanese beat them, starved them and beheaded two sergeants.

Of the Marines captured on Bataan and Corregidor, 239 officers and men died from the brutality of the Japanese.

When Carlson's Raiders withdrew from their surprise attack on Makin Island, nine marines were left behind and captured. The Japanese beheaded them, all.

In 1945, Navy and Marine pilots who were captured by the Japanese were beheaded.

When the Marines re-captured Guam in 1944, they found the graves of groups upon groups of civilians who had been used as laborers by the Japanese and then beheaded.

The hatred that pervaded our group was not only something taught to us, but also was the prevailing attitude carried over from World War II.

Toward the end of that war, only a few years before, most military planners were convinced that we would have to invade Japan itself to end the war. They also were sure that the Japanese would fight to the last man. Consequently, US Intelligence figured that this invasion would cost a minimum of 100,000 American lives. So President Truman dropped the bomb.

After four long bitter years of war, facing the Japanese infamy, brutality and atrocities, we hated them with a vengeance. And vengeance is what we sought even five years after the war. These attitudes form the background for my next letter.

March 4, 1951

Dear Folks,

I told you in my last letter that we weren't going to stop at Kobe. Well, we changed plans. We stopped there and had liberty ashore. We left our seabags in a warehouse and they let us go on liberty. Tomorrow, Monday, we dock at Pusan. There, we get bandoliers of ammunition and get on a train that takes us up to the front.

I am in the 1st Marines (1st Regiment), 1st Marine Division, now. Ross is with the 5th Marines. We finally got split up. They let us know our orders, yesterday. Meek was sent to the 7th Marines (7th Regiment). Yellowhead to the 1st Marines, also. Haven't seen Bailey, yet. So, the five guys that started out are really getting split up.

Kobe is a pretty large city. When we arrived, there was a band playing the Marine Corps Hymn. Real Gung Ho! The Japs along the dock would smile and wave but nobody aboard ship smiled or waved back. We had been thoroughly indoctrinated with Marine Corps lore of World War II in bootcamp. But, when we got on liberty, and got to know them, everybody's mind changed. I believe the Japs like their life better, now. They say MacArthur treats them pretty square.

Kobe was bombed in the last war; but, it is built up new again except a few buildings that are still rubble. The town and the people are a strange mixture. The buildings are quite different. One will be a modern building; but, right next to it will be an ancient one. The people still live in houses with straw floors and low ceilings. You even have to take off your shoes when you go inside.

You see all types of people. One may be dressed like we dress and right next to him is someone dressed in an ancient oriental way. Then, there are the Geisha girls. They always dress in flowing robes that are embroidered.

The 1st Marines that I am to join are on line, now. They are spearheading "Operation Killer." So, it looks like I will be in combat very soon. I try to laugh all the time. In fact, one of the guys said he was glad he was going with me because I keep everybody's morale up. But, trying to laugh all the time isn't easy. I'm scared to death, although I haven't shown it yet. I guess fear is like seasickness; it's all in your head. I didn't get seasick because I talked myself out of it. So, I'll sing the Marines Hymn and try to keep from being scared.

Right now we are in this channel at the lower part of Japan. There are a lot of junks, oriental boats, here, with their paper sails. They sure are funny looking. I'm on deck about to freeze. It sure is cold.

Well, write a lot but don't expect many from me. I'll be busy, you know.

Love,

Burton

I hadn't gone into much detail about the Geisha girls because I could hardly describe my Geisha encounter to my parents. On liberty, of course, Phillip Meek and I had gone to a Geisha house. This was our last liberty before combat; we looked for adventure. It unfolded like this:

"Hey, Meek, you want another beer?"

I had finished my can of Pabst "Blue Ribbon" and was ready for another, trying to make this into a "good" liberty before going back to the troop ship and the overpowering reality of war.

Because our liberty had been granted based on the "port" or "starboard" side of our assigned bunk aboard the USNS Randall, Ross was not with us. He had the next liberty, "starboard." Meek and I were "port."

"Meek, let's order another beer." No response.

At this Japanese bar, he sat there and stared into space.   And my mind wandered, also.   I thought,"Hey, what's next?"

Meek sat there looking into space. All 5'7"of him, if he stretched his most erect "at attention." He was impeccably dressed if that were possible. Nothing out of place. With shining black hair, his complexion was dark, mirroring his Indian ances- try. His black eyes shone above a sharp and chiseled nose.

He finally spoke. "Let's get the hell out of here," he said.

It was cold outside and I wondered where he might want to go from here. I wanted to get to a warm somewhere and have another beer.

"Andy, let's find a whorehouse."

So that's what was bothering him. That really hadn't been in my immediate plan and I didn't give him a reply. Just thought about it. And while I was thinking, I realized I was looking with shocked

Western eyes at an unbelievable sight.

The light from the bar illuminated the street in front. The street had a deep gutter on the side with water flowing along it and pissing in the water was a young Japanese fellow of 19 or 20. It was surprising to see this in public, on a public street, but a real shocker to see him talking to a girl as he pissed. This was my first encounter with the Oriental "mystique."

As we stood there, watching, she left and he noticed us.

"Hi, G.I."

"Hi." We said in unison.

"You Marines?"

The "r" was slurred.

"Yes." Again, in unison.

"I like Marines."

In my best "pigeon" English, I asked, "You live around this place?"

"Oh, yes. I live here during war. B-29 come. Boom! Boom!"

Haltingly, we communicated. He told us that Kobe had been heavily bombed; but now the city was being rebuilt. He said the schools were bombed and had not been rebuilt; so he hadn't been to school since the war.

Meek was so impatient. "We want girls. We want Geisha girl." He butted into the conversation.

"Ah! OK. Numba One Geisha for you. OK. You follow, Marine."

As we followed, Meek gave him a pack of cigarettes for being our intermediary and we continued to the next corner. At the intersection we turned and saw a bright light down at the end of the street. Our new friend indicated that was where we would find the Geisha house. Meek rushed us down the street; our friend made arrangements, and Meek negotiated the price. Tonight was going to cost 3 packs of cigarettes.

It was the custom to remove our shoes and leave them in the entrance way. In stocking feet we were ushered into separate rooms by an older Geisha. The room was lit only by candles giving a soft warm glow with shadows. Perhaps, it was the pervading scent of incense which caused a feeling of relaxation and physical well-being, a warm coziness.

Shortly, a very young Geisha, certainly not over 15 or 16, dressed in a flowing embroidered robe, entered the room and knelt down to remove my uniform. She was like a large porcelain doll wrapped in gorgeous robes.

In the center of the room on the floor was a pallet, the soft pad and comforters which made up our bed. The Japanese houses were heated by indirect heat from under the floor, so that the bed was warm and inviting.

She did not remove the robe immediately. We snuggled in the warm bed and as we came together she opened her wrap, like the unfurling of the petal of a radiant flower. The incredible warmth of her body transcended all thought of war. The amazing petiteness of her sexual being captured my mind and held it prisoner. The incredible sexual explosion she caused would remain as a bright memory long after.

That evening I had experienced the second

Oriental "mystique." And in my half-dream after, I
pondered the Western fantasy of the Geisha "mystique"—of an anatomical difference, of a "cross-
wise" aperture.

But screams jarred me from this reverie.

Being concerned with his personal cleanliness,
Meek had used a "rubber" for protection during his
sexual activity. Afterward, as his Geisha left the
room, he searched for a place to deposit this used arti-
cle. Finally, spying what appeared to be a rectangular
receptacle in the corner, he tossed the condom into
what he supposed was the trash.

Not so. It was a habachi containing hot coals.
The smell propelled a number of screaming Geishas
into the room.

***

Our adventures came to an end on Saturday, March 3rd,
when we embarked for Korea. We arrived in Pusan, Korea,
on Monday, March 5.

Now, as combat approached, our thoughts of war became
an obsession. For me, two pictures of war dominated: a
World War II newsreel of incessant artillery fire in Egypt
and *The Red Badge Of Courage* by Stephen Crane. At the
time, I had nothing else with which to compare war.

During World War II, I watched movie newsreels of the
tank and artillery battles in the Egyptian desert. Those images
and the never ending roar of the sound track are still with me.
Probably several films were spliced together to give the
effect of a continuous cannonade. I wondered how anyone
could stand the incessant barrages. However, actual combat
was not like that movie.

Likewise, *Red Badge* depicts a false picture of combat.
Although his brother was at Chancellorsville, Stephen Crane,

the author, was born in 1871, seven years after the Civil War ended. He had no first hand knowledge of war or combat.

The story is what a skilled writer might conceive the "fog of war" to be—dream-like events abounding in imagery and illusion. It does not depict combat as I know it.

And why is this important? Because no one can prepare another for combat, psychologically. Nothing you will read or view can prepare you. But as I rushed to combat, I thought incorrectly that I knew what it was like.

***

In Pusan we disembarked and boarded a train north to the fighting. Rumors spread of guerrilla attacks on troop trains and guards were placed between the cars, rifles at the ready.

The land was brown where not covered by snow, and bleak—a montage of dull sky and drab land. A view from the windows was so uninviting we quickly found other means to pass the time. Playing cards, discussing our plight or sleeping shortened the monotony.

Each side of the train car contained two rows of wooden "shelves" as wide as a man. These were hard wooden bunks on which to sleep or if not overly tall from head to butt, to sit for other activities. An oil stove heated each car. Our meals were the 5-in-1 or 10-in-1 rations which we managed to heat on canned Sterno "stoves." These were not the individual C-Rations that we soon would receive in combat.

At one end of each car was located the "head," a small room with a round fitting which evacuated directly to the tracks beneath. Standing or squatting over the hole was the necessary method of use.

We traveled north approximately 170 miles from Pusan towards Wonju. Sometime on March 6th on a siding replete with trucks, we left the train and boarded the trucks. We continued north to a snowy field outside of Hoengsong where we set up our shelter halfs for the night. In the early evening, bright red flashes from artillery in the distant black sky and dull thuds from their cannonades told us that we were close to the lines and caused considerable apprehension before sleep overcame us.

The next day we waited for transportation. Finally in late afternoon my truck came to take me to "Dog" Company, 1st Marines. Again I waited until my guide, Andy, came to pick me up. He was from a machinegun squad, where I was to be the new ammo carrier. That came as quite a surprise. I thought I was a rifleman.

As I followed Andy to my foxhole, a figure in the winter dusk said "Hi." He asked questions about the states and home folks' attitude toward the war which had been such a debacle so far. The voice was calm and somewhat authoritative; but the individual was dressed in a completely unofficial uniform.

He wore no helmet, but rather a "piss cutter," the Garrison Cap from the dress green uniform. His trousers were from the same dress green uniform. Yet his "dungaree" blouse was hanging out over the trousers and a .45 caliber pistol hung strapped in his shoulder holster. I wore dungarees, termed a utility uniform, that was authorized for combat and I was mildly shocked at his out-of-uniform condition.

He asked, "How are things in the states?"

"Fine. Camp Pendleton is gearing up. I think they will start sending drafts over each month, now." I thought that was what he meant.

"Actually, I was wondering about other things. What's on the Hit Parade." He talked about a radio program that presented the most popular hit music each week.

I didn't know. "Since I was in bootcamp and then in advanced training, I really don't know. I just haven't kept up with it. But coming over on the ship, they played Armed Forces radio and 'Tell Me Why' by the Four Aces was really popular."

"Oh, guess I haven't heard it." Changing the subject, he asked, "Well, what do your folks think about your being in Korea?"

"Well, that's kind of strange. They agree with Truman. But they are rather unhappy about MacArthur. On the other hand, some of the neighbors don't think we even should be here."

At this point, he let me know his opinion in no uncertain terms:

> MacArthur is an ego-maniac. He was in World War II and he still is. He is personally responsible for thousands of boys getting killed in the last few months—both soldiers and marines. If it hadn't have been for General Smith not believing MacArthurs' analysis of the Chinese and planning for their attack, the Marines would have lost the whole division.

> And, another thing! Truman is no friend of the Marines. Why, just last September, when congress asked him to give the Commandant a voice on the Joint Chiefs of Staff he said something like, "The Marine Corps is the Navy's police force and as long as I am President that is what it will remain." He even said, "They have a propaganda machine that is almost the equal of Stalin's."

> Why, there's been trouble with the Army—and Truman was in the Army—almost from the beginning.

There is a story about the end of the American Revolution when they were disbanding the military forces and all that remained was a corps of mules and two battalions of Marines. The Army and Navy tossed a coin to see who would take the mules or the Marines. The story goes that the Army won the toss and took the mules—that's their mascot, isn't it.

Well, maybe it doesn't go back that far. But it really does go back to World War I. The Marine 2nd Division held at Belleau Woods in France. They decimated the Germans. The Marines stopped the enemy and drove them from the woods. The French were so grateful, they renamed the woods for the Marines. They were even praised by a special holiday declared by the French parliament. This made the Army so mad that an envious rivalry broke out and lasted for generations. It even kept the Marines out of Europe during World War II.

So, don't trust the Army. Except maybe Ridgway. He seems to be a straight shooter. He believes in making the enemy pay an immense price for any gain. We like his style.

The conversation ended and Andy led me to my foxhole. Mildly perplexed, I wondered who this disheveled, opinionated character could be. So I asked Andy who that scruffy person was. Andy replied, "Oh! Him. That's just our Lieutenant."

Officers did not wear insignia or clothing that might identify them as officers. This oddly dressed lieutenant led his troops into battle firing his Colt caliber .45 M1911A1 pistol and carrying his walking stick, called an "Ede Wa" stick. And, in fact, he did lead and we followed.

In the dusk, I jotted down the following note:

March 7, 1951

Dear Folks,

I'm on the front lines, now. It's snowing cats and dogs, this evening. Although I was trained as an infantryman, I'm in a machinegun platoon, now.

A machinegun platoon is made up of three machine gun sections. Each section is composed of two squads, each with a Browning .30 caliber light machinegun, a squad leader, a gunner, assistant gunner and five ammunition carriers for each gun or 16 men per section. Each section is attached to each of three rifle platoons, that make up "Dog" Company.

We're eating rations and digging foxholes* for tonight. Tomorrow we move out into the attack, heading north. It's about dark so I don't have time to write more.

Love,

Burton

---

*The World War II "foxhole" became the Vietnam "fighting hole".

CHAPTER FIVE

FRIEND AND FOE ALIKE

O n our way to war we the 6th Draft were transported in different manners. After striding off the ship amid a tunnel of Korean well-wishers, then grabbing ammunition bandoliers, John Camacho, Ross and I boarded the same train. Later John disembarked from our train and boarded another, hauling boxcars, which took him to the outskirts of Wonju. At this location he was initially housed in a pyramidal tent with "Charlie" Co., 1st Battalion, 1st Marines. Similarly, Ross left our train and was transported to the 5th Marines.

Gene Burnett did not board the train at all. Conveyed by truck to a seaside town, Pohang-Dong, a short distance from Pusan, he joined the 1st Amphibian Truck Co. Gene became the driver of a Dual Utility Cargo Water (DUKW, pronounced "duck") vehicle. These were six wheel drive (ground) or propeller driven (water) amphibious trucks designed to carry a World War II 105 howitzer and its crew.

Likewise, by various means of transportation, others of our group joined their respective companies.

Indeed, as we became a part of this new environment, we also became aware of our surroundings—the mystic Orient and the inscrutable Oriental, friend and foe alike. To us, they all looked the same. How could you tell the difference between Koreans—North or South—or Chinese? Who was friend? Who was foe?

Admittedly, we looked upon all Asians with disdain. Perhaps the Japanese were not sub-human as we had expected. But we still heartily maintained our voice of derision in any reference to the Mongoloid race. We called them, "gooks" or "Chinks," friend or foe alike. It was common practice to describe any debacle as, "Fucked up like a Chinese fire drill." Even MacArthur's sycophant, General "Ned" Almond tried to deride the vulnerable Chosin marines at Koto-ri with a contemptuous, "Scared of a bunch of Chinese laundry men?"

We marines viewed the gooks and Chinks with scorn that would not diminish during this war. In fact, the complete incompatibility of our cultures caused misunderstandings by both the Peoples Republic of China and the United States that contributed to the deaths of thousands.

One notable military difference between western and the communist armies was structure. Their organization was extremely simplified in comparison. Termed with Chinese nomenclature incomprehensible to us, the Chinese People's Liberation Army (PLA) established enlisted leadership with a "squad leader" like our sergeant. The officer ranks were led by "Unit Commanders"—like a captain at the lowest command, a colonel for a battalion, a general for a division, an army or an army group. For the staff there were majors, and a Commissar or political officer at every unit level. Communist armies were notable due to so few in leadership positions. Nevertheless, after the Korean War, the PLA changed to a western-style organization.

Cut from the same cloth, communist armies were quite similar in tactics. The cardinal one: surround, encircle and exterminate.

Nevertheless, within these armies, differences did exist, the chief difference between the PLA and the North Korean People's Army (NKPA) being discipline. The NKPA practiced physical violence against its troops—slapping, beating and brutality. The PLA did not condone physical abuse against its soldiers and applied it only as a last resort.

In fact, for thousands of years, both discord and harmony have prevailed between these Far Eastern people and in these ancient lands.

Korea derives its name from the Koryo dynasty which ruled from the 10th to the 14th century. From the 14th century to the mid 20th, the country was called Choson in Korean or Chosen in Japanese, "land of the morning calm." Other references have been "the Land of 3 Kingdoms" and "the Hermit Kingdom." The former because of the three dynamic dynasties—Koguryo, Silla and Perkche. The latter, "Hermit Kingdom," because of the countries extreme policy of isolationism during the 1800s.

Korea is largely a mountainous country with only about 20% of the total area suitable for farming. The north is predominantly mountainous; the south has the lowlands. It is situated between the Yellow Sea and the Sea of Japan. On its northern landlocked border, Korea sides with China's region of Manchuria, separated by the Yalu and Tumen Rivers. In the northeast, a 10 mile border frontiers with Russia's Siberia. Korean animal life is similar to that found in China and Siberia: tigers, lynxes, leopards, bears and wolves, especially in the north. (See Map 1)

Belonging to the Mongoloid race, the Korean people may have first inhabited the peninsula some 5000 years ago. They spoke many dialects, but these were unified with political unification in the 7th century.

Legend reveals several possible beginnings of Korean

history. One states that around 2000 years ago, a semi-divine figure, Tan'gun, founded the ancient state of Choson at the site of modern Pyongyang in northern Korea. Another legend recounts the tale of a refugee band of Chinese loyalists who followed their leader, Kija, to Choson after the fall of the Shang dynasty around 1028 B.C. And this Kija line ruled northwestern Korea until overthrown by a Chinese military figure, Wiman, in 194 B.C. The Wiman Choson flourished with its capital at Pyongyang and transmitted its Chinese culture to the loosely knit Korean tribes.

The first truly Korean state, the kingdom of Koguryo, emerged around 100 B.C. It consolidated power in an area encompassing today's northern Korea, the Yalu River and along the Manchurian border. Before 500 A.D., tribes from the southern half of the peninsula were coalescing, the Silla kingdom appearing in the southeastern region and Perkche kingdom in the southwest.

From the ensuing struggle, Silla with its capital at Kyongjue merged triumphant over the Perkche. With Chinese help, Silla was able to consolidate its fortunes and introduce a golden period of prosperity for art, literature, law and government in the 6th century. These rulers adopted the Confucian system of social relationship, whereby the rulers assumed the role of sons or younger brothers to the Chinese emperors.

Unfortunately, by 935, Silla had peaceably surrendered to a new master, Wang Kon, founder of a state called Koryo (thus Korea), with its capital at Kaesong. In 1392, the Koryo dynasty was overthrown by General Yi who ascended the throne as King Taejo. This dynasty returned to the old name Choson for the country and moved the capital from Kaesong to Seoul. The dynasty lasted until 1910.

Despite Manchu attacks from the north and a Japanese

invasion during the 16th century, Choson remained faithful in its relationship to China. In the first half of the 19th century, amid drought, famine and sporadic peasant insurrection, Choson stood firm against any sort of contact with the West. Although Western trading ships and missionaries tried to "open" Choson as well as Japan and China, the Yi system under the Taewon'gun (Prince Regent) displayed a consistent belligerent attitude toward the West. This belligerence extended to the United States.

In early 1871 two American gunboats were fired upon and the ship General Sherman was burned on the Han River. The Sherman's crew was massacred. On 10 June, the marines landed with 109 men commanded by CAPT McLane W. Tilton. They attacked three forts along the Han and PVT James Dougherty killed the Korean commander. In this reprisal action requiring hand-to-hand combat, he was among five marines who earned the Medal of Honor.

In the last decade of the 19th century, the Japanese began to move on Choson, competing with China and Russia. In the Sino-Japanese War of 1894-95, they effectively eliminated China. And then in 1904-05, decisively defeated Russia. During the next five years they strengthened their grip on Choson. Destroying all vestige of independence, Japan ordered the army of Choson to be disbanded in 1907. By 1910, Choson was annexed to Japan as a virtual Japanese colony, Chosen.

During the next 35 years of occupation, Japanese became the official language of the government and courts. Japanese policy deluged the peninsula: administration, officials and police were completely in Japanese hands. The Japanese governors actively controlled all aspects of life through the use of spies, police and the army. Culture was suppressed. Use of the Korean language was prohibited. Efforts to preserve

Korean identity were stifled.

Koreans came to hate the Japanese and named them, "dwarf pirates." Koreans did adopt the language, however. They had no choice.

This dominance by the Japanese was so lasting that in 1950 when we marines needed to learn the rudiments of the language to communicate with the people, often it was the Japanese phrase that we were taught by the Koreans. Five years after the occupation, Japanese still was prevalent. In fact, even geographical locations might have two names, such as the Chosin Reservoir, also called the Changjin Reservoir, the region of the 1st Marine Division's noble winter battle.

At the end of World War II in 1945, after the Japanese defeat, Russia and the United States agreed upon occupation spheres of influence regarding Korea (the Japanese colony) and partitioned the country. The Japanese troops surrendered to the Russians north of the 38th degree parallel north latitude and to the United States troops south of that dividing line.

In the fall of that year, Soviet forces arrived at the 38th parallel and proceeded to sever roads, railways and telephone lines. Even more ominous, movement of people and commerce was stopped and a fortified frontier was established. They set-up a communist administration in Pyongyang and appointed a very youthful Kim Il-sung, the leader.

Kim, a life-long Korean Communist, had sporadically participated in hit-and-run fighting against the Japanese in Manchuria during the mid 1930s. His complete biography, however, appears to be clouded and the subject of myth and fantasy. Legend says he spent many years in the Soviet Union. Legend says he led massive Korean Communist resistance during Japanese occupation. Legend or not, he was exceptionally young, 33, when the Russians chose him in 1948. No matter what countless official tales recount his heroic deeds, the fact remains that the Soviet forces occupied the northern portion of Korea and they installed Kim Il-sung and his youthful cohorts as the communist puppet rulers.*

Perhaps Stalin considered the country rather inconsequential; yet he installed a readily compliant, fully indoctrinated disciple to make sure his orders were tacitly followed. Most definitely, in the next five years Stalin trained and armed these Korean puppets until they were strong enough to storm across the 38th.

Again at this point in history a mystery arises surrounding Kim's attack. Some believe he may have been struggling with rivals for power in his government and thought a fast invasion of South Korea, a uniting of Korea, would bring him the ultimate advantage over his rivals. Certainly, his army was superior to that of South Korea. Other accounts indicate that he visited Stalin in1949 to secure Stalin's sanction and backing. Stalin, however, told him to go back, to rethink his plan and to only return with a more concrete strategy. This he did—the consensus being that a swift strike by the North Koreans would avoid any move by the United States to rescue the South Koreans. As a result, the North Koreans quickly prepared for invasion.

Prior to the attack, the Russians trained and outfitted a modern army for Kim: automatic weapons, heavy artillery, T-34 tanks, trucks, 40 YAK fighters and 70 attack bombers. The Koreans could boast eight infantry divisions at full strength, two divisions at half strength, a motorcycle reconnaissance regiment, an armored brigade equipped with T-34 tanks, and

---

*Kim Il-sung died on July 9, 1994. He was 82.

five brigades of border constabulary. A force of some 135,000 troops.

Meanwhile, since 1945, an elderly but vigorous anti-Communist Korean patriot, Syngman Rhee, gained power and became president over the South Korean government organized by the United States. (Probably because he lived most of his life in the United States, this westernized version of his name is used in US history and by our press. Correctly Korean, his name is Rhee Syngman.) The old man was an irascible curmudgeon, a fact which led to frustration and stormy relations with American officials. Although the US supplied military weapons to Syngman Rhee, planes and tanks were not included for fear he would invade the north.

Following a policy which found Korea outside our defense perimeter, the US began withdrawing troops from Korea and by 1949 only 500 military advisers were left. Privately, the advisers did not believe that the South Koreans could repulse an invasion from the north.

Thus the events played out to war.

Yet the people, the land and the tradition remained oblivious to man's folly. As people, Koreans were the nationality that other Orientals looked down on. They were considered rustic, backward and uncultured.

Traditionally, women wore a short blouse tied together by a bow, and a high-waisted, long, full skirt. For men, bloomer-like trousers and a loose jacket also tied with a bow were traditional. In summer, however, the blouse and jacket were replaced with a white vest, and in rural areas only the open vest was worn above the waist by both sexes. On their feet were rubber shoes with pointed slightly turned-up toes.

The typical house in rural areas (Korea was mostly rural) had two to four rooms with walls of clay, wood or pounded earth, topped with a thatched or tiled roof. It was either

L-shaped or U-shaped. Similar to the Japanese, the interior walls and ceilings were paper; windows were made of semi-transparent paper but sometimes of glass. The heating system was unique and indirect. Through a system of flues connected to the stove in the kitchen, heat was passed under the floor, keeping rooms toasty; the dwellers slept in sleeping pads and covers on the floor. Fuel was wood collected from the mountains, and the collecting had continued for centuries. By 1950 the hills and mountains were practically de-nuded. (Fortunately, today, a reforestation program and modern heating methods have caused a greening of Korea.)

Sanitation by our standards was wretched. The fertilizer used in the fields on the crops was human. This waste was collected in a small out-building adjacent to the house, similar to "outhouses" found in the backwoods of this country. The convenience of stationary seating, however, was not available. Standing, straddling or squatting was necessary. Transportation of the waste to the fields was provided by "honey buckets." The farmer carried a beam of wood or a yoke across his shoulders from which on each end was suspended wooden buckets by ropes. In summer, the pungent odor was enough to make a toughened marine turn green.

Rice tea was their favorite beverage. Rice was the staple food, steamed and eaten with a wide variety of side dishes. Among these kimchi, fermented white radish and Chinese cabbage, was paramount. Obviously, this not only guaranteed flatulence but also acrid, odoriferous bowels. Perhaps this was best described by one of my squad members while on patrol one day. It had started to rain on this warm spring afternoon and the platoon leader stopped the patrol. Passing by the source for a farmer's "honey buckets," my buddy and I were stopped near it. Undecided as to whether to brave the stench and get in out of the rain or stay out and get wet, he said succinctly, "God, that fuckin' gook shit stinks."

The Chinese, on the other hand, held a higher position in the Oriental hierarchy.

For the last several thousand years, China had maintained a relationship with Korea—sometimes as ruler, sometimes as benefactor or both. Although a few cadres of Koreans had fought for Mao Zedong's Communist Chinese forces against the Japanese, the occupation of Korea by the Japanese in the first half of the 20th century effectively severed any Chinese relationship. Moreover, at the end of World War II, the Russians instigated an agreement with the United States to partition the country and gain control of the north. Watching with concerned interest the Soviet building of the North Korean Peoples' Army (NKPA), Mao's government became even more troubled with the Soviet-backed invasion of the south.

Despite their chasm of differences—chief among which was that Mao could hardly tolerate Stalin's complete indifference to him, the Chinese and Russians still maintained coldly tolerant speaking terms. Much more important to these leaders was the real uncertainty whether the Americans would resort to use of the atomic bomb. They believed this to be a viable option. So with great caution, they approached the events taking place in Korea.

Crossing the 38th parallel, the NKPA quickly seized Seoul. Bulldozing all before them, they swept the peninsula and surrounded Pusan, the port at the southern end. At this Pusan Perimeter, the invasion that had commenced in June 1950, was finally stopped. Now came the events of August. (See Map 1)

To gather the impression that the Chinese lacked intelligence gathering and contact with the Koreans as well as the Russians would be incorrect. In fact, Chinese liaison officers were accepted "observers" in the North Korean Army. Such an observer was Colonel Wong Lichan. He accompanied Korean Colonel-General Kang Kon who led the drive south.

The General, surprisingly tall for a Korean, was a personal friend of Kim Il-sung. They had been guerrillas together since age 16. Surely this aided Kang's winning the leadership of the invasion. And on August 4, he was poised to wipe out the remaining Pusan resistance.

This was not to be. At last, the Americans put up not only a stiff defense but also out fought the NKPA on the ground. US airpower incessantly pounded the NKPA as well as their extended supply lines. Then General Kang Kon (King Kong to the Americans) was killed by a land mine. The death of North Korea's ablest leader seemed to incapacitate the army, making it temporarily leaderless and vulnerable.

The NKPA suffered 40% casualties, some 50,000 killed and wounded. Even with Kim Il-sung's continued mobilization and supply of fresh troops, this enormous attrition could not be sustained. In the view of the Chinese Peoples Liberation Army (PLA), 30% casualties brought a combat unit close to disintegration—a 40% loss, untenable.

The Chinese observer, Colonel Wong Lichan, reported this NKPA calamity to the PLA command in Peking.

On August 6, Mao Zedong summoned his generals to conference. Among them were General Zhu De, Commander in Chief, Peoples Liberation Army (PLA), and General Peng Dehuai, Commander in Chief, of the yet to be formed Chinese People's Volunteers (CPV). Mao wanted to move a sizable army through Manchuria and into Korea in the span of three weeks. Others of his staff argued that it would take up to four months. Nevertheless, entering the war was the subject at hand.

A number of reasons underlay this determination of Mao.

After driving out the Japanese, he turned to fighting Chang Kai-shek and the Nationalist Chinese. Defeating these armies, Mao drove Chang off the mainland to Taiwan. At this point, the PLA felt invincible, now burgeoned by Communist Chinese forces, former war-lord armies, and even Nationalist armies, who changed sides. Most of these survivors had been fighting for upwards of 20 years—most all of them soldiers from their 'teens. With this mighty force, soldiers and generals, alike, wanted to invade Taiwan and unite China under the communist banner.

But President Truman had dispatched the Seventh Fleet to the Taiwan Strait to protect the Nationalists. In no position to challenge this naval force, the Chinese were held impotent.

Again, in Mao's view, a unified Communist Korea was vital; but disaster loomed. The Russian created NKPA had faltered in its bid for re-unification. They had shot their bolt on the Pusan perimeter. And Russian policy dictated that satellites should do the fighting—a policy that lasted beyond Vietnam until Afghanistan. They, doubtlessly, would not send back-up troops.

In fact, the South Korean and US sponsored United Nations troops might even push the NKPA north, up the peninsula. What about an amphibious landing behind the NKPA? What about the atomic bomb? The Chinese might tolerate Syngman Rhee's lack-luster forces close to Manchuria, but not those of the Western nations.

The Revolutionary Committee, Mao's group at the meeting that day, spent a great deal of time pondering the subject and all of its aspects. After lengthy consideration, they decided to prepare a contingency plan to back-up the NKPA in case the battle front deteriorated even more.

Indeed, General Peng Dehuai was dispatched quickly to Shenyang, Manchuria, to prepare plans as soon as possible for any eventuality. Ironically enough, Peng arrived and began his preparations on September 4th, just about the time we Oklahoma boys were joining the Marines. As Mao's choice, the General was to lead the People's Volunteer Army (PVA), composed of regular units from throughout China ordered to Korean service. Of course, the "volunteers" were in name only, ostensibly to imply little or no support from the Chinese government or the People's Liberation Army (PLA).

Although only half could be considered combat ready, the strength of the PLA totaled some 5,100,000. Four field armies were the principal units for selection. In northwestern China, the First Army comprised 34 field armies. Poised for an invasion of Tibet, the Second Army consisted of 49 field armies. Charged with the initial attack on Taiwan was the Third Army with 72 field armies. The Fourth Army, totaling 59 field armies, was divided between Manchuria and southern China. Another 39 field armies were stationed under the North China Army. (Chinese field armies numbered between 10,000 and 11,000 men.) Additionally, another 2.6 million men were located in local defense and construction corps.

Gargantuan in size, the Chinese People's Liberation Army's greatest problem was mobility. Logistics and communications were gigantic, almost insurmountable constraints. In fact, the inadequate rail network would be the limiting factor deciding the number of troops, the quantity of supplies, and their time of arrival for any massing of troops in Manchuria before crossing the border into Korea.

Perhaps of only slightly lesser importance to mobility was the unsophisticated weaponry. The PLA was not a modern army by any sense. Mao's army fought, for the most part, with captured Japanese weapons. The typical soldier carried a Japanese .25 caliber rifle. But 20% carried no weapons. It would be necessary for them to pick up a weapon from the dead and wounded on the battlefield.

By 1949, the PLA had captured millions of rifles, several hundred thousand machineguns, thousands of artillery pieces, hundreds of tanks, armored cars and airplanes from the defeated Nationalists. And although some of the weaponry was American, most of the captured equipment was junk, worn-out, or scrap.

In any case, replacement parts were not available. The obvious solution: purchase new arsenals from Russia, transport the plants to China and fabricate military hardware. This was a plan for the future. It could not be a reality in time to benefit the People's Volunteer Army. They would fight with what was available.

Each Chinese soldier in combat carried a ration of cooked food consisting of rice, beans, and corn as well as adequate small arms ammunition in amounts to last him four or five days. He was self-sufficient. He needed no fire to cook his food. Indeed, he traveled light over rugged terrain and left no sign of his presence.

Peng's plans were flexible. He did not recommend an all-out assault nor a strictly guerilla campaign. Although some of his officers thought the Americans could be lured north into the vast mountains and deep ravines, he doubted the Americans would be that stupid and chose the plan of stopping any invasion of North Korea at the narrowest neck of the peninsula, north of Pyongyang.

Additionally, his specialists reasoned that three regiments of porters or coolies would be needed to move food and ammunition from Manchuria to the PVA, wherever they fought. Thus the plans were laid for China's entrance into the war.

On 15 September, the American Marines landed at

Inchon. By 29 September, Seoul was retaken and the NKPA rout headed north brokenly past the 38th. The effectiveness of the North Korean Army had ceased. They were no longer a viable force; only remnants fought on.

Now, the United Nations forces (mostly US) conducted a limited operation centered on the capture of Pyongyang, the North Korean capital, as well as the industrial cities of the eastern coast. To this end on 15 October, the Marines sailed for Wonsan and subsequently in late October to Hungnam. MacArthur's cautious policy at this time was to take these areas and leave the territory bordering China to the South Korean troops, so as not to alarm Peking. Only a few weeks later, he changed his mind and pushed all his troops toward the Yalu.

Similarly, at first the Chinese were cautious. But on 14 October, the first Chinese troops crossed the Yalu River on old Japanese built bridges which connected Andong, Manchuria and Sinuiju, Korea. These were the advanced troops of General Peng's People's Volunteer Army (PVA), known as the 13th Army Group, commanded by General Li Tianyu. Taking up blocking positions along the Chungchon River in North Korea, the field armies of the 13th faced the US Eighth Army some 60 miles south of the Manchurian border. Other field armies of the 13th would advance to the east coast.

In November the 9th Army Group, commanded by General Song Shilun, entered Korea, 120,000 strong, to move against the U.S. Marines at the Chosin Reservoir. With this force the strength of the PVA totaled 380,000 men.

To hide their movement the PVA set forested mountains afire. And this great conflagration created a pall which hovered over the peaks and covered the movements of the Chinese. The troops marched at night, slept during the day in deep ravines or forests and covered their tracks. They maneuvered in the wild mountainous vastness between the UN commands.

Hoping the Americans would stop and evacuate North Korea, the Chinese failed in their signals. Some few Chinese were captured and caused far-reaching confusion. They wore North Korean uniforms and were the early contingent of some 2000, supplied by North Korea. Unfortunately, this Chinese message to stop, discreetly sent to the American command, was misunderstood. The Americans saw only a few Chinese, dressed in Korean uniforms, joining the last-ditch efforts of the North Korean Army.

The American command did not get the picture after capturing soldiers who could understand neither Korean or Japanese. Even a South Korean general who had served with the Japanese army in Manchuria, upon inspecting the dead of one battle, declared them to be Chinese. MacArthur, however, refused to believe the Chinese would enter the war.

To the Americans, the Korean war was strictly military. To the Chinese, the impending elimination of North Korea by Western forces was not only a threat to their internal security but also a threat to their emerging leadership in Asia. The Chinese decisions were politically motivated. The decisions of MacArthur were an attempt to regain past glories.

The Chinese attacked around October 26th, and the ROKs, Republic of Korea Army, broke first. By 1 November, the U.S. Eighth Army was in retreat before the Chinese 13th Army Group. The Chinese employed their usual successful tactic: surround, encircle and exterminate.

At the combat level, company and battalion commanders utilized buglers to relay commands. Additionally, each commander carried a whistle for the same purpose. As he went into battle, both of these options were available to direct the orders of the leader. On the PVA side, it served the same purpose as our radios. On the UN side, as the ones being attacked, this cacophony was frightening.

As the U.S. Eighth Army broke, the PVA were successful beyond their wildest dreams. As they thrust south this ragtag army that lacked modern weapons and was not properly clothed or equipped for winter was supplied by the American taxpayer. First, they were supplied uniforms, weapons and food obtained from the fleeing ROKS. Of course, these supplies had come from American support. Later, boots, watches, heavy weapons and assorted supplies as well as C-rations were captured from the retreating Eighth Army. Even radios, tents and maps became available. The Chinese soldiers now carried the weapons of the U.S.Army—M-1 rifles, .30 caliber Browning machineguns, bazookas, sleeping bags, ponchos, backpacks, even meat and Sterno stoves. Tons of supplies lay about abandoned just for the taking, all litter from the retreating Americans.

Promises of guns, ammunition and food from Manchuria were voiced by commanders. But there was no need. Superior quality equipment was at hand. Persistently, however, rumors maintained that artillery batteries for reinforcement of the Chinese had crossed into Korea but were heavily bombed, adding that Major Mao Anying, Chairman Mao's eldest son, was among those killed. Yet heartened by fast and easy victories, armed, warmly clothed and fully fed, the soldiers unanimously agreed that the Americans were not only made out of soft stuff but also were truckbound. For them, wheels were a necessity. The Americans were not made of the stuff required to trudge up the mountains and fight real battles. The British, Australians and Scots agreed and made their derogatory remarks generally with more ribaldry and scorn, one of the less derisive being, "You barstards can't fight your way out of a paper bag."

Unfortunately for the Chinese, the ecstasy of looting the U.S. Eighth Army abandoned supplies was short lived. Although extremely mobile on foot, the troops could not carry what might hamper their long marches. They traveled extremely lightly. So, eventually, they threw away much of their booty.

Having liberated Pyongyang for Kim Il-sung, General Peng commanded more than 300,000 troops by early December. His 9th Army Group of 120,000 men under General Song Shilun were attacking the American X Corps beachhead, the 7th InfantryDivision and the 1st Marine Division, in the northeast. General Li Tianyu and the 13th Army Group of 180,000 men pursued the U.S. Eighth Army down the west side of the peninsula.* **

For perspective, a review of the battle order reveals that the PVA commanded by Peng consisted of the 9th Army Group commanded by Song and the 13th Army Group commanded by Li. The 9th with120,000 men, consisting of the 20th, 26th, 27th and 30th field armies, opposed the Marines and the X Corps. The 13th, 180,000 men strong, with the 38th, 39th, 40th, 41st, 42nd, 50th (former Nationalists) and 66th field armies were advancing down the west side of the peninsula against the U.S. Eighth Army. Finding no source

---

*A divided UN command existed during this period. MacArthur exerted direct control over Major General Edward Almond and the X Corps. Thus, the UN force in the northeast was not under the command of Lieutenant General Walton Walker, commander of the Eighth Army.
**An interesting point should be mentioned here. From the many accounts of the Chinese entry into the war, a curious revelation in the references is notable. The Chinese general's names appear to be different. Chinese oriented references refer to the People's Volunteer Army commander as General Peng Dehuai. In Western and Marine Corps oriented texts, he is Lin Piao.

to the contrary, apparently the reinforced field armies of Peng's PVA numbered some 30,000 troops, more than the 10,000 to 11,000 men of the regular Chinese PLA field armies.

The Marines had inched their way some 70 miles up the narrow gauge railway tracks from Hungnam to the Chosin (Changjin) Reservoir when new orders came to strike inland toward Kanggye, the new hiding place of Kim Il-sung. Apparently, this was an attempt to draw the Chinese away from the disaster they were inflicting on the U.S. Eighth Army. But the Chinese attacked the Marines in strength.

The subsequent Marine breakout from the Chinese trap, bringing out their dead and their weapons in December 1950, is history. This running fight has been described as a battle unparalleled in US military history. The 1st Marine Division had beaten off at least seven Chinese divisions and left the 9th Army Group prostrate with crippling losses of over 40,000 troops dead and thousands more wounded or suffering from frostbite.

Although the Marines were praised, Gen. Walker's U.S. Eighth Army was skewered by the media. Some called their debacle America's worst military beating since Pearl Harbor; others termed the disaster the worst defeat the United States

---

Because the Korean and Chinese orientation bears examination in this chapter, the Chinese names are utilized. Nevertheless, it seems journalists and historians were attempting the same sounds. The last name, Peng and Lin, require a beginning consonant or hard sound followed by an "in" sound. Likewise, his first name begins with the same consonant, D or P, followed by sounds of "ee" then "o." To some extent, similar differences between texts occur regarding Generals Li Tianyu and Song Shilun who, for example, appears as Sung Shin-lun. And, of course, the positioning of names is the opposite of Western names. In Asia, the family name or surname comes before the given name.

had ever suffered.

On the other hand, the Chinese were praising General Li of the13th Army Group; but General Song of the 9th Army Group, graduate of Whampo Military Academy and veteran of Mao's Long March, offered to resign because of his unsuccessful attack on the Marines. His man responsible for the attack, General Zhang, threatened suicide.

Startling to the generals was the fact that not all the soldiers were killed in the battle. From reliable sources was drawn a picture of uncountable numbers of snowmen in the fields and mountains surrounding the Chosin Reservoir battle. Upon inspection of the snowmen, investigators found frozen people inside. Whole platoons, rifles on shoulders, were found squatting in squad order. Coolies pressed down by their heavy A-frames, women refugees with their children, even old men sitting upright were frozen hillocks in the snow.

Peng and his generals formulated a face-saving summary of excuses: the terrible weather, supply problems, air attacks, lack of firepower. The soldiers' clothing in the 9th Army Group was issued for a Taiwan invasion. They maintained more men died of cold than bullets. This included coolies hauling supplies; thus few supplies were delivered. Combat was continuously broken off because ammunition had been depleted. Of course, air attacks were constant. In self-criticism General Song admitted his overdispersal of troops denied the opportunity to strike the Marines in force along their route of withdrawal.

One division was unable to outflank and split the enemy, taking heavy casualties when it attacked from the front. Another was repelled because it had mistakenly thought the enemy had been completely destroyed, and did not take advantage of the enemy's confusion. Other troops were criticized

for being unfamiliar with the terrain and moving so slug-
gishly that an attack was postponed for four days. They
refer to US troops breaking out of the trap because of the huge
number of air attacks and the intense firepower from sea
and air.

But weather and inadequate supplies are blamed for cre-
ating the worst losses. The troops carried only seven days'
worth of food and ammunition. (Other sources say four
days.) No winter uniforms were issued and grain and ammunition supplies were delayed.

Armed with his summary, General Peng flew off to
Peking to convince Chairman Mao that it was time to supply
the People's Volunteer Army with modern weaponry. He
proclaimed that to prevent any future fiasco similar to the
northeast Korea disaster, Mao should purchase and equip
Peng's army with modern Russian equipment. Mao must
have agreed. For, apparently, during the next three years,
much of the output of Soviet arsenals went to China. And, on
face value, this was not surprising. China had taken the
place of North Korea in the unification attempt or, at least, to
save the Communist north. And Russia continued its time-
tested policy—help the satellites, but let them fight the war.

Abundantly clear, however, is the fact that unlike the
13th, the 9th Army Group at the Chosin Reservoir was not
able to re-supply themselves from the Marines, which contributed to the Chinese catastrophe. In this case the American
taxpayer did not lose. With the 9th Army Group a skeleton,
with the coolie supply lines over-extended from Manchuria
to the 13th Army Group invadingSeoul, with transportation
and movement limited to darkness because of air attacks,
the war took another dreadful turn for the PVA.

In late December, while riding in his jeep, the U.S. Eighth
Army commander, General Walton Walker was killed in an

accident. MacArthur selected 55 year old, Lieutenant General Matthew B."Matt" Ridgway as his replacement. He also abolished the divided command. (X Corps, including the 1st Marine Division, and the U.S. Eighth Army) At this point, the entire United Nations force was placed under Ridgway's command—some 365,000 men. MacArthur never again dabbled in Korean field operations.

After turning around his troops' defeatist attitudes, Ridgway inaugurated his new military philosophy. He got his troops off their butts. They abandoned the road columns of trucks and met the enemy at the mountain tops. They brought to bear all the fire power possible on the enemy and that was considerable. As these "bugle blowing, whistle shrilling" Chinese charged in their engulfing tactics, Ridgway concentrated his fire on their masses. The concept was called the "meatgrinder." In the new year, Ridgway's concept worked well. The Chinese began to suffer huge loses.

Another tragedy developed in Seoul. Syngman Rhee's death squads were at work. Before the Chinese drove through the South Korean capital, these murderers were ruthlessly executing thousands of political prisoners, not necessarily communists but rather political opponents of the South Korean president. British troops came across truckloads of abject men and women with their hands bound behind their backs with electrical wire, who were forced to kneel in trenches and executed, shot in the backs of their heads. When the city was retaken in February, the squads renewed their work.

In January, Ridgway's "meatgrinder" cost the Chinese enormous casualties in taking Wonju. And that was as far south as General Peng's People's Volunteer Army penetrated. Like the Koreans at Pusan, the Chinese had shot their bolt.

Describing the Chinese attack in October through December, the *U.S.Marine Operations in Korea*, Vol IV, maintains:

—the blunt fact remains that the United Nations forces had been beaten in spite of an overwhelming superiority in aircraft, artillery, armor, and transport as well as command of the sea. Stateside Americans can scarcely be blamed for asking themselves why their well-equipped divisions had been defeated twice within six weeks by an Asiatic peasant army using semiguerrilla tactics and depending largely on small arms, mortars, and light artillery.

The answer cannot be given in simplified terms. Although the Chinese Reds were represented by a peasant army, it was also a first-rate army when judged by its own tactical and strategic standards. Military poverty might be blamed for some of its deficiencies in arms and equipment, but its semi-guerrilla tactics were based on a mobility which could not be burdened with heavy weapons and transport. The Chinese coolie in the padded cotton uniform could do one thing better than any other soldier on earth; he could infiltrate around an enemy position in the darkness with unbelievable stealth. Only Americans who have had such an experience can realize what a shock it is to be surprised at midnight with the grenades and submachine gun slugs of gnome-like attackers who seemed to rise out of the very earth.

Nevertheless, in the aftermath of the Chosin fiasco, the 13th Army Group spread its forces across two-thirds of the peninsula from the Yellow Sea. The depleted 9th Army Group, re-enforced by three newly formed North Korean corps, attempted to hold the eastern front next to the Sea of Japan.

At this juncture both countries, China and North Korea, began intensive recruiting for their armies with a "Hate America" campaign. These men who filled the ranks of the armies were little more than cannon fodder. Recent recruits, charged up by the hate campaign, experienced little more than three weeks training. Some came to the front who could not fire a rifle.

As described in China's "Hate America" drive of early 1951, the Americans were accused of practicing all manner of bestialities, including cannibalism. Not only the illiterate peasant masses but also the soldiers in Korea were indoctrinated with this propaganda by their political commissars.

North Korea's attack was more concrete than ideological. It took the form of a museum, which contained the "atrocities" committed by the American soldiers during the 52 days they occupied the country between October and December 1950.

Blond, blue-eyed American soldiers with wolf-like grins, claws for hands and long, hooked noses leer from the walls of this war museum. Glass cases hold fire-charred cloth shoes said to be from women and children locked in storehouses without food or water and eventually burned to death. Other cases hold swatches of black hair, some still braided and caked with mud, said to have been recovered from corpses of women weighted down by stones and thrown into a reservoir. And still another contains a dagger said to have been used to cut out eyeballs of civilians, and a gasoline can with USA on the side that was alleged to have been used to start the massacre fires.

American soldiers are charged in general, but one officer in particular is the center of hate. This officer, D. Madden Harrison, it is claimed, ordered his troops to bury alive everyone in the country. The museum officials maintain that he was very cunning and while the Americans retreated south in

November and December 1950, he escaped by boat to an off-shore island, becoming an intelligence commander who organized agents to send against North Korea. There is one photo of him—or rather his back.

(The museum exists, almost a half century later, to hand down accounts that the North Koreans accept as history.)

A final vignette or two to this "alternate look" at our enemy. The former Nationalist army that changed sides and became the 50th field army of the 13th Army Group under General Li was virtually wiped out in the final battle for Seoul as Ridgway and his troops fought back up the peninsula in January 1951.

Lastly, General Peng Dehuai (Lin Piao), the esteemed hero and commander of the Chinese People's Volunteer Army, became a Marshal of the People's Liberation Army of China in 1955. Later, during the Great Leap Forward, he criticized Mao and was stripped of his command. In 1974 the Red Guards of the Cultural Revolution grabbed the poor old marshal and tortured him to death. In 1980, however, he was posthumously rehabilitated as a Chinese hero.

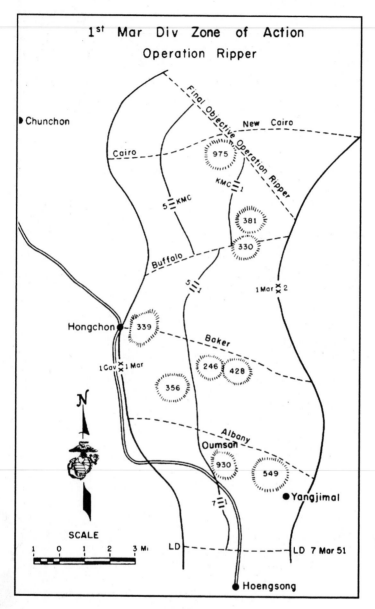

MAP 2

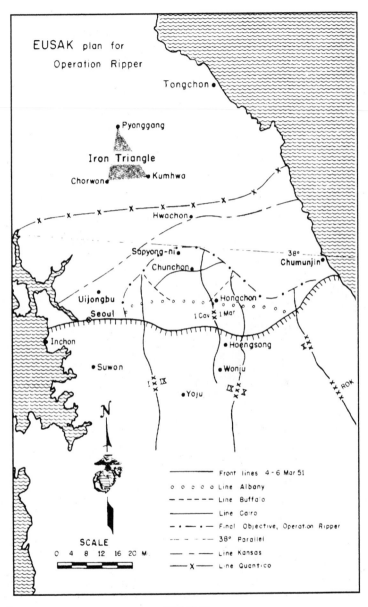

EUSAK plan for
Operation Ripper

Tongchon•

•Pyonggang

Iron Triangle

Chorwon• •Kumhwa

×—×—×—×—×—×—×—×

Hwachon•

Sapyong-ni• 38°
Chunchon• Chumunjin•

Uijongbu•
Seoul Hongchon•
1 Cav ×× 1 Mar

Inchon• •Hoengsong

•Suwon •Wonju

N

I ×× IX •Yoju ×× ×××ROK

SCALE
0 4 8 12 16 20 Mi.

——————— Front lines 4 - 6 Mar 51
o o o o o o Line Albany
— — — — — Line Buffalo
——————— Line Cairo
—·—·—·— Final Objective, Operation Ripper
—··— — — 38° Parallel
— — — — Line Kansas
—×— Line Quantico

MAP 3

CHAPTER SIX

OPERATION RIPPER

When the North Koreans assaulted the South in June 1950, General MacArthur was the Commander in Chief in the Far East. His below strength occupation army in Japan, the Eighth Army, included four divisions of some 12,500 men—an extreme reduction in strength from wartime. Quickly he ordered contingents to Korea commanded by Lieutenant General Walton Walker. Through the summer and into the fall, U.S. Reserves, Airborne Divisions, Regimental Combat Teams as well as the 1st Marine Division, ROKs, and the armies of UN members augmented MacArthur's army in Korea.

Detached from the Eighth Army in September and ordered to the landing at Inchon, the X (Tenth) Corps under Major General Edward Almond became the immediate command of MacArthur, not General Walker, who continued to command the remainder of the Eighth. At the Chosin Reservoir, the X Corps included the 1st Marine Division and the U.S. Army 7th Infantry Division. Later the U.S. Army 2nd Infantry Division joined the Corps. Nevertheless, a divided command existed until Walker's accidental death in December.

With the appointment of General Ridgway to ground commander in Korea, MacArthur relinquished his control of the X Corps and Ridgway assumed command of all UN forces. His command, the Eighth United States Army in Korea (EUSAK), was unified. On the evening of 7 March 1951, I joined "Dog" Company, 2nd Battalion, 1st Marines (Regiment), 1st Marine Division, IX Corps, EUSAK.

When I joined the squad, the "Andys" doubled in number. The other Andy, CPL James Anderson, the gunner of our squad, took me under his wing since I was the new man. That dreadful first night on the front lines required the protection of an experienced marine. He showed me how to dig my foxhole and how to set up my shelter half for protection against the elements.

He explained to me what was happening:

> You see, Andy, when we set up, we form a perimeter defense. Now, you can't see it all from right here 'cause our line goes 'round the hill. But just imagine a horse shoe. We're set up in a semi-circle. Now, every platoon is in that type of defense when they set up. You see, they can be self-defending. They don't have to connect to the next platoon or company. And you can occupy more ground that way with space in between.
>
> Now, you see, we're on the right side of the horseshoe. We're not facin' the front, exactly. So tonight what you'll be doin' on first watch is to look for movement out in that rice paddy in front of us. You're an ammo carrier; but when we're set up, it's your responsibility, along with the other ammo carriers, to protect and defend the machinegun with your rifle fire.
>
> And another thing. We all smoke on watch. But there's a right way and a wrong way. I want

you to cup both your hands around the cigarette.
Particularly when you take a drag. When you light
up get your head in your sleeping bag. 'Cause a
cigarette ember can be seen at 300 or 400 yards at
night. And those gooks will zero in on you.

Now, mind what I told you and you'll live longer.

"OK; I will," I said with real apprehension for
fear I might forget something.

Oh, if you have any questions, anytime, just ask
me.

He went back to his hole. Then I was alone and
on first watch.

My foxhole was extremely uncomfortable and the next
few hours became a restless, doubting time. Was that some
movement out there in the moonlight? Should I call to the
next hole for help? Did I really dig my foxhole deep enough?
What would combat really be like? Could those gooks see the
glow of my cigarette?

Finally, my wristwatch indicated that my watch was over
and I crawled halfway out of my hole and in a low voice
called Andy for his watch. When he answered, I crawled
back into my hole and went deeply to sleep, except to be
awakened once by rifle fire from around the hill to the front.

The morning came with the smell of coffee and cook
fires, as well as the crunch of someone walking past to
Andy's hole. Whoever it was laughingly remarked to Andy
that last night Arch got it right through the horns.

I stretched and rose up out of my hole to see Andy standing by his. So I asked him, "What does getting it right
between the horns mean?"

"Well, you heard that firing last night, didn't you? That
was around in front. The gooks will come up in scouting
maneuvers to see where we are. They're not attacking.

They're just feeling us out. So there was a skirmish and ol'
Arch, over there, got a bullet right between the eyes.'

"Right between the horns," he repeated, shook his head
and walked off to the breakfast fire, chuckling.

Obviously, ol' Arch, whoever he was, had been killed; but
the way he had been killed was a joke.

With these crusty veterans, compassion and sentimentality
were reserved for their personal group and friendships were
cautiously formed. Arch was from another platoon of the
company. This seemingly insignificant fact went unnoticed
on my first day, for I did not yet understand war. But combat was learned quickly and my new awareness appeared in
my next letter.

***

March 16, 1951

Dear Folks,

Well, I'm a combat veteran, now. I went out on
patrol and I wasn't scared. I haven't been scared
from the time we hit Korea. Bullets flying around
don't bother me a bit. They say old veterans are
scared when they go into battle but I don't think so,
because I'm not.

Although when we went out on patrol, I think
somebody back home was praying for me because by
all rights I should have been hit.

I was the last ammunition carrier for our squad's
light .30 caliber machinegun and I was carrying two
cans of "ammo." We just got up to the knob of a little hill outside our lines when a bullet whistled past
my head. I just laughed about it. Out here when you

get shot at, you keep going because the machine-gun has to have the ammunition and, also, a moving target is hard to hit. It appeared, however, to be a random shot. Thank God, these Chinese are bad shots.

We were pushing out on patrol, searching for where the gook's were. Anyway, we went down the hill and continued across some rice paddies. (There is no cover at all in a rice paddy.) My platoon went up behind an old gook house for some protection; then quickly moved out across some more rice paddies leading up toward the notch between two wooded hills.

All of a sudden we were ambushed. We were caught in the crossfire of two Chinese machineguns set up on each of those wooded hills. And, I was right out in the open. After a few shots ripped past my feet, I was jerked behind a huge mound, fast, by our corpsman. (The Koreans bury their dead sitting upright at a prominent point overlooking their land. These round graves are earthen mounds above ground, maybe 4 feet high and 4 feet across, which provide good cover. I don't believe they have cemeteries.) So, our squad set up the machinegun by the mound and began to fire back. The Chinese finally got the range of our machinegun and the gunners jumped back down behind my mound for cover. Since we were just on a reconnaissance patrol, our platoon leader, the lieutenant, signaled to pull out.

Because we were providing covering fire for the rest of the platoon and the gunners were using my ammunition, I was left with the machinegun and our machinegun squad was the last to leave. When the platoon moved back and reached the safety of some hills to our rear, then we pulled out.

To escape the enemy gunfire, I ran as fast as I could, carrying two cans of ammo; but the rice paddy was down hill and muddy. I became overbalanced, went head over heels, splashed right into the muddy water between the furrows, and wallowed in the mud. I jumped up laughing so hard I now could hardly run. I wished someone could have taken a picture.

We headed around some more hills until our platoon got hit again. This time it was the column ahead of my squad that got hit; but, while I was moving up the road, I saw one of our guys in the mud in the rice paddy, shot in the back. I hear he lived. Generally, very few get killed. Usually the wounds are in the arms and legs.

When I saw him, I felt no sensation or sickness in my stomach. The things I expected like getting scared and getting sick from seeing people wounded hasn't happened to me. Combat doesn't bother me a bit. But, I wish the people back home could see that bloody guy in the mud. This is war; we need support from all the people, back home, not indifference. And, I wish they could see us as we really are over here. Just animals. Just existing.

You would hardly recognize me, now. I have a beard. I'm grimy with dirt. My fingers are orangy-brown, stained from the nicotine from cigarettes that I smoke on watch at night because I cup my hands closely around the cigarette so no light will get out. I wish the people back home could see the guys whose faces are discolored from dirt because it has been so long since they washed. Our only water is to drink. I haven't had my clothes off in weeks. I must smell awful because I can smell the other guys. There's dirt on and in everything because the ground, your foxhole, is your home. I wonder how it feels to take a nice hot shower? I wonder why some of the people back home don't care?

For some reason combat is not altogether fighting. We went through that skirmish and then the next day moved out into the attack. The Chinese must have fallen back because we didn't meet any resistance. With occasional light snow flurries, the first day we covered about four miles. I was carrying close to 100 pounds, counting my pack, my sleeping bag, parka, my .30 caliber M1 rifle and two cans of machinegun ammo. Each can weighs 20 pounds and has 250 rounds of ammunition in it.

That night we dug in on a steep sixty-degree slope on the side of a hill. The next day, cloudy and cold, with tanks in front of us, we pulled out, again, and attacked without resistance through a wide valley between ranges of mountains.

That afternoon, my squad stopped to rest in front of a Buddhist shrine, and some of the guys went inside to investigate. Some of them found straw prayer mats to line their foxholes that night. Others got silk scarves. But, one guy brought out a scroll with a picture of Buddha on it. Everybody got a big laugh out of that because there wasn't much he could do with it.

When we moved out, my back felt like it would

break. The ammo belts around my neck were biting in terribly. But, finally, we stopped and I rested while our tanks knocked out some gook machinegun emplacements on a hill some 200 yards away. That night, we set up our perimeter defense on that hill where those gooks had made their final stand.

The next few days, we patrolled with little or no resistance. Down mountains, up mountains, always with that ammo holding me back. Then, my feet began to pain me. They felt raw. I knew I had not looked at them or had my socks off for some time. Over here, we wear Sno-Pacs. The tops are leather, laced halfway up to the knee; but, the bottom part, the "shoe," is rubber. Just like wearing galoshes without shoes. They are supposed to keep water out, but no air circulates inside. So, my feet sweat.

Usually, we set up our defenses on the highest pinnacle around, of course. We had just gotten our foxholes dug, one day, when we got the word that we were going back to regimental headquarters. We jumped to one conclusion. This is what we had been waiting for, Division Reserve—a chance to shave and wash up, a chance to lie around.

Although a few trucks appeared in the valley below us, we still had to walk five miles down this long valley to the road where we would board the truck convoy which would take us to our reserve. As we began our hike out, we piled our ammo and packs on the available trucks below our perimeter. On this five mile march, my feet caused so much pain that I hobbled most of the way and was one of the last to get there.

When we finally got to the road, we found out

that the 5th Marines were going to take our positions and we were going to go up and help out the 7th
Marines. I could hardly walk and turned myself in
to the corpsman.

I hear the 7th Marines (those we, the 1st Marines,
went to help) really got hit. So, it looks like I'm
missing out on a battle.

Now, I'm in a field hospital 40 miles behind the
lines. I've got the first stages of trench foot. They call
it hyperhydrosis. The bottoms of my feet are raw in
places. But, the Doc just came around and said I
would go back to duty tomorrow but not up to the
lines. That means, I'll probably be going to Division
casual company. That's a holding company for those
awaiting orders to go back to their regular outfit.
The Doc says I won't go back until supply can get me
some field boots instead of Sno-Pacs, which cause
my feet to sweat and blister.

So that's where I am, now. Write soon, I haven't
gotten a letter yet.

Love,

Burton

Although I commented on my feeling of bravery in my
letter, I had not seen real combat. The Chinese were re-
grouping and the skirmishes we encountered were mere holding actions. During the month of March, I thought I was a
part of "Operation Killer." That was the original name given
to this operation, the purpose of which was to move the UN
line north, recapture Seoul, and reach the 38th parallel once
again. But it caused enormous consternation when that title
reached Washington. The State Department was trying to
devise ways to negotiate with the Chinese to end the war

and this title implied killing Chinese. The Joint Chiefs of Staff protested to General Ridgway, who changed the name to "Operation Ripper."

Also my letter did not reveal other aspects of combat that I had learned quickly. In combat the nervousness of the veteran is directly related to his time in the field. Generally, the less time, the more nervous. This trauma manifests itself in increased frequency of bodily functions.

On patrol or in the attack, everyone must urinate, but the newer the person, the more frequently he must relieve himself. Korea was hilly and mountainous with endless trails on the ridgeline. Normally the combat team moved along the trails single file with members jumping out to piss then jumping back in line. The real problem that slowed the advance would occur if too many had to take a "crap."*

Another point in my letter alluded to "digging in" at night. It said nothing, however, about standing watches. Of course, that was a necessity. The gooks might come to feel out our lines. They wanted to know where we were just as

---

*Bodily functions alone among the obvious reasons are basic to why women are unsuited for combat. There is no privacy in war. It is natural survival, even barbaric. Women have never taken a major part in combat—in any culture, in any country, in any period of history. Certainly they may have appeared in rebellions, in revolutions or insurrections. But once a movement or government is established, the state does not send its women into combat—for they provide procreation of the species.

Because men are basically stronger than women, in hand to hand combat, the odds are that a woman is not going to win. And love liaisons would be disastrous. Each man needs to rely on his buddies and he needs everyone's attention. What must not be condoned is two lovers (heterosexual or homosexual) with their own agenda.

In combat men are excited, apprehensive and nervous. Thus a reaction occurs; they have to piss incessantly. A man can remain standing. He can even continue to walk, urinate and be alert to his surroundings. Even if prone, taking cover from fire, he can still piss in that position if necessary.

much as we wanted to know where they were. The striking difference was that they patrolled at night; we patrolled during the day. The reason was our airpower.

Winter died hard that year. Snow flurries, gray skies and cold nights lasted until April. In the late gray afternoon our platoon leader would set up our perimeter defense, usually on a hillside or mountain top, anchored by machineguns at strategic positions. Of course, my squad dug holes on each side of the gun hole—two men per foxhole. Operationally charted at eight men per squad and two squads per section, our squad seldom numbered more than five or six, the section seldom more than 11 or 12.

Most of the time our squad front consisted of three foxholes, two foxhole buddies in each.

The first order of business required digging the foxholes. Often we had to help dig the gun hole before digging our own. Certainly the machinegun was to be protected. And at times, quickly. We accomplished the digging with our entrenching

---

Unfortunately, in her quest for equality in combat, the feminist must expect equality in pissing also. A woman cannot see much squatted down and immobile. The man standing, watchful for the enemy; the woman, squatting, unable to be cautious. What a wonderful picture of equal opportunity—pissing together in combat!

After Desert Storm, the media presented the case for women in combat by presenting a female soldier's version. She maintained that although she was in a support unit, it was like being in combat because she was close to the front and subject to SCUD attacks. She and another female soldier sacked in a tent with four males. She said they worked things out because the males left when it was time for the females to change their uniforms or night clothes.

I believe she missed the point! There are no tents in combat. No privacy in combat; no civility in combat!

Combat is primitive man. Combat is back to basics—survival of the fittest.

It's a man's game, not meant for women.

tool. Each marine carried one attached to his pack.*

After "humping" the ridgeline for eight hours carrying close to 100 pounds and after digging foxholes, none of us felt like light hearted conversation. Actually, comment was almost non-existent and relegated to absolutely necessary grunts. Bone weary, we gathered twigs and branches for a fire. Although small individual Sterno stoves sized to heat our ration cans were a part of our C-rations, for some of the troop our bonfire served not only for warmth, but also for cooking rations and warming coffee.

Surprisingly, in spite of our exertion we were not ravenously hungry and we hurried our meal, stomped the embers down, and covered them with sand scraped up with our helmets.

When darkness came we either went to sleep or went on watch, our shifts usually lasting two hours. Obviously, with 12 hours of darkness a squad of six could handle the job. Fewer squad members or threat of imminent attack, however, might require longer watch schedules.

A mid-watch was the least desirable. Being awakened from a sound sleep left us clouded and dreamy minded. After the watch, finding sleep again became difficult. But as the morning wake-up call came down the line, the mid-watch was usually sound asleep again. Thus the mid-watch was reserved for the new guys. And, because sleep went uninterrupted,

---

*The tool itself consisted of a short wooden handle approximately two feet long attached by a swivel to a pointed spade, which could be placed in three positions. When digging, the spade was extended straight out and used as a shovel. When positioned perpendicularly to the handle, the tool became a pick. In either of these positions, the spade was locked in place with a screw nut. When folded next to the handle, it was ready to place in the entrenching tool cover that attached to the top middle exterior of the pack.

first or last watch was the prerogative of old timers.

In retrospect, many mid-watches during Operation Ripper become a montage. Etched in memory, the harsh whisper awakes me now as it did then from my dreamless sleep or a dream which had become reality. In either state, my awakening was accompanied by disbelief. In this cramped hole in the earth, I awoke again to the dream of Korea and to a breathy low voice, demanding, "Andy, it's your watch."

The sentry, making sure his replacement was awake, waited for me to sit up before he passed the watch. Only half awake, I would place my rifle on the foxhole parapet, then, reach for my canteen. Usually filled before nightfall from 5-gallon water cans, a canteen was our daily ration unless we found a clear stream. From this we could fill our canteen after we had purified the water with chlorine tablets. As usual, when filling the canteen it overflowed and was full up to the screw cap. And in the Korean cold, ice formed up the neck of the canteen at night. So I would chip away the ice with my bayonet to get a cold drink of water.

Then I would sit up in the hole or stand up and sit on the edge of the hole, depending on its size, my lower half, clothed in long-johns and pants, still in my "mountain type" sleeping bag. Of course, my boots are in the hole beside the foot of my bag; I had used them for my pillow. My upper body would be clothed in an undershirt, cotton shirt, wool shirt, dungaree jacket and field jacket. Unofficially condoned by our leaders, I could stand watch completely inside my sleeping bag with just my face exposed if weather became exceptionally cold. The bag had an inside quick release.

Next for a stimulant and awake up jolt I down a hunk of chocolate candy supplied with the daily C-ration. Then, pulling the bag up and crouching down, I light the first cigarette of the watch, cupping it in my hand to prevent enemy detection. I take my drags inside the pulled-up bag to expose no light from the bright ember. Indeed, to stay awake I consume more chocolate and smoke more cigarettes for the rest of my watch.

The gun hole is at the apex of a small glen, extending down in a crescent from the juncture between two wooded hills. Our troops range along the ridgeline across the tops of both these hills, but the placement of the gun hole commands the most likely spot to repel a probing attack up this depression to our ridgeline, certainly, the easiest access for scouting gooks.

Although offering the cover and concealment of trees for us, the hills were not densely forested or thicketed; during the day light and snow easily filtered through the sparse foliage and the tree trunks. At night, however, we were concealed.

The tiny crescent ravine, in contrast, bore no vegetation and was a perfect field of fire. The ground of both ravine and hills revealed a mottled aspect of black and white as the patches of snow melted during the day and froze at night. Unfortunately, this caused deep contrasts between black and white, dark and light, shadow and bright.

When not actively employed the mind wanders. Cigarettes, chocolate and cold water may bring dull consciousness. But reality is still back in the dream. The mind wanders as the eyes slowly move from shadow to snow patch to shadow, again. The open eyes move, but the mind inches back into dream reality....

Did I see movement? Movement!

I come awake with a start. My stomach tightens; it isn't panic, yet it isn't quite fear. With apprehension I scrutinize the shadows once more.

The alternatives were many. A breeze might rustle a

branch causing its shadow to move. Rumors maintained
Korean deer and even tigers had been seen. But could it be
gooks creeping up at this very moment? Should I whisper to
Andy? Should I wake him? What should I do?

Be watchful. Be alert. Keep both eyes peeled!

Drink water, eat chocolate, light another cigarette. But
reality is still back in the dream. The mind wanders as the
eyes slowly move from shadow to snow patch to shadow,
again. My open eyes stare; my mind inches back into dream
reality....

It is Sunday afternoon after the papers are read;
my family and I listen to "One Man's Family." I
try to understand the story, I listen more carefully....

I am lying on the rug, ...listening to the radio. A
far off voice speaks a word, "Awake...."

Awake!

"Hey, are you awake?" The voice of the dark figure
beside me is gruff and a hand shakes my shoulder. Again, he
says, "Are you awake? Come on, now, stay alert. You've got
to stay alert." The last exclamation was pointed and commanding.

Suddenly I'm in Korea again.

"Yea. Yea. I'm awake. OK, I'll stay alert." I answer
plaintively.

My God, that was the lieutenant, making his rounds. I
must stay alert. Get the water. Ice in the canteen, again.
Grab the bayonet. Where's the chocolate? Light the cigarette.
Stay alert. I've got to stay alert!

Seldom if ever were the nights pitch black. Without the
moon even when cloudy, some details might be seen in the
night. And this I must do. Inspect the vale from side to
side. Check the tree line. Stretch. Move around, but the

hole is restrictive. No matter, stay alert.

Drink water, eat chocolate, light another cigarette. But reality is still back in the dream. The mind wanders as the eyes slowly move from shadow to snow patch to shadow, again. Open eyes glaze and blankly stare: my mind inches back into dream reality....

The smell of the cookies baking tells me that Grandmother is making goodies. On the stool in the pantry she sits and rolls out dough for the oven. She lets me taste a hot cookie. Grandmother has always been very special.

Why are firecrackers popping outside? This is not the Fourth of July. Why is somebody shooting off firecrackers? Firecrackers!

Jumping almost straight up, I realize that a firefight is erupting on a hill a half a mile away. Tracers shoot across the sky. The thump of mortars jar the ground. Machineguns rattle.

I hear the sporadic static of rifle fire.

I watch the firefight during the length of a cigarette and a drink of water. Then I check my wristwatch; I find my tour of duty is ending. In a loud whisper, I call, "Andy. Andy. Your watch."

He straightens up in the gun hole and awaits the dawn; I pull the sleeping bag over me, zip it up and try to go to sleep.

It was a watch played out time and again.

Perhaps, unknowingly at the time, my youth captured the wisdom of Ernest Hemingway, who believed, "A good soldier does not worry. He knows that nothing happens until it actually happens and you live your life up to until then. Danger only exists at the moment of danger. To live properly in war, the individual eliminates all such things as potential danger. Then a thing is only bad when it is bad. It is neither bad before nor after. Cowardice, as distinguished from panic, is almost always simply a lack of ability to suspend the functioning of the imagination. Learning to suspend your imagination and live completely in the very second of the present minute with no before and no after is the greatest gift a soldier can acquire."

***

On 11 February 1951, a Chinese counterattack on the central front began northeast of Wonju. Apparently, this movement was designed to take UN pressure off the Chinese forces around Seoul. Elements of the 39th, 40th and 66th field armies of General Li Tianyu and the NKPA V Corps struck north of Hoengsong and two ROK divisions were overcome and withdrew. This force threatened Wonju.

Now General Ridgway initiated his new tactical concept for the UN forces. He believed it more important to inflict maximum punishment on the enemy at a minimum cost in casualties, rather than holding ground to the last ditch. Moreover, he conceived a counterattack toward limited objectives in the hill country north of Wonju to staunch the thrust of the communist forces. He wanted to throw them off balance; and, he called on the Marines to lead what was still termed "Operation Killer."

Although the communist forces had reached the outskirts of Wonju by 18 February, patrols discovered a subsequent general withdrawal along the front. As planned, however, the new Ridgway offensive jumped-off on 21 February. The Marines, becoming a part of the IX Corps under Major General Bryant E. Moore, were integrated with the army's 24th Infantry Division, the 1st Cavalry Division, the ROK 6th Division and the 27th British Commonwealth Brigade. The

1st Marines and the 5th Marines moved into action attacking northeast of Wonju to cut off the enemy forces that had penetrated southeast of Hoengsong.

As the Marines moved out, Generals Moore and Ridgway observed them from an embankment above the rice paddies. Ridgway spotted one marine, heavy radio communications on his back, stumbling along with his boot lace untied. The general slid down the embankment, stopped the marine and tied his boot lace.

Correspondents on the spot had a field day. Foes of the war in general and foes of military theatrics in particular gagged in protest. But General Ridgway insisted no theatrics were intended.

Moving in mud along miserable roads, through narrow valleys and rocky hills, the Marines encountered complete lack of resistance until 23 February. Then the 1st (1/1) and 2nd Battalions (2/1) of the 1st Marines fought for two hills of a ridge south of the first phase objective. By 24 February, they had reached that objective, a ridgeline about three and a half miles south of the high ground dominating Hoengsong. (See Map 3)

On the same day Major General Bryant E. Moore, commanding IX Corps, was a passenger in a low-flying, small helicopter which struck a telephone wire and crashed into the Han River. He was rescued, but died of a heart attack a half hour later.

General Ridgway chose the commander of the First Marine Division, Major General Oliver P. Smith, to be the interim commander of IX Corps. He commanded this major unit of the U.S. Army for nine days. At this point in Marine Corps history, that had only happened twice before: Major General John A. Lejeune commanded the 2nd Infantry Division once in World War I and in World War II, Major

General Roy S. Gieger, who commanded the Tenth Army on Okinawa after the commander, Lieutenant General Simon Bolivar Buckner was killed by Japanese artillery fire.

Brigadier General Lewis B. "Chesty" Puller took command of the division while Smith commanded the corps. On 25 February, fighting was called to a halt as ammunition, fuel and supplies were replenished. But on 1 March, the Marines renewed fighting along the central front in the Hoengsong area. The second phase of "Operation Killer" proved tougher; they had to take the hills to the north of the battered town and across the muddy plain. Yet, by 4 March, the Marines occupied that line of hills and were mopping up.

Captain Robert P. Wray's Charlie Company of 1/1 had entered Hoengsong on the 25th but an aerial observer had discovered a communist ambush and he was recalled. In fact, during the second phase of "Killer," Charlie Company did enter and remain in Hoengsong where John Camacho joined them as a replacement.

The troops as well as the central front were pelted with snow on 4 March. The ground was still covered on 6 March when trucks left us at night in a snowy field outside Hoengsong.

Dissatisfied that "Operation Killer" had not produced his objective of killing masses of enemy troops and at the same time placating the Joint Chiefs of Staff, Ridgway developed "Operation Ripper." Since the enemy seemed more interested in retreating than fighting, he kept in close pursuit. Now Ridgway pressured the communists with Phase One of "Ripper."

In his book, *The Korean War*, General Matthew B. Ridgway describes the operation: "The aim of Operation Ripper, however, was not merely to recover the capital city [Seoul] or occupy new ground. It was primarily to seize or destroy enemy personnel and equipment. In this respect it was not wholly successful, for the enemy fought delaying actions only, as he pulled his forces rapidly northward. Weather and terrain gave us more trouble than enemy action, particularly in the central zone, where mountain peaks thrust into the clouds and precipitous slopes dropped into valleys hardly wide enough for a cart road. Enemy strong points, perched high on the barren summits, had to be enveloped and carried by assault."

On Wednesday, 7 March 1951, the dawn was cold and clear, but later a light snow began falling. On the central front, the assault regiments for the operation were the 1st Marines on the right and the 7th Marines on the left. The 5th Marines remained in the Hoengsong area continuing to patrol. But by mid-afternoon both assault regiments, achieved their objectives, advancing toward Phase Line ALBANY, five miles beyond the line of departure (LD). The 2nd Battalion (2/1) prepared their perimeter defenses; and in the late afternoon I reported to the machinegun section of the second platoon of "Dog" Company (D/2/1) under the protection of "Andy." (See Map 2)

The next day, 8 March, resistance stiffened and die hard pockets of the enemy were encountered. The second day of the operation was my first day of combat; we were ambushed and I saw my first wounded marine. On the 9th, we continued the attack through a wide valley supported by tanks.

Then the advance came to a halt to wait for Army units to catch up. Although the 2nd Battalion (2/1) took up blocking positions, Dog Company (D/2/1) continued daily patrols. On the 11th, the Army had caught up and the attack began again. Resistance was light. And by 14 March, all Marine units were dug in along Phase Line ALBANY. Dog (D/2/1) came off the hill and boarded trucks. Suffering from raw, painful feet, I turned-in to the corpsman, who sent me back to the field hospital.

Dog Company (D/2/1) mounted up, along with the rest of the 2nd Battalion (2/1), and moved from the right flank where no enemy was encountered to the extreme left flank. The battalion circled to the rear, then moved by truck through the 7th Marines, dismounted and struck out across rolling country toward Hill 246, later attacked by 3rd Battalion (3/1). Moving on Hill 428, Fox (F/2/1), under Captain Goodwin C. Groff, and Dog (D/2/1) under Captain Welby D. Cronk assaulted enemy resistance. But the Chinese bunkers resisted stubbornly until dusk when the companies were ordered by battalion (2/1) to withdraw to defensive positions around Hill 246. The battle cost the Second (2/1) and 3rd Battalions (3/1) 7 killed in action (KIA) and 86 wounded in action (WIA). Counted enemy dead, 93.

Also on the 15th, the Eighth Army in the west marched into Seoul. After changing hands four times in nine months, the capital city had been pounded into rubble.

With several layers of skin worn off the soles of my feet, I could hardly walk and was transported 40 miles back to a field hospital in order to let my feet dry out and raw places heal.

The corpsman had directed me to the battalion aid station and from that point I was tagged, literally, for the field hospital. Aboard the casualty truck headed to the hospital, we traveled the Hoengsong-Hongchon highway. A highway in name only, the connotation was completely incorrect. This was a rough dirt road, barely wide enough for two trucks to pass. Engineers, however, were attempting improvements.

Nevertheless, it was along this hazardous road that two bizarre sights appeared to me during that journey. The first was the scene in the valley of Hoengsong beside the river. From the six-by truck bed, I could see completely across the town. No building was standing. The town was devastated. And as we drove through, the most lasting picture in my memory displays the steel buildings or warehouses that were only twisted sheets of metal. Pounded into rubble, the town supported only a name.

As we crossed the river and curved up and over the hill to the south, the second bizarre sight came into view. In the oncoming lane of the road was a larger than life sized "ginger bread" man. A gook had been run over and lay smashed as flat as a pancake in the road. Unlike animals struck on the highway, there were no visible viscera. Like a bug smashed with a flat iron, he appeared to be steamrollered. No loss, we thought. He wore a North Korean uniform.

Perhaps, that shape had soldiered with the rapidly dwindling NKPA V Corps. At any rate, we faced an old enemy, General Show Shui Kwai, commanding the PLA 66th field army under the 13th Army Group of General Li. His 196th and 197th Divisions in defensive positions with the 198th in reserve comprised about 24,000 men. The opposing Marines numbered over 25,000 men. At this time the enemy forces, both Chinese and North Korean, were estimated at 504,000 men, defending across the waist of Korea. The total UN force opposing them was 493,000 men.

But the Chinese were withdrawing, offering only occasional resistance along the central front. In fact, on 15 March, UN forces intercepted a Chinese radio message: "We cannot fight any longer. We must move back today. We will move back at 1400. Enemy troops will enter our positions at 1300 or 1400. Enemy troops approaching fast."

Quickly attacking past Phase Line ALBANY, the Marines began the second phase of Ripper on 14 March. In the push to Phase Lines BAKER then BUFFALO, mud, flooded streams and wretched roads constantly hampered progress. The 7th Marines on the left took Hongchon without a fight. But, as mentioned, the 2nd (2/1) and 3rd (3/1) Battalions of the 1st Marines on the right ran into a fight around Hills 246 and 428. By 20 March, however, the Marines had reached Phase Line BUFFALO. (See Map 2)

On the same day, the 5th Marines attacked on the left, the Korean Marines (KMC) in the middle and the 1st Marines on the right. This contingent of the Eighth Army continued north toward Line CAIRO. The most rugged resistance was encountered by the KMC on Hill 975. After three days of bitter combat, resistance slackened and the objective taken. The 1st and 5th Marines had already pushed to Line CAIRO, meeting light opposition from NKPA troops who had relieved the 66th Chinese army. As the Chinese armies moved north, massing in the rear for a new offensive, the North Koreans were used as expendable delaying units. Additionally, an old tactic was used to shroud the front in haze—a smoke screen from burning green wood.

The Marines advanced to the new Line CAIRO on 26 March. (See Map 2) These units of the Eighth Army had gained about 35 miles in the last three weeks, while pushing nearly to the 38th parallel. On 29 March, Operation Ripper gave way to Operation Rugged in order to extend the front north to Line KANSAS. (See Map 3)

By 2 April, General Smith commanded a 20 mile front. The 7th Marines were attached to the 1st Cavalry Division. And the 5th Marines and KMC were attacking across the Soyang-gang river. Finally, at this point, the 1st Marines and Dog (D/2/1) were directed into Division reserve near Hongchon.

***

With an occasional patrol to keep the troops in shape, Dog Company (D/2/1) relaxed. Easter, in reserve, was a time to recuperate. In the pouring rain marine cooks brought hot Easter dinner to the men by truck. After religious services on Easter Sunday, chow lines formed. Hot ham, yams, mashed potatoes, creamed corn along with cake were ladled into their mess kits. Tarps kept the rain out of the food being served, but the run back to the tent was time enough for the rain to drench our chow.

This reserve was not totally rest and relaxation. Dog (D/2/1) maintained a perimeter defense of foxholes manned by three guard watches of three hours each, at night. This defense surrounded the company area in which were the tents of the troops. Each marine carried a shelter half and two wooden poles and stakes. On the long edge the shelter half had metal buttons and button holes, so that two of them could be joined together to make a tent for two. Generally, each marine had a bunk buddy. If, however, there was no one available, one shelter half could provide a half tent which was better than nothing.

In the attack, Marines did not put up tents but dug foxholes. Sometimes the marine slept on a straw mat but more often on air mattresses that were being issued. He ate "C"*

---

*The box contained a day's rations consisting of three cans of meat and vegetable, a can of fruit, hot chocolate and coffee mixes, creamers, crackers, cookies, can opener, cigarettes and toilet paper. These were surplus supplies from World War II. The box also contained a can of Sterno and matches. The Sterno can was mounted on a stand and lighted. Open cans of food could be placed on top of the stand over the flame and heated. However, it was usually easier to gather twigs and branches and make a bonfire.

rations that came in a cardboard box and fit in his back pack.

I told my folks what I could of the situation yet tried to keep a cheerful mood. Indeed, it was an honor to be the personal war correspondent for my family, my neighborhood and my church. In fact, many of my letters were passed around the neighborhood and a few read in church by the pastor.

March 24, 1951

Dear Folks,

We are back in battalion reserve—rest and relaxation—and living is easy. Of course, we go out on patrols. I just came off of one; but the patrols are easy, too.

Before I came back to the company, I was issued field boots, boondockers, and got rid of those Sno-Paks. The new boondockers are the wrong size and have worn blisters on my heels. My feet sweat so much that they swell from water under the skin of the soles. The doctors called it hyperhydrosis. They say not much can be done but to stay off my feet. In an infantry outfit! So, I hobble around on sore raw feet. The guys call me Hopalong. But, Hopalong Cassidy had a horse. I wish I did.

You can bet that we always set up our defenses on the hilltop. So, the hot shower tents are at the bottom of the hill. I am about to go take my first shower since I left the troop ship over three weeks ago.

Tomorrow is Easter. Easter in Korea. We are getting all shaved and showered and cleaned up for church. We are putting on our new spring clothes for the Easter parade. (They brought new dungarees up from the rear to issue to us.) I think I will be in style with my goatee and my moustache, which is always getting in my food because it's a handlebar. They both are rather dirty blond and I do mean dirty.

The Army is on both sides of us, Marines, and squeezing us out. When they come together, then we will go into division reserve, I hear.

Everybody has a buddy to dig in with at night. That is, a buddy to live with. Mine is a guy named CPL James Anderson; and, of course, anyone named Anderson is called Andy. Since we bunk together, it really fouls things up. We never know who is being called. In the other squad is PFC Leo Andrews. He is called Andy, too. So, in our machine gun section, we have three Andys.

I pal around with one of the "acting" squad leaders from another section, PFC Gordon Harbison. He is a true marine with quite a few years, last war and this one. He has got brains and brawn, just like the Hollywood Marines. With two and a half years of college at Wayne University in Wayne, Indiana, we get into big bull sessions about college and current events.* His buddy, Little Jake, joins in. The intellectuals, of course.

I still haven't received any mail. I will be so glad to get a letter. Well, hope the letters find me, soon.

Love,

Burton

As we moved out daily either on patrol or in the attack,

*Gordon Harbison was only a PFC. In WWII, however, he had served at a higher rank in the Army.

our supplies were transported by the Civil Transport Corps. The members were those South Koreans who lacked military training. Since these indigenous laborers received pay as well as rations and clothing, no shortage of them existed. Working with wooden "A-frames"—because of their shape— used since ancient times in Korea to carry heavy burdens, companies of porters, individually, could carry a load of 100 to 125 pounds over ground too rugged for vehicles. Hauling ammunition and supplies, they accompanied us into combat, although at the company rear. Several hundred were attached to each regiment during Operation Ripper.

Utilizing these porters allowed the companies to operate at minimum strength—certainly, in the machinegun section—and to achieve greater mobility.

However, these were not the concern of a marine in reserve. The following newsy letter of March 25, 1951, put the "R&R" in perspective.

I was sure glad to get your letter. Today, is Easter Sunday and the rainy season has started. I've been in my tent all morning because it has been so cold and wet, outside. From time to time, a barrage of artillery or mortars will go over us. Other than that, it is a fairly quiet day. We're about four miles south of the 38th parallel.

I finally got some mail. You said in your letter that it was cold at home. Well, this place is colder. When we are on line or in the attack, we always dig in on a mountain at night and we stand watches all night long. It is so cold that water freezes in the canteens and you have to break the ice before you can get a drink.

Yesterday, I met some New Zealanders. They

wear tams, berets, just like the British. I wanted
one for a souvenir; so, I tried to trade my utility cap
for their hats. But, they wouldn't trade. They said
that they had to wear helmets if they didn't wear
their tams. And, "The bloody 'elmuts are too
bloomin' 'eavy."

The other day, we found a "burp" gun. This is
the personal machinegun that the gooks use. It's a little like the old "Tommy" gun in the gangster movies
except it is smaller and has a perforated barrel like
our light .30 caliber machine gun. In other words, it
is air cooled and the real barrel has a metal jacket
around it that has holes in it. It shoots something like
a .25 caliber, just a little bigger that a .22. It sounds
like ping, ping, ping, only really fast.*

Not all of the gooks carry these. And, its use
would compare to our BAR, Browning Automatic
Rifle, and BAR man. The BAR is like a machinegun,
really, and is a .30 caliber. In each marine rifle squad
of four, there is one BAR man and three riflemen,
one of which is the squad leader.

I almost forgot the most important thing. The
other day I was sitting by the camp fire and I looked
out on the road that goes past us and I saw a company
coming off patrol. I just looked up and there was
Ross. We saw each other at the same time. He's

---

*Actually, the North Korean "Burp Gun" was supplied by the Russians and
identified as a 7.62-mm Shpagin, PPSH M1941 submachinegun. The
receiver and perforated barrel jacket were made of a simple stamping.
The barrel jacket incorporated a simple built-in muzzle break compensator.
The bolt assembly had a fixed firing pin and a one piece extractor.
Workmanship was rough with little machining except on working surfaces.

just down the road from me about a half mile. He's in "Item" Company; the same regiment as I am. He only was with the 5th Marines three weeks. Because of heavy casualties in the 1st Marines, he was transferred. And, Ross is an ammo carrier just like me.

He hadn't gotten any letters so he read mine. But, your letter only mentions that Ross' baby was born. You didn't say whether it was a boy or girl. You didn't even tell us the name. Since the Red Cross hasn't contacted him, he only knows that he is a father. I think I'll go see him this afternoon to see how he is doing. [See Figure 5]

Incidentally, you probably have wondered about these funny company names. Well, over a walkie-talkie radio, "A" Company could be misunderstood. So, our companies have names for their alphabet designations. Like Able, Baker, Charlie of the 1st Battalion; Dog, my company, Easy, Fox of the 2nd Battalion; and George, How, and Item, Ross' company, of the 3rd Battalion.

Well, one more patrol, tomorrow, and, then, the whole division goes way back behind the lines to Corps reserve. The Army is relieving us. In fact, some Army units came by in trucks just a while ago.

Everybody started yelling. The old marines who are still left from the Wonsan landing have not

---

The overall length was 33 inches. The drum capacity was 71 rounds with an effective rate of 30 rounds per minute, semi-automatic, to 70 rounds per minute, short burst. The effective range for a short burst was 220 yards. Otherwise, fully automatic, the rate was 500 rounds per minute.

forgotten how the Army routed in the north last December and left the marines to fight their way out. Finally, there were cat calls from all over and it was getting out of hand. I thought we were going to have our own private little war between the Army and Marines, right there. But, our company commander made us stop.

Seriously, the Army is a disgrace. We take an objective and turn it over to the Army and before you know it they have bugged out, run, and we have to take the ground, again. In fact, every time they set up, they designate the MBR, which means the Main Bugout Route. They plan on running.

Just the other day, an Army artillery company set up across the road from us when we were set up in a rice paddy. This was a Negro company commanded by white officers. They had a mess hall and hot showers in tents as well as the large six man pyramidal tents; while we were in our shelter halves, eating "C" rations. They fired their 155 howitzers all day and these guns really have a wallop. They just about bounced us out of our foxholes.

That night was quiet. After I had guard duty, I went to sleep and remember sometime in the night that I heard some firing to our front. This could have been a gook probe to find out where we were or some trigger happy new marine who heard a noise and fired. I went back to sleep.

The next morning when I woke up, I looked across to an empty field where, yesterday, there had been a company. They had bugged out. Those few shots had scared them and they ran. They even left some of their equipment. Well, marines tend to be scavengers, anyway. So, we had a good time....

Now, I began to receive mail. At one mail call, I received 10 letters. And not all from my folks. At least one was in answer to a letter and picture that I had mailed before I sailed. It came from the University of Oklahoma at Norman.

March 7, 1951

Dear Burton,

"She wears the golden anchor, ..." At long last. Our pledge class was initiated Sunday. I sure am glad to get that little ol' anchor pinned on me. I've been floating around on a little orange, pink and blue cloud ever since.

Well, how is the Pacific by now? Hot and blue? Just think what a traveled man you're going to be by the time you're through. Give the Marines my love. I was impressed by your picture. Thank you very much. You're very nice looking.

I'm glad you don't feel like you are wasting your time in Korea. I don't quite understand it all, but then I suppose no one does.

School at present is very busy. We're having four weeks' tests. I had one in Greek drama, today. I'll say this for it—it was inclusive. 20 spot passages! I knew about eight; and, then, the essay questions. Give defects in Sophocles' dramatic techniques! Men have just spent the last 1300 years describing him as the perfect dramatic writer. I just about choked.

We're working on a modern dance program we have to give this spring. Right now I'm listening to records, trying to pick one out that'll fit our carnival theme. Do you like Copland's "Rodeo"? I'm doing the choreography.

My friend, Sally, and I went to New York between semesters. What a riot! We liked to never made it up there (two weeks), but when we got there, we lost our minds. Ahh-me. Times Square on Saturday night. There's nothing like it. I've been sitting listening dreamy-eyed to the recording of "Manhattan Towers" ever since.

You should have a big time in Tokyo. Watch out for those geisha girls. Don't get ensnared!

Since you are, shall we say, definitely involved in this here war, I shall send you a poem I wrote entitled: Poem for War

POEM FOR WAR

It does not matter that the rose-dust falls softly
from the tamarack
That the blood-red summer moon is yet not full,
That black flocks of crows rustle close between
the weeping willows,
That the honeysuckle has choked the orange black
tiger lily
For the gray of twilight stalks swift sure footed,
And night comes all at once.

Well, off to the books. The war news is rather depressing tonight, but then we can't win all the time. Write and tell me how goes the war and if we are winning.

Take care of yourself.

Love,

Mona

Her attitude and perception reflected the vast majority of

Americans who were not personally involved. Being perplexed by this perception, I reviewed her poem with my
"intellectual" friends. I mentioned it in this April 4, 1951, letter.

> I'm getting in a rut. I'm in the hospital and, of
> course, it's my feet again.
> Here, we are in a big wide valley between two
> mountain ranges with a river a little ways off. We are
> close to this town that is now rubble called
> Hongchon, I think. Today is a beautiful day. It's
> warm and feels like spring. And, I have the urge to
> go someplace, to travel. I really feel good. But I
> don't guess I can with these feet and being in the
> hospital.
> A few days ago, I went over to see Ross. We
> read his letters and got a big laugh about his being a
> papa of a boy. The next day, we went on our last
> patrol and didn't meet any resistance. I hardly made
> it back because I couldn't walk. Once again, I went
> to Sick Bay and the corpsman sent me down to the
> hospital.
> I can't wear a shoe on my right foot because it's
> so swollen. I hobble around in my socks. I get three
> shots of penicillin a day and soak my feet in some
> solution three times a day. I haven't walked nor-
> mally in so long I wonder how it feels.
> I guess the guys are going into reserve today. I
> ought to be with them in a week. We'll be in division
> reserve for quite awhile, I think.
> Well, I've gotten another name besides Hopalong
> in our machinegun squad. I am the only one in our
> squad who ever went to college. So they call me

"Intellectual Boy." Have I got them snowed! They
ask me to spell words or answer brainy questions. I
told them I almost was selected for Officer Candidate
School and that did the trick. I'm intellectual now.

Mona is writing me now from OU [Oklahoma
University]. She's taking Greek drama and she
writes poetry. She sent me a poem entitled "Poem for
War." It's symbolism, I guess, and you'd have to be
Greek to appreciate it. It's certainly Greek to me. I
can't find anything about war in it. But, at least,
the guys got a big laugh out of it.

It starts with something about rose dust falling
from the tamarack. Now, we, machinegunners no
longer fire bullets. It's rose dust. Can't you see us
yelling at the gooks, "Here's some rose dust from our
tamarack." Her poem went to war, but instead of
being serious it's quite a comedy. I'll write her that
everyone really "enjoyed" her poem. The guys call
her "Our Intellectual Woman."

                              Your Intellectual Son,

General MacArthur was sacked on April 10th and for the
next few days, the war came nearly to a stop. My letter of
April 14, 1951, revealed the feeling of Marines regarding
the event as well as my youthful naivete about life.

I got your package, today, and the cookies were
great. I am back from the hospital and we've been
having some wonderful weather, lately. The days are
really beautiful. We're set up in pyramidal tents with
stoves with six guys per tent. We are so far in the rear
that division headquarters is 30 miles up closer to the
lines than we are. And Ross is just down the road a little ways. I haven't seen him, yet, because we aren't

supposed to go out of the battalion area; but, I think I can sneak off one of these days.

Well, everybody is really happy about MacArthur's being relieved. The new commander (Ridgway) believes in saving as many lives as possible. He thinks the Marines need to go home because they have done a lot of hard fighting in this war. So, we're all for him.

Tell the people that you mentioned in your letter that I appreciate everyone's thinking about me. I feel more than a little important. I feel I have the backing at home. Thanks to all of you for your prayers. Give Grandmother special thanks.

Please send me a small notebook that I can keep in my pocket so that when I see something that I would like to write about I can. Here is one instance, but I've probably forgotten some of it.

As usual, we were climbing up a path to the top of a ridge. When we got to the top, suddenly, we rounded a turn and displayed before me was Utopia. The path started downward,and there before me, gleaming in the morning light, lay the most beautiful valley I've ever seen in Korea. It was beautiful beyond description. As our patrol filed singly down the trail into the valley, I was filled with thoughts of the ultimate attainment, of scenes in grandeur.

I've always had the urge to travel west. Always west. But, here, I thought, this surely is the place of my reverie. The perfect place.

As I continued through this Utopia, I became accustomed to it. Perhaps it wasn't so different from other valleys. Had I really found my goal?

Across the valley lay another range of mountains.

Another adventure. Perhaps it was curiosity or search for more knowledge; but, with no remorse, I left this valley that had once been Utopia.

Isn't this like the life of man? He works. He strains throughout life to achieve his goal. But, as he becomes acquainted with his new surroundings and as he becomes familiar with his new life, he wonders if this is really his goal. He sees new mountains to climb. New opportunities and challenges. He has a choice: to stop or to continue on. Some men will stay; some men will continue on.

I hope that through my life I will continue on.

Perhaps, I'll find the highest peak. But, if I don't, I still will have enjoyed the journey along the way.

***

Little Jake liked to build fires. And he was quite good at it. A master fire maker was Jake. When we set-up in the field, as soon as he could get to it, he would find the twigs and wood for his craft. As his buddies, we always waited for Little Jake to build our cook fire, because being from the wild west plains of Texas, he had to be a cowboy and know about these things.

Even reserve duty with the mess halls and showers did not deter Little Jake from building a fire in our machinegun section area and making coffee from the single packages left over from his C rations.*

---

*During Operation Ripper, the Marines were a part of the UN IX (Ninth) Corps along with other Army units, Korean Marines, and ROKS. These units alternated recuperating off line in Corps reserve, which had not only amenities of tent showers down by the river and hot chow from mess halls but also movies and live USO shows.

Little Jake yelled, "Fire's hot!" "Come make your coffee!"

From our two pyramidal tents which slept six men each, the other members of the group came with either their packaged coffee or cocoa. This togetherness time had started on the front line at chow time, but now continued in reserve usually after evening chow.

Generally there were four or five of us: Little Jake, "Harby"Harbison, Andrews, and me. Sometimes Andy (now SGT James Anderson) would join us.

We filled our canteen cups with water from our five gallon water can and set the cup in the hot embers. When the water boiled, we stirred in our powdered coffee or cocoa, and prepared for the highly philosophical discussions of our extremely sophisticated members.

Our section leader was Staff Sergeant Louis Pellizzari, an Italian career marine. The first squad leader was (new) SGT James (Andy) Anderson who had been my gunner when I first joined the section. But when the squad leader was wounded, Andy was promoted to that position. He never had much to say and was a loner. Occasionally, when he felt like it, he would join the group.

My squad gunner and assistant gunner were bunk buddies. PFC Carl Krauss was the gunner and from Chicago. He and assistant gunner PFC James McGrath had their own agenda—sports—and rarely joined our group. In the field they lit their own fire and discussed nothing but sports, sports, sports. (See Figure 6)

That left Andrews and me, the two ammo carriers of the squad, to bunk together. Oddly, however, we were a part of an unconnected cook fire group consisting of the acting squad leader and gunner of one squad and the ammo carriers, us, of another with occasional visits from our squad leader.

"Little Jake" from Texas had been in the Marine Corps for awhile. His history was not readily discernible although he had mentioned Okinawa and the Naval Base at Subic Bay in the Philippines. Nothing was holy to little Jake. He was profane; but he was everybody's buddy. He sacked in with Harby and was his gunner.

An acting squad leader of the first section, PFC Gordon "Harby"Harbison came from Ft. Wayne, Indiana. After almost three years of college at Wayne University, he ran out of money and rejoined the Marine Corps. Harby was a philosophy and sociology major. Here in reserve with the rudimentary refinements of civilization, this relationship— Harby, Little Jake, Andrews and me with SGT Andy, some- times—worked out fine. As like souls search out like souls, our group coalesced.

We made our coffee over Little Jake's fire and relaxed.

"Did you see Jennifer Jones' eyes when she saw me pissin' in the piss tube." Little Jake was laughing.

Harby asked, "When was that?"

"Just awhile ago. She probably hadn't seen anything like mine."

"Little Jake, you're impossible. What happened?" I was fired up for the story.

Jennifer Jones, the movie star, had been entertaining the troops in USO shows and had been traveling between camps in a khaki painted Buick along with a colonel and a driver.

Lining the road into camp were artillery shell casings that had been partially buried in holes lined with rocks for per-colation. They were called "piss" tubes and were used for that purpose.

When Jennifer Jones left camp, Little Jake had been purposely standing at one of the tubes, using it as she passed. He saluted her with one hand, the other directed his stream.

Everyone roared. Little Jake had done it again.

"OK. OK." Harby had enough of that subject and was interested in something more serious.

He said, "Now, we know why I joined the Marines. And we know Little Jake, here, is a career Marine."

At this, Little Jake yelled as if he had been stuck with a pin.

"Andrews and kids of 17 are too young to know any better. And when they see 'The Sands of Iwo Jima,' they naturally join up. So, Andy, after two years of college, why did you join?"

He wasn't talking to SGT Andy. I was being skewered.

I said that I had seen John Wayne movies like other guys and got patriotic. But, really, my best buddy, Ross, and I had decided to join the Marines because it sounded like the most exciting service to be in and we wanted action.

There was another reason also. All my family had been Air Force and before that the Army Air Corps and before that The Air Service. (The Air Service was a part of The Army Signal Corps in World War I.)

My father was an Air Service mechanic at Orly Field in France and had learned to fly during the casualty depleting and waning days of that first world war when pilots became few.

I wanted something different.

"But, this is not flying. You're right here where you can get killed at any time. Is this exciting?" Harby bored in.

"Yes. This is war. It makes men out of boys." I strongly felt this was true.

Harby had to inject his philosophy.

"I suppose you're right. I suppose in some way or another, man has always had to find his manhood. Some primitive tribes still have elaborate rituals—a rite of passage. And, perhaps, war provides a rite of passage."

"It's said, Biblically, that there will be war and rumors of war until Armageddon. So, until world peace without end comes, man's rite of passage will be war. I can believe that."

"But, I wonder what the home folks think about war. What does your girlfriend say in her letters, Andy? Tell us what good old Mona has to say about war."

"OK, here's what she says." I took the well worn letter from my dungaree pocket and began to read excerpts. This impressed them. Carrying her letter around.

"Well, how is the Pacific by now? Hot and blue? Just think what a traveled man you're going to be by the time you're through. Give the Marines my love. I'm glad you don't feel you are wasting your time in Korea. I don't quite understand it all, but then I suppose no one really does. The war news is rather depressing tonight, but then we can't win all the time."

"God, she has no concept of war, at all." Harby was disappointed in her. "But I'll bet few people do in the states. They're just going on with life and trying to ignore the terrible news reports as best they can. No concept."

"No fucking concept," Little Jake seconded the motion.

"You're probably right." I said. "Because she goes on talking about her Oklahoma University and her Greek drama classes and her modern dance class and about going to New York City between semesters. You know her dad is loaded."

"My God, Andy. You can't take her seriously. Here you are, just a poor ass marine in Korea and this girl is on another plane in life. Certainly not yours." Harby was not encouraging.

"But wait. There's more." I began to read, "Poem For War,"ending with...

"For the gray of twilight stalks swift sure footed,
And night comes all at once."

"No fucking concept." Little Jake yelling again, adamantly.

"No concept, at all," from Andrews, laughing like an idiot.

But Harby changed his mind, abruptly. "Hold it. Wait a minute. She's got something. I think maybe she is more intellectual than the rest of us. 'And night comes all at once.' I like that. Yea, she's deep. Andy, we're going to call you both our intellectual boy and his intellectual girl. From now on, it's Intellectual Boy for you."

For a moment, that pronouncement silenced the rambunctious group.

"Hey, let's go to the movie," a bored SGT Andy finally got a word in. And everybody roared with laughter.

I guess I went along with the gag because they continued to call me "Intellectual Boy" from that time. And when they fired the machinegun, they talked about the "rose dust" falling.

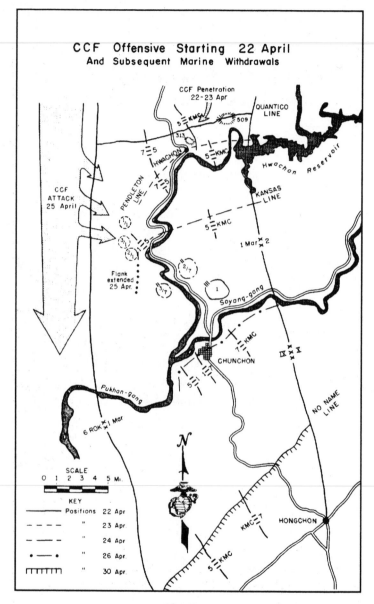

CCF Offensive Starting 22 April
And Subsequent Marine Withdrawals

CCF Penetration
22-23 Apr

QUANTICO
LINE

5 KMC

509

313

7 5

HWACHON

5 KMC

Hwachon Reservoir

CCF
ATTACK
25 April

PENDLETON
LINE

7 5

KANSAS
LINE

1/7

5 KMC

1 Mar 2

3/1
2/1

Flank
extended
25 Apr.

2/7

3/7

1

Soyang-gong

7 KMC

CHUNCHON

5 1

Pukhan-gong

NO NAME
LINE

6 ROK 1 Mar

SCALE
0 1 2 3 4 5 Mi.

N

KMC 7

HONGCHON

KEY
—————— Positions 22 Apr.
—— —— ——   "   23 Apr.
—— —— ——   "   24 Apr.
•——•——•   "   26 Apr.
⌐╥╥╥╥⌐   "   30 Apr.

5 KMC

5 KMC

MAP 4

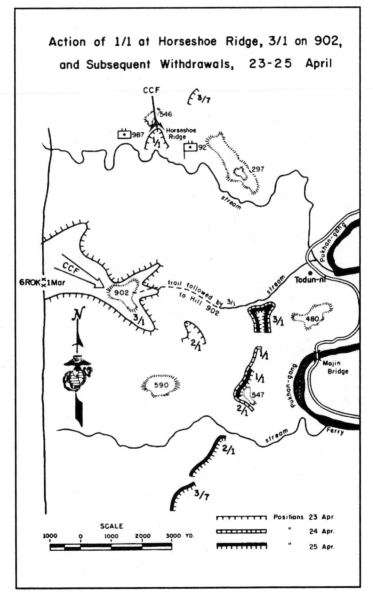

Action of 1/1 at Horseshoe Ridge, 3/1 on 902, and Subsequent Withdrawals, 23-25 April

MAP 5

CHAPTER SEVEN

THE CHINESE
SPRING OFFENSIVE

As April and spring began in the "land of the morning calm," President Truman relieved General MacArthur of his command, explaining, "General MacArthur was ready to risk general war. I was not." MacArthur had miscalculated from the beginning and caused horrendous defeats. Even more, Washington could no longer control his actions. Therefore he was replaced. General Ridgway assumed command of the United Nations forces and LT General James A. Van Fleet replaced Ridgway as commander of the Eighth Army.

One of the first acts of General Ridgway, the new UN commander, was to notify Korean President Syngman Rhee that a major replacement of leadership in Rhee's military organizations was necessary. General Ridgway was distressed with the consistent failure of ROK units to stand fast on line; they broke and ran, leaving their equipment. Consequently he intended to withhold any further equipage until Rhee shaped-up the ROK command. Compliance was not soon enough; another ROK disaster was in the making.

In Ridgway's *The Korean War* he recounts that he sent "...a message to the effect that Rhee's primary problem was to secure competent leadership in his army. This he simply did not have, and I wanted him to be told so flatly and specifically—

that from his Minister of Defense on down there was a serious weakness in command, as had been too often evidenced
by repeated battle failures of major ROK units. Until he
developed proper leadership, I felt he should be told that
there would be no further talk of equipping additional ROK
forces. Too many major items of badly needed equipment had
already been abandoned without justification."

Obvious, also, was the Chinese build up of forces across
the 38th parallel. Air Force intelligence officers had con-
firmed heavy troop concentrations. But the most highly reliable reports of this impending offensive came from prisoners
captured by Marines.

The new Chinese tactic recently employed was to shoot
and withdraw. They wanted to draw the UN forces out on a
limb and chop it off as they had in November and December.
Actually, this was an ancient tactic—draw your enemy out by
making him pursue you because he believes you are defeated and on the run, then surround and destroy him.

No matter what tactic they might use, the Chinese had no
plans for individual surrender. Supposedly each soldier
fought, escaped or died, but was never captured.
Consequently, these communists did not teach their soldiers
the proper conduct of prisoners. And surprisingly, they even
informed their troops of command battle plans. When captured, the troops promptly spilled the plans for the Chinese
spring offensive to the readily available Marine intelligence
officers. As a result, the UN forces knew the attack was
coming on 22 April, and they presumed that the command
was ready.

In fact, the 1st Marine Division resumed its advance up
the center of Korea on 21 April before the offensive. The 5th
Marine Regiment was in the center, the 7th Marines on the left
and the Korean Marines (KMC) on the right. The 1st Marines

(including John Camacho's Charlie Co., my Dog Co. and Ross' Item Co.) were in reserve—set up just outside Chunchon in a dry, abandoned rice paddy, quartered in pyramidal tents, eating hot chow. To the west of the 1st Marine Division and in the center of the Korean battle line was Rhee's vulnerable 6th ROK Army Division. In front of the Marines, the enemy was burning forests to mask its troop movements, casting a pall of smoke over the line of advance. It was a precursor of things to come—a change in Chinese tactics from hit and run to a direct frontal assault.

Although some Washington bureaucrats believed that a stalemate was near because the Chinese were quickly withdrawing across the 38th parallel, General Ridgway cautioned that this could be a re-grouping for a new drive south. Of course, he knew the Chinese were mounting their spring offensive because prisoners captured in March had revealed the plan.

In the line of advance of UN forces, the weakest segment was the ROK Army. On 21 April, the 6th ROK Division on the left of the 1st Marine Division failed to maintain contact. By day's end there was a mile and a half gap in the line between the ROKs and the Marines. On 22 April, the ROKs never succeeded in closing the gap.

On that night the Chinese attacked and slammed full force into the weakest link. Within minutes the 6th ROK Division began to collapse and by midnight they were routed. The gap opened by the Chinese was 10 miles wide and 10 miles deep, exposing the 7th Marines flank. The offensive opened by moonlight after artillery and mortar fire on the ROKs in the central sector; by daybreak it had spread across the whole peninsula.

(See Map 4)

The Chinese field armies in this central sector were the

20th and 26th, both from General Sung's 9th Army Group and the 39th and 40th field armies from Li's 13th Army Group. Their estimated strength was between 20,000 to 25,000 per field army, totaling over 90,000 troops in the offensive. The Marines totaled over 25,000 plus the Korean Marines.

The 20th and 26th field armies opposed the Marines during the Chosin Reservoir breakout. Evidently they needed three or four months to reorganize and get back into action. In reserve until needed, the Chinese held the 42nd and 66th field armies of the 13th Army Group in the Iron Triangle to the rear. (See Map 3) The 42nd was mauled by the Marines in November. Apparently they were still recovering.

As the ROKs "bugged out," trucks, troops on foot, and fleeing civilian women and children intermingled and clogged the Main Supply Route (MSR). There was no leadership; the troops were listless and apathetic. In confusion thousands straggled along the road.

The first Marine units to be hit were the Korean Marines (KMC), who had recently taken their objective, the Hwachon Reservoir, and held Hill 509 when attacked. Next attacked was the 1st Battalion of the 5th Marines (1/5), who climbed and battled their way to the top of Hill 313 in heavy fighting to defend the town of Hwachon. Subsequently, however, the KMC and the 5th Marines in the center of the line were ordered back from the QUANTICO Line to the PENDLE-TON Line. (See Map 4)

Quickly, the 1st Marine Regiment was called out of reserve to plug the gap. Now the 1st Marine Division not only held the line facing north but also curved the line west to cover its flank. By 2130 on the night of 22 April, the 1st Marines were alerted and the 1st Battalion (1/1) with John Camacho's Charlie Co. was selected to be the first to execute the "gap plugger" order. By midnight, they were aboard trucks rolling north through thousands of straggling ROKs.

Before the 1st Battalion, 1st Marines (1/1) arrived, the 3rd Battalion, 7th Marines (3/7), battled 2000 troops of the 358th Regiment of the 120th Division of the Chinese 40th field army through the night. They bent but held until the 1st Battalion, 1st Marines (1/1) came up as reinforcements. The next day 3/7 was able to disengage and withdraw through 1/7, who replaced them.

Since the early morning of 23 April, First Battalion (1/1) (including Charlie Co. and John Camacho) bitterly fought the Chinese from a hill called Horseshoe Ridge across a wide valley and over 5000 yards to the north of 2nd Battalion (2/1) and 3rd Battalion (3/1). (See Map 5) This heroic action of CAPT Robert P. Wray's Charlie Co., holding a curve of this horseshoe-shaped ridge against hordes of Chinese, has become a Marine Corps legend. On the ridgeline of Hill 902, facing the west and the Chinese, was 3/1 (including Item Co. and Ross). On the same ridgeline further east, 2/1 (including Dog Co. and me) backed up 3/1.

During that night, the enemy troops attacked and decimated Ross' 3rd Battalion (3/1) on Hill 902. By the morning of 24 April, 3/1 began withdrawing along the ridgeline through the 2nd Battalion (2/1). Late that afternoon, my battalion (2/1) also withdrew to the next ridgeline and connected with the 1st Battalion (1/1) as well as 3/1, who faced west on the same ridgeline. Likewise, all Marine elements moved back to the KANSAS Line.

That night the enemy attacked Dog Co. at the center of 2nd Battalion. An awesome firefight lasted throughout the night with fiery tracers pouring from two opposing machine-guns. The gooks attacked, blowing bugles, shouting,"Marines, you die," and trying to assault the ridgeline, a surrealistic scene bathed in the eerie glow of parachute flares dropped from Marine planes.

On 25 April, Dog Company moved back to another ridgeline and awaited another attack which did not come. During the next day the Marines moved across the Pukhan River and established a temporary line at Chunchon.

Eventually, the fifth Chinese offensive failed and by 29 April, they had been halted all along the NO NAME Line. The 5th Marines had moved to the left sector with the KMC in the middle and the 7th Marines on the right. The 1st Marines were squeezed out and sent into Division Reserve. (See Map 4)

***

John Camacho from our bootcamp Platoon I-65 joined Charlie Co., 1st Battalion, 1st Marines (C/1/1) at Hoengsong at the beginning of Operation Ripper. He too had been in Division Reserve with the rest of us in the 1st Marines when the Chinese attacked the ROKs to begin their spring offensive.

More importantly, however, was his maturation between the beginning of March and the end of April—the time between when he joined Charlie Co. and 23 April. But then the baptism of battle, facing Chinese suicide assaults is, in itself, maturing.

Charlie Co. was manned primarily by combat veterans, not only from World War II, but also troops that had experienced the Inchon landing as well as the Chosin Reservoir in December. This manning by blooded veterans may have produced a philosophy in Charlie Co. which made sure that each new green kid had an old veteran to guide him.

John Camacho's mentor was CPL Gerald Castagnetto from Redding, California. John, as a machinegun ammo carrier, was put under the wing of the corporal. And John, still a new marine, needed his help as we all green kids needed a mentor. Most of us got that kind of support. We needed a mentor to tell us what to do, what to watch out for, what to expect. We needed to know the sounds of war. We needed to learn the sounds of artillery, mortars and bullets—the sound of everything in battle. How close is that bullet or mortar or artillery shell? When should we dive for cover? The veteran taught us.

Although Gerald Castagnetto was John's mentor, he was reticent. He didn't readily divulge information. He wasn't a particularly outgoing person. But John followed him diligently during his first days of combat and found out from him about surviving in war.

The first Battalion (1/1) boarded trucks around midnight and arrived across the Pukhan River at their disembarkation point in the early morning of 23 April. Under orders from IX Corps, both the 5th and 7th Marines began to withdraw to consolidate their positions, while 1/1 moved in to plug the gap and face the enemy to the west.

In the valley, the Chinese encircled an Army artillery battalion that had backed up the ROKs. The first action saw Baker Co. mount an attack at 0130, advancing 1000 yards to relieve the pressure. In fact Baker Co. advanced another 1500 yards and relieved a second Army artillery unit which was under an assault. Upon the return of Baker, 1/1 occupied a horse-shoe shaped hill southwest of the new lines of the 7th Marines. (See Map 5)

Charlie Co. was dug in along the nose of the horse-shoe, with Able Co. on the right and Baker Co. on the left. In the morning light John Camacho was allowed to use field glasses and observed the Chinese peering down on his company as the Marines dug in. The gooks just sat and waited.... At dusk on 23 April, the 1st Platoon leader, LT Neil Mills of John's platoon spotted advancing gooks and called in mortar and artillery fire. Charlie Co.'s machineguns opened fire. Despite this devastation to their forward elements of the attack, the Chinese kept coming.

The real attack came at the hour 2000 at the nose of the horse-shoe with LT Reisler's third platoon holding an advanced outpost. Hundreds and hundreds of gooks came in wave after wave, blowing bugles and shooting green flares, screaming, "Awake, Marine, you die!" Throwing grenades and firing their "Burp" guns, the Chinese swooped down from their higher ridge line. Under intense mortar, machine-gun fire and grenade attack the 3rd platoon fell back.

Through the hole the gooks struck head-on into John Camacho's 1st Platoon; LT Norman Hicks' 2nd Platoon shifted to help out. The waves of Chinese were so numerous that the company had to give ground. But Charlie Co. did so stubbornly and set up its positions again 50 yards behind the old line. If Charlie Co. collapsed, the entire battalion would be overwhelmed. Realizing this full well, CAPT Wray ordered, "Everybody, forward!" And John's squad thrust the machinegun ten feet forward.

He remembers that all night long bullets were flying all around him. For four hours the relentless Chinese continued their attack on Horseshoe Ridge, but the Marines held. Charlie Co. was reinforced from time to time by squads from the other companies. Men carrying back the wounded returned to the line carrying ammunition. With such determination the line held.

On the morning of 24 April, IX Corps ordered the Marines to withdraw to a new line. The 1st Battalion (1/1) moved off Horseshoe Ridge, leaving Charlie Co.'s 2nd Platoon as a rear guard. The decimated 1st Platoon led the attack downhill and across the rice paddies back to the river, then up the ridgeline some 5000 yards to the rear to tie in with my 2nd Battalion (2/1). Coming off the hill, they followed a stream bed down to the river then followed the road around the mountains to come up the next ridgeline from the rear. It took all day, but they were tied in with us by nightfall.

As a member of the rear guard, John remembers that day well. Coming down from Horseshoe Ridge, his platoon had to cross a rice paddy filled with water from recent rains. The water prevented him from running. He sloshed through the mud. The slow dash of the rear guard across the paddy provided shooting targets for the Chinese. John's platoon was desperately exposed. And the men of his platoon were dropping on each side of him as the Chinese picked them off.

Finally the survivors made it to some trees for temporary cover. Then they pushed on crossing a road—the Chinese had it zeroed in. Fortunately tanks and Corsairs came to the rescue. And John made it across, but several others were wounded.

This terrible event matured John almost overnight. This experience where he seemed to go unscathed with others dropping around him had a tremendous effect on the young marine. In fact, his greatest trauma occurred during the night long battle when his mentor, CPL Gerald Castagnetto, was killed.

John felt the anguish, deeply. He never again became close to anyone in Korea. He knew many men of Charlie Co. and became one of the "fixtures." But he never became close. Later in his tour he moved from the 1st section, machineguns, to radio man with the SCR 300 Radio on his back. No more personal contacts, though. John stayed in Charlie Co. for the rest of his tour, but those three days in April haunted him.

A footnote to John Camacho's story: Dusk had come as he was digging in that night on the new ridgeline. He heard a familiar voice in the dark and John called out, "Rosser?" Coming down the path trying to find new positions on the line was 3rd Battalion (3/1). John heard an answer, "Is that you, Ka-me-ko?"

***

When the ROKs broke on 22 April, my 2nd Battalion (2/1) and Ross' 3rd Battalion (3/1) were set up in rice paddies outside of Chunchon, following a training schedule in order to integrate new replacements into the battalion. On the morning of 23 April, Ross' battalion had only 30 minutes notice to prepare to board trucks and head north On the road the trucks moved through the still milling, leaderless ROKs.

Around noon they disembarked in an assembly area and received the order to move out to Hill 902 about 1345. The hill designations were adapted from map elevations. This objective was 902.4 meters high, thus the nomenclature, Hill 902. Since a meter is 3.2 feet, this hill translated into an elevation of 2880 feet—a more proper term would be mountain.

After they assembled near the river, the objective was only five kilometers or 3 miles away but the crest was over 2500 feet high. Winter had finally passed; it was a hot day. The significance of this vantage point was its domination over the approaches to the bridge crossing the Pukhan River—the passageway through which the 1st Marine Division must withdraw.

Aerial intelligence indicated that the gooks were closer than 3/1 to this objective. Obviously, they also urgently wanted Hill 902.

The Marines were carrying their rations, sleeping bags, shelter halves, their individual weapons as well as mortars, machineguns and rocket launchers with accompanying ammunition. Each man was carrying a load from 45 to 90 pounds.

Even rugged old-timers found the trail rough. The men were pushed to the limits of human endurance. The First Sergeant of George Co. philosophized, "It'll be rougher if the Chinamen get to the hill first. Now, move out."

Third Battalion (3/1) made it to the ridge first, but it was almost dark. Hill 902 was a natural fort, a bare outcropping of rock. Several ridgelines ran from the prominence. 3rd Battalion had just climbed the first before digging in. Another led down southeast and the 2/1 sector. The third led to an even higher elevation on Hill 1010 in the direction of the Chinese.

(See Map 5)

George Co. straddled the rocky peak of 902 and sent a short spur out in the direction of 1010. How Co. tied in on George's left, extending down the southeast ridge. Item Co.(and Ross) was on the right flank, essentially along the ridge just climbed.

Around 2200 that evening an artillery liaison team and three forward observers arrived. They were the spotters for the 11th Marines (artillery) and the U.S.Army's 987th Armored Field Artillery, the heavy weapons in support of 3/1.

Shortly after midnight, the 360th Regiment, 120th Division of the 40th Chinese field army attacked not only with blistering small arms fire but also with one of the heaviest mortar barrages 3/1 had received since arriving in Korea. Having overrun the 3/1 outpost, the Chinese began slipping down hill from 1010 and came into hand grenade range. This cataclysmic barrage of bullets, mortars and grenades continued through the night.

In George Co., Technical Sergeant Harold E. Wilson performed heroically. As he rallied his troops to prevent the line from buckling, crawling from foxhole to foxhole, gathering ammunition from the wounded and passing it to the able bodied, he was wounded in the right arm, then the leg, the left shoulder and forehead. A mortar blast knocked him off his feet and a fragment cut his cheek. Although wounded in five places, at first light Wilson helped to drag back the bodies of four dead marines who were killed in the outpost. Finally, he allowed himself to be taken to the rear. He not only won the Purple Heart but also the Medal of Honor.

The next morning on 24 April, 3/1 attempted to disengage and move down the roller-coaster ridgeline southeast through 2/1. The trail seemed to swoop down and up every several hundred meters. The Chinese were close and nipping at the heels of the rear guard units. The day was hot again. The trip back was worse than the trip up. The Marines ran out of water but they trudged on carrying everything out: dead, wounded, guns, ammunition.

First Sergeant Edgar H. Lee of Item Co. carried six rifles on his back. He said, "They are not expendable yet." And, one way or another, they made it out. As they neared 2/1, we sent out carrying parties to help with the dead and wounded. They moved through us and then took up their new positions.

In a 48 hour period, 3/1 had taken extremely heavy casualties, but they had not broken.

***

Weldon (Ross) Rosser remembers his combat initiation, as well as the Chinese offensive:

I remember a time during the last of March or

first part of April when we started running into
stronger forces of North Koreans. One day we called
in napalm and that performed great. Then we started up this valley heading up to some hills and as
we neared the top, a gook with a .50 caliber came out
from a cave. He had me "dead-to-rights" in his
sights, but this guy over to my left was ready and shot
him just before he fired. I really feel Don Shone
from Ohio saved my life. I won't forget it. Lots
more hills and lots more rain. Lots more losses and
lots more close calls. But by the time we went into
reserve, I felt as I was getting seasoned and felt comfortable going to the next hill. By now I was first
ammo carrier. I still watched closely to cover my ass,
however. At night I kept a cigarette going to keep
awake. We had lost several men at night—they just
vanished. So I threw lots of grenades.

Our next major assault was to stop the Chinese
offensive. We came out of reserve and set up on Hill
902. I'm not sure, but I think we were trying to beat
the gooks who were coming from the other way, to
the top of 902. "Item" Company got about half way
up the ridge and dug in around midnight. Rather
we tried to dig in, but the ridge was too rocky. I
tied my sleeping bag between two trees and tried to
sleep. Couldn't sleep, so left my bag and crawled to
the ridge under a large tree.

After midnight the gooks attacked and we called
in our artillery. They got the coordinates wrong and
the artillery shells started hitting our company. It
was a nightmare—we lost around nine men to our
own guns. The next morning, I went to get my
sleeping bag, but it was gone—nothing but the ties

left where the bag had been. I had been tremen-
dously lucky that I could not sleep and moved up the
ridgeline the night before.

We started collecting the dead, then kept going
to take this tall hill. After an all-morning fight, we
got to the top facing the gooks about 200 yards away
and coming on again.

We disengaged and started down the hill firing
behind us at the gooks. We were low on water and
everyone was thirsty as hell. We were still carrying
all our gear and our dead. We were supposed to
have stalled the gooks when we assaulted that hill and
then come down another ridgeline. And we did.
But we didn't stall them for long. The gooks were
right behind us. Right on our ass.

As I remember, three guys and I were carrying a
dead marine that must have weighed 225 pounds,
but still when necessary, dropping him and firing to
the rear at those gooks. And we were dying of thirst.

Half way down the hill, I saw Anderson, who
had joined the Marines with me. I stumbled over to
him and asked for water. I was never so glad to see
someone I knew in all my life.

We finally got to the bottom of the hill where
there was a lake and I just fell in. Then, we headed
up to another ridgeline. That night, before we set up,
I saw Ka-me-ko. [John Camacho]

This was the worst battle of my time in Korea.

***

My parents learned of the battle from their "war correspondent" who went on at length in this April 29, 1951,

dispatch. (See Figure 10)

Everything is fine. Please realize that I feel fine
and I'm probably in the best shape I've ever been in
my life, except for my feet, which are minus several layers of skin. In fact, I simply wore my feet out.
The bottoms are absolutely raw. I'm in the hospital
and I'm in a bed with springs.

During the last few days, I've ridden in almost
every type of transportation: ducks, trucks, ambu-
lances, planes, trains, buses and now a ship in Pusan.
I'm drinking coffee and listening to the Phil Harris
show. I'm in a bed with springs and have a bedside
table to write on as well as a radio with earphones at
the side of my bed.

I'm aboard the hospital ship, The Haven, in
Pusan harbor. And, there are real live nurses, here.
The first American women I've seen in a long, long
time. They even tickle my feet.

It seems that I definitely have hyperhydrosis or
too much water under the skin and walking tends
to wear off layers of skin on the soles of my feet.
And, I'm in the infantry!

But, I would like to remember what I've been
through, so I'll write it to you. Now, remember, I'm
OK; so, don't worry.

Last Monday morning we got the word to move
out from reserve. The Chinks had hit the ROKs and
they had run. These Koreans won't even fight for
their country and I have no use for them whatsoever. That left a big hole in the lines above Chunchon
and we were to plug the gap. We were taken up
north in trucks across a large river called Pukhan-

Gang, above the 38th. Then we were dropped off
and started up into the mountains to set up a defense.

It was really rough going. We were soft from
reserve. The mountains seemed higher and steeper
than in South Korea. Even worse, by the time we
got to the top, we had drunk most of our water and it
was too far to go down to a stream to fill our canteens. So we did without.

These mountains have Chinese trenches dug in
a continuous line on all the ridgelines. I wonder
how many thousands of Chinese or maybe North
Korean laborers it took to dig this never ending
trench? That night we fell into the trench dog tired
and tried to sleep. But, all night we could hear firing
to the west of us where our 3rd Battalion was. Across
the valley to the north, the light of flares and the
flash of artillery showed us where our 1st Battalion
and the 3rd Battalion, 7th Marines were in a terrible
fight.

About noon, we heard that our 3rd Battalion
(Ross' Battalion) was going to be moving through us
down to the bottom of the ridge. They had been hit
hard and had many casualties. One platoon of one of
the 3rd Battalion companies was almost wiped out
when some Army artillery that was supporting the
company fouled up and dropped shells on them.
Also, our own planes mistook them for Chinese and
strafed the platoon. The Chinks were in close pursuit
when the battalion withdrew. But, like Marines, and
unlike the Army, they brought all of their gear back
with them. They left nothing for the Chinks.

As they moved through our position, I saw
marines carrying 3 rifles or 2 sleeping bags or 2

packs. They brought all their dead and wounded except a few. In the confusion of battle, four wounded men were left behind; but, six men went back to get them. The Chinks were so close that all ten were killed before they could get back to our lines.

Our 3rd Battalion moved through us all morning and they were a sorry looking lot. They were tired and beaten. And, all we could do was offer them what little water we had. I saw Ross' machinegun squad or rather a few guys from it. They said they thought he was OK.

I stood by the path all morning and into the afternoon, waiting for Ross. The word came that we were to move down the ridge as soon as 3rd Battalion had moved through us. We were ready to leave as the last of the stragglers were coming down, when I saw Ross. I wanted to run up and grab him and shout, "Thank God, you're OK." But all I did was smile and say, "How's it going?" Then I looked closer and got quite a shock. He wasn't the Ross I had always known. He looked years older. All the life was out of him. He looked like he had given up. He just didn't care, anymore. His face was drawn. I thought he was going to burst into tears at any moment and his voiced cracked when he talked.

He said, "Pretty rough. We lost 3 men out of our squad, last night. Some from the Chinks and some from that damned Army artillery."

"Sit down and have some water." I said.

"Thank God; I haven't had any since last night." He said.

"Have you got any mail?" He asked.

"Yes." And, I gave him all my mail.

Since we didn't have time to read all the letters, we traded. He gave me his. Then, he got up.

He said, "I'll see you." And, he started down the trail.

(See Figure 10)

I felt the most helpless I think I have ever felt. All I could do was give him that little bit of water. It about broke me up to see him like that.

But, all I said was, "Play 'er cool, Ross." Just like I did when we were growing up.

Only, I really meant it because there were Chinks on three sides of us. He looked back kind of sad and went on down the hill.

We moved out behind the 3rd Battalion and went down the trail to the valley. The weather was hot and the trail, dusty. We found a stream, there in the valley, that was partially dammed, forming a small pond. But, big enough to get wet and fill our canteens. Some of the guys actually went in. Then, we started across the valley and up the path to the next ridgeline. This was the mountain behind the one where we had been. Always higher. You'd think, "Surely, we'll get there, soon," but we'd round the next bend in the trail and still have to go higher. We were moving faster, now, because the Chinese were firing on our rear. They were right on our heels. Seemed like thousands of them.

Now that I had filled my canteen from the stream, I swore that I would not take a drink until I got to the top. I was soon completely exhausted. My tongue was swollen. It felt like I had cotton in my mouth. It was so dry that I couldn't even spit. And, I cursed those two heavy ammo cans.

Finally, we made it to the top and I sat down below the ridgeline, exhausted. The machinegun section leader came over and said that I'd better go over the ridge and dig in but I had better keep low. Snipers, you know. I was too tired. I didn't care if there were snipers. But, fortunately the ground was not hard and I did dig a deep hole.

The mountain ridgeline was like a T. We were on the top bar of the T and the Chinese were trying to come up the trail that was the leg of the T. Where the trail intersected with the ridgeline was one of our heavy machineguns. As my luck would have it, my squad's machinegun [manned by Krauss and McGrath] was set up in a hole right next to mine. Machineguns attract a lot of attention.

It was dark when I finished digging. I ate some canned fruit for the juice and got ready for first watch. We were going to have 50% watch that night, which means half the troops would be up the first half of the night and the rest would have the last half. I was faced not toward the trail but straight over the rim. There was a gentle slope for some15 yards as far as I could see; then, the slope became much steeper down to the valley.

I could hear the Chinks crawling up the hillside in front of me. Their leader kept yelling and blowing a whistle. My M1 rifle was ready, pointed down the incline and I had two grenades ready. Then things quieted down.

After midnight, everything exploded. In the darkness, the Chinks had set up a machinegun down the trail at the bottom of the T and began to fire into our positions on the ridgeline or the top of the T.

Our machinegun, the one at the head of the trail, began firing back. Quickly, a battle began between the two. Further down the trail, the Chinks began firing rockets into our positions. They had captured one of our bazookas from the ROKs or the Army and were firing it against us.

My machinegun, out on the ridgeline of the T, started firing at the gook machinegun and that drew fire. Bullets and rockets were hitting all around my hole. One bullet thudded into the side of my hole right next to me. And, this battle kept up all night. One continuous nightmare.

One of our planes took up a station above us and dropped parachute flares that lit up the whole area. But, of course, the Chinks could see, too. They had climbed to a point right below us; just over the gentle slope. Perhaps, only 25 yards away. Just below sight level. They were shouting, "Marines, you die," and blowing whistles and bugles. Then, they began tossing grenades uphill at us. Some rolled back down but some caught in soft earth and exploded close by.

While most of the machinegun battles were taking place, I was in the deepest part of my hole trying to be as small as possible as the bullets and rockets whizzed overhead or thudded around my hole. But, when it sounded like the Chinks were coming over the rise at any time, someone threw a grenade and everyone in our squad followed. We rolled them downhill. We threw them straight out so they dropped down on the gooks. We lobbed the grenades until, I think, we had thrown all we had.

For the first time, I got scared. I got the shakes

and shook all night. I shook so hard I could hardly light a cigarette. But, they tell me that no matter how long you have been in combat, you get the shakes every so often.

Incidentally, the next morning we found that we had slaughtered the Chinks below us that night.*

The hill we moved onto the next day was the worst. Guys were exhausted from lack of sleep and the strain of climbing. This ridge of mountains was the highest, yet. I thought we would never get to the top. The tortures of the climb are indescribable. It was one living hell.

But, that night we got rest. I guess the Chinks didn't know exactly where we were. Somehow, I missed guard duty and slept all night. But, the strangest thing happened. I dreamed that I was back home and it seemed absolutely real. I walked from downtown out Maine Street to Pierce Street and then home. I remember every block and every house. Now, that has to be 19 blocks. When they woke me up, I could not believe I was there in Korea. My dream had become reality and reality had become a dream.

On that day about noon, we got the word that we were moving back, again. And, in the late afternoon, we pulled out down the mountain. Half way down, my legs were shaking from the strain. My feet felt raw. The weight of my pack and ammo cans

---

* The *U. S. Marine Operations In Korea*, Vol. IV describes the event thus, "Only minor patrol actions resulted except for two attacks in company strength on 2/1 at 0050 and 0150. Both were repulsed with total CCF (Chinese) losses of 25 counted dead."

forced me downhill and I couldn't stop. My legs and feet ached and ached. We, finally, stopped for a break.

One of the Fox Company machine gunners went mad. Completely crazy. He was frothing at the mouth. Mucous was coming out his nostrils. His face was streaked with sweat, tears, and dirt. And, he screamed, "Marines are supposed to stand and fight. But, all we do is run. You dirty cowards! I'm going back and kill those Chinks." He kept yelling, "Kill those Chinks."

The Corpsmen took him on down the hill.

We went down into the valley. I thought how easy it would be to quit. No more terrible ammo cans to weight me down. If I could just pass out! There's a thought. My feet were on fire. I was in a daze, but I saw a duck (an amphibious truck) in front of me. I thought, "I'll put my ammo on it. That wouldn't be throwing it away."

But something said to me that the squad won't have it, if I leave it. And, then, I was past the duck. I hadn't quit.

One of the squad leaders from a rifle platoon came up and noted that I had fallen behind quite a bit. And, he took my ammo and carried it for me until I caught up with my squad.

By the time I reached the river I could barely walk. My feet seared with pain. So, I turned-in to sick bay.

They took me across the river on a duck. I got on an ammo truck with other casualties and was taken back to the field hospital at Chunchon.

As we left, it was dark and the mountains were

on fire around us. All the troops were coming across the river. Some were wading across waist deep in the river. Everything was getting mixed up and there was complete turmoil on this side.

The field hospital at Chunchon was moving back so the next day we, a group of lightly wounded or injured casualties, went down to Hongchon by truck where we spent the night. It rained and the weather was too bad to get planes out, so the next day we went by ambulance to an Army hospital at Hoengsong. Then, today, we caught a C-47, a four motored plane, to Pusan. [incorrect, probably a C-54] We took a train from the airport to Pusan, then a bus to the hospital ship.

This hospital ship is really fine. I'm so glad to be here rather than in an Army hospital. There's nothing like the Navy for good care.

This letter to my folks didn't mention that during the battle I was so scared I had to urinate copiously; that I rolled out of my foxhole many times to "piss downhill on the gooks," while lying on my side; and that, just as quickly, I rolled back into my foxhole. Nor that I tried to get my whole body in my helmet when the gooks started firing rockets at us from a captured American bazooka.*

Ross and John Camacho made it to the other side of the river also and were not casualties. Gene Burnett was driving

---

*The "bazooka" was a 3.5 inch rocket launcher with a smooth bore tube, 60.25 inches long. A high explosive anti-tank rocket loaded into the breech end completed an electrical circuit. When ignited through this circuitry, the rocket was propelled through the launcher tube by the jet action of the rocket motor. The "bazooka" was a crew served weapon, primarily used as an anti-tank device. The crew consisted of a gunner and loader.

a DUKW (duck) across the Pukhan River that night, ferrying
casualties across.

When next I wrote my parents on May 9, 1951, I was
leading the good life in the hospital.

> There's nothing like this life of leisure. When I
> first got here, the nurses wheeled me to the head in
> a wheelchair. But, now, I'm allowed to wear house
> slippers and shuffle to the head. I get foot baths
> twice a day and have to elevate my feet and keep
> them uncovered so they can dry out and grow skin.
> At first, I was getting shots of penicillin, also.
>
> Just across the ward is a wounded guy who
> wrote one of my favorite songs, "Somehow." Billy
> Eckstein sings it. He's a colored guy named "Duke"
> Upshawl and he has written several popular songs.
> He works for MGM in civilian life. Now, it's the 5th
> Marines.
>
> Then, there's a Frenchman from Paris. He has
> helped me to brush up on my French. This hospital
> ship takes care of casualties from all the U.N. forces.
> But, I can't get around much to met others in our
> ward. They won't let me.
>
> I'm answering about three of your letters, now.
> The fellows in the ward are really envious of me. I
> have received seven letters since I have been here.
>
> I'm glad that everybody likes what I write. It
> really makes me proud. Thanks for the notebook and
> mechanical pencil.
>
> I don't know how long I'll be here. Something
> new broke out, today. I have raw places under my
> arm pits and a breaking out on my posterior. You
> know what I mean. I wonder if it isn't from lying in

bed for so long. I haven't been out of this ward for ten days. The doctor won't let me get up on my feet except to go to the head. He cut the dead skin off of my heel. I've got a hole about three layers of skin deep in my heel, now, but its healing fine.

I hate to write such a short letter, but nothing really is happening here.

To my knowledge the Navy medical service was exemplary. Few Marines would find fault with the Navy Corpsmen who were by their side in battle. We owe a tribute to these Navy personnel who wear the uniform of Marines. They are to be honored, for they are the first to tend the casualty.

In Korea, the Battalion Aid station was next in line to receive the stricken. This was the first line for stabilizing the patient. Navy field hospitals, miles behind the lines and, generally, out of artillery range, performed necessary surgery and stabilized the patient to be transported. The more seriously wounded were transported to Japan and, when recovered sufficiently, sent home to the states or back to Korea. Some patients remained at the field hospital until recovered to be cleared to return to combat duty.

From the field hospital, certain patients with long term but not serious incapacities were sent to the hospital ship. I was in this group. I had an injury that would take an indeterminate time to heal.

The hospital ship became boring because of the transient population. The troops, as I got to know this patient and that, were always leaving to go back to their companies. New troops did arrive, but that was no great solace. They usually were too sick to talk at first.

So I had plenty of time to write...like this letter on May 16, 1951.

Well, I have been aboard this hospital ship over two weeks, now. I don't know how much longer I will have to stay. I've stopped taking foot baths. I'm not getting any treatment. I guess the doctors are just waiting for the old skin to come off and the new skin to get tough enough to walk on.

Every day's about the same. I've read about every book in the ship's library. We have sick call in the morning, when the doctor looks at everybody. Then the rest of the day we read, sleep, play cards or listen to the radio. Sometimes we get to go to the show. It's pretty dull.

To answer your question, I can't send money home in the mail. We get paid in military script. Not dollar bills. At home, these bills would be just so much paper. I thought that I sent you some of this script one time so you could see what it was. Anyway, the smallest money order that I can send is $50. I may just let my pay ride on the books and just keep the money I have to last me until I come home. I think that will be in October or November.　[It turned out to be March 1952]

Good news! The doctor just came around and told me that I can get up now. They're going to give me new clothes and he said to put on my boondockers and walk a lot. I guess that's to toughen my feet and to strengthen me up after being in bed so long.

I suppose one of these days I'll be leaving for casual company in Mason. Then from there I'll go back up to the front.

Soon, it would be time to return to the lines. And, again,

would the affliction of my feet return? So few go to the lines; so few have ever been in combat; so few have known the battle. So, "Why me?" The thought, the worry crept in. But I was young and did not dwell on the dark side of life. An inspirational note was written on May 22, 1951—so typical of a very young man. I wonder how my parents received it.

I left Pusan and the hospital ship on May 20th, going to Mason where the airfield is located. We flew from Mason to Wonju. That's where I am now. Tomorrow we're supposed to go up to the lines. Today our division jumped off in the attack. So I guess I'll be ridge running soon.

Before the Chinese offensive, when we were in reserve and going on patrol each day, I experienced one particular beautiful day but have forgotten to write about.

On this brilliant morning, it had been a tough and arduous patrol up the long path to the top of this hill. But, at the top, in the morning calm, the strain was over. The path downward was easy. The pack on my back seemed lighter.

The morning mists rose from the valley. On mountain and in valley, emerald green pervaded all the plush vegetation. I, too, was invigorated. I felt exhilarated, magnificent, invincible. This was the end of another combat patrol in Korea. And, I had survived!

Since I'm going up to the front, I'll write when I can.

***

During the Chinese offensive of 22-25 April, the casualties for the 1st Marines numbered nearly 300. As the crises passed, so did the command. In a simple ceremony on the afternoon of 24 April, General Smith was relieved by Major General Gerald C. Thomas as 1st Marine Division commander. General Thomas had been a marine since 1917. He won a Silver Star and was wounded in France during World War I. He served on Guadalcanal and Bougainville in World War II. Later he served in China. He would now lead the Marine offensive against the communists.

The Marines pulled back east of the Pukhan River around Chunchon and then continued to withdraw south to the new NO NAME Line northwest of Hongchon. As the plan began, four battalions—1/1, 2/1, 3/5, 3/7—had taken up positions on the west bank of the Pukhan to protect the bridge and ferry sites while other units crossed. Thus protected, the withdrawal went smoothly.

It was apparent by this time that the enemy had been mauled by the IX Corps in this sector. Now the communists shifted their drive to smash the I Corps and capture Seoul by May Day, the world-wide Communist holiday. They were soundly repulsed. The Eighth Army had found new spirit with Ridgway and Van Fleet.

A shortage of vehicles slowed the withdrawal to Hongchon, but by 30 April the 5th Marines, KMC Regiment, and 7th Marines were deployed right to left on the Line northwest of Hongchon. The 1st Marines were in reserve closer to Hongchon.

Although this Spring Offensive had been a resounding defeat with UN estimates of enemy casualties ranging from 70,000 to 100,000, intelligence officers warned that this was only the first round. The Chinese had 17 fresh divisions waiting for the second round.

As Van Fleet again shuffled the 1st Marine Division to the X Corps, the Chinese attacked the eastern front on 16 May. They broke through 5th and 7th ROK Divisions and penetrated 30 miles. Now directly in the path of the enemy, the 7th Marines were attacked by the Chinese, slashing behind their lines to cut the MSR. Item Co. (I/3/7) held and in the counterattack sealed off the Chinese escape route and slaughtered the enemy force.

This second phase offensive in May is best described by *U. S. Marine Operations In Korea,* Vol. IV:

> On the 18th the 1st Marine Division, carrying out X Corps orders, began a maneuver designed to aid the U.S. 2d Infantry Division on the east by narrowing its front. The 7th Marines pulled back to NO NAME Line to relieve the 1st Marines [now out of reserve], which side-slipped to the east to take over an area held by the 9th Infantry. The 5th Marines then swung around from the Division left flank to the extreme right and relieved another Army regiment, the 38th Infantry. This permitted the 2d Infantry Division to face east and repulse attacks from that direction.

> By noon on 19 May the enemy's renewed ... Offensive had lost most of its momentum as CCF (Chinese) supplies dwindled to a trickle along a tenuous line of communications. That same day, when Colonel Wilburt S. Brown took over the command of the 1st Marines from Colonel McAlister, all four Marine regiments were in line—from left to right, the KMCs, the 7th Marines, the 1st Marines, and the 5th Marines. A new NO NAME Line ran more in a east-west direction than the old one with its northeast

to southwest slant. Thus in the east of the Marine sector the line was moved back some 4,000 yards while remaining virtually unchanged in the west.

At the end of the line the Marines had the second of their two fights during the CCF offensive. Major Morse L. Holliday's 3/5 became engaged at 0445 on the 20th with elements of the 44th Division. Chinese in regimental strength were apparently on the way to occupy the positions of the Marine battalion, unaware of its presence.

This mistake cost them dearly when 3/5 opened up with every weapon at its disposal while requesting the support of Marine air, rockets, and artillery. The slaughter lasted until 0930, when the last of the routed Chinese escaped into the hills. Fifteen were taken prisoner and 152 dead were counted in front of the Marine positions.

From 20 May onward, it grew more apparent every hour that the second installment of the CCF ... Phase Offensive had failed even more conclusively than the first. The enemy had only a narrow penetration on a secondary front to show for ruinous casualties. Worse yet, from the Chinese viewpoint, the UN forces were in a position to retaliate before the attackers recovered their tactical balance. The Eighth Army had come through with relatively light losses, and it was now about to seize the initiative.

***

My next letter on May 28, 1951, digressed into obvious emotional depression. Outwardly, the five day flu had taken it's toll on my good humor. Inwardly, something more troubling.

I'm still in division casual company. So far, I've been gone from Dog Co. for a month. I've been here about six days because of diarrhea. But, I'm getting over it now. So I'll probably leave here in the next few days.

We hear we have about 50,000 Chinese in a trap, now, and I also hear around here that things will soon be over. [Not so. War would continue two more years.] Anyway, one of these days, the division is supposed to go into X Corps reserve. At that time, all the reserve Marines will be sent home and will be replaced with regular Marines. [Completely untrue rumor.] I hope to spend maybe June and July in reserve someplace.

I don't think I'll even try to get a transfer. Although my feet are so unreliable, I'm still going to try one more time on the lines.

Three months ago today I landed in Japan. I believe this has been the longest 3 months of my life. It is a very strange feeling. It seems like all of this is a dream. When I do dream it's always about home. I completely forget about Korea. But, when I wake up, it's hard to realize that I'm really here. And, it seems like home is so far away, then.

I remember I still felt sick when I left casual company. Probably, more deep in my psyche was the fact that every time I had been on line for any length of time and had to carry those ammo cans that weighed almost 20 pounds each, my feet became raw in short order. Two or three layers of skin would quickly disintegrate. I had been either in a field hospital or the hospital ship on three occasions during the past three months and could not help but wonder if it would happen a fourth time.

Indeed, even more immediate questions existed. I had been in bed for almost a month. Was I in shape for combat? Did I have the strength and stamina to carry the ammo cans up and over the ridgelines once again? In my youthful despair, these questions deeply troubled me. For a marine prides himself on being able to do the job. I pondered that I might not be able.

Figure 4 ABOARD TROOP SHIP
PFC Weldon (Ross) Rosser and PFC Burton (Al) (Andy)
Anderson on the "purple" Pacific

Figure 5 IN RESERVE–KOREA
PFC Weldon (Ross) Rosser and PFC Burton (Al)
(Andy) Anderson in reserve prior to the Chinese
Spring Offensive

Figure 6
IN RESERVE–KOREA
PFC Carl Krauss (gunner) and PFC Burton (Al) (Andy) Anderson (ammo carrier) in reserve prior to the Chinese Spring Offensive

Figure 7
BURNETT AND DUKWs
CPL Floyd (Gene) (Smiley)
Burnett and a DUKW from the
1st Amphibian Truck Company

Figure 8

CAMACHO AND
HORSESHOE RIDGE
PFC John (Ka-Me-
Ko) Camacho, 1951,
and Horseshoe Ridge,
1991

Figure 9

ONTIVEROS AND SWARTZWELDER

PFC John Ontiveros (acting squad leader) at bunker where he earned the Bronze Star

PFC James (Swartzy) Swartzwelder, now James Forrest

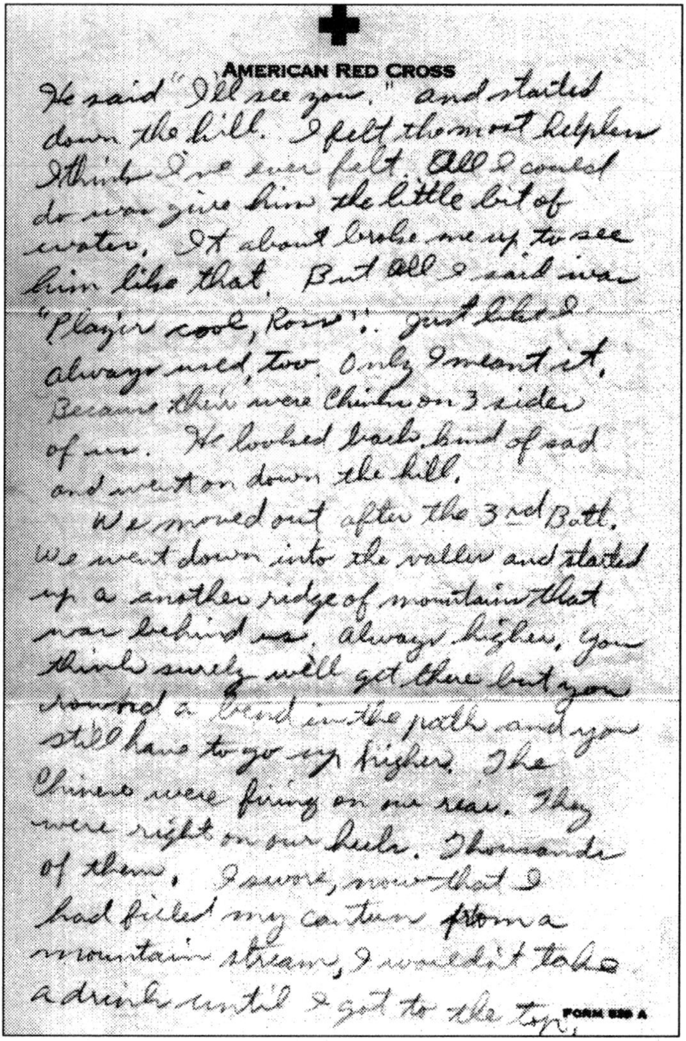

AMERICAN RED CROSS

He said "I'll see you." and started down the hill. I felt the most helpless I think I've ever felt. All I could do was give him the little bit of water. It about broke me up to see him like that. But all I said was "Play'er cool, Ross". just like I always used, too. Only I meant it, Because there were Chinks on 3 sides of us. He looked back kind of sad and went on down the hill.

We moved out after the 3rd Batt. We went down into the valley and started up a another ridge of mountains that was behind us. Always higher. You think surely we'll get there but you round a bend in the path and you still have to go up higher. The Chinese were firing on our rear. They were right on our heels. Thousands of them. I swore, now that I had filled my canteen from a mountain stream, I wouldn't take a drink until I got to the top.

Figure 10 A CORRESPONDENT'S PAGE
Copy of a page from a letter written aboard the hospital ship, The Haven (See Page 180)

1st Marine Division

CHAPTER EIGHT

IN THE AIR,
ON LAND AND SEA

Depending on the sector in which we were located, the lead units in the attack might have as many as three forward observers—air, artillery, naval gunfire. Most often, the artillery observer was present to call in artillery coordinates to the 11th Marines for that support. In fact, 3rd Battalion (3/1) was supported by both Marine and Army artillery observers on Hill 902 when blocking the Chinese offensive.

On many occasions, the forward air controller on the ground talked directly to the pilot overhead. When within range in the eastern sector, Navy observers assigned to our forward units called in coordinates for heavy naval gunfire from ships off shore in the Sea of Japan. This was the long-standing Marine Corps doctrine of close support. Specifically, the Navy, the Marine artillery as well as the Marine Air Wing, supported the troops on the ground.

Differing military philosophies opposed this doctrine as well as others of the Corps. From a less strident viewpoint, it might be observed that basic differences in tactics between the military services cause a multitude of problems, particularly when combining services with different strategies.

The Marines are assault troops, a mobile attack force. In a fast aggressive offense, they strike straight ahead as fast as possible, taking as much enemy ground as quickly as possible. They do the cleaning up later. However, the Army does just the opposite. The Army mops up all resistance and secures the area before moving out to the next objective. The one tactic is a fast maneuver, the other a slow operation. When Marine units are combined with other armed forces, these differences may cause horrendous problems.

Close air support of Marine ground troops was such a problem in Korea. The Air Force doctrine of strategic warfare was at odds with the Marine Corps doctrine of close air support. The commander of the Fifth Air Force administered the air war as the Army Corps commanders administered the ground war. The Marines, undoubtedly the best troops and pilots in Korea, were under the command of other services. Make no mistake then, the 1st Marine Air Wing was under the command of the Fifth Air Force.

From the Fifth Air Force commander's viewpoint, his control system provided a flexible means of controlling and directing air power as well as providing priority as needed. He did not intend to change it.

His system divided the enemy-held territory into 22 sections. Squadrons of the Fifth Air Force were required to make hourly flights, every day, over the same sector until the pilot was so familiar with the area that he would immediately notice any change and report it.

From the ground the forward air controllers (FACs), carrying their back-pack radios and attached to the infantry, would request close air support.

The Fifth Air Force used special airborne controllers called tactical air coordinator, airborne (TACA), were used by the Fifth Air Force when the FACs were unable to control airstrikes from the ground because of terrain and battle conditions. Known as "Mosquitos," they flew the World War II low-winged trainers, T-6 or Navy SNJ, built by North American. Locating the target from above, they would then direct the air strike.

From these two points, all information was funneled back into the Tactical Air Control Center (TACC) of the Fifth Air Force-Eighth U.S. Army Korea (EUSAK), Joint Operations Center (JOC), code name "Mellow." At the discretion and direction of JOC, planes were dispatched for interdictory attacks on the enemy deep in his territory or for close air support to the ground troops.

The Marine air controllers on the ground were separated from their air power. They had to request support from JOC, who might or might not send support. Likewise, no assurance of Marine air was possible. It was first come first served. At any given time the Marine pilots might be supporting the ROKs in the west and the Air Force supporting the Marines. As far as the Marines were concerned, they were totally at the whim of JOC and the Marines did not like it. They felt they were losing their established system of close air support and more specifically that which came from Marine air.

The official history, *U.S. Marine Operations in Korea,* Vol. IV comes right to the point:

> Operation KILLER was the first real test of the JOC system as far as the Marines were concerned, and both the flying and ground-force Marines felt that it had shown grave shortcomings. Air support on 1 March proved so disappointing that General Puller, as temporary commander of the 1st Marine Division, reported the situation to General Shepherd, commanding FMFPac [Fleet Marine Force, Pacific]. His letter is quoted in part as follows:
>
> "We are having very little success in obtaining

Marine air for CAS {close air support} missions
and practically no success in having Marine air on
station for CAS missions.... Most of our CAS missions in the current operation have been Air Force or
Navy Carrier planes. They do a good job and we are
glad to have them, but our Marine air, with whom we
have trained and operated, can do a better job. We
have attempted to insure that Marine air would support us, and to cut down the delays in receiving such
support, as evidenced by the attached dispatches.
We have received no decision relative to our requests.
Apparently, the answer is no by default."

General Puller's report was obviously written
for the record, since General Shepherd was present
at the 1st Marine Division CP at the time. He witnessed personally the Marine attacks of 2 and 3
March and the air support they received. On the 3rd,
the day of heaviest fighting in the entire operation,
there could be no complaint that few Marine aircraft supported Marine ground forces. The Corsairs
flew 26 CAS sorties that day and cleared the way
more than once for the 2d and 3d Battalions of the
7th Marines. The trouble was that air support as
administered by JOC was so often late in arriving,
even when requested the evening before. More than
once the infantry had to go ahead with only artillery
support. Such delays threw the whole plan of attack
out of gear, for air and artillery had to be closely
coordinated to be at their best.

General Shepherd had a series of talks with
General Harris [Commander, 1st Marine Air Wing].
Both then conferred with General Partridge, com-
mander of the Fifth Air Force. They requested that

he authorize the 1st MAW to keep two planes on station over the 1st Marine Division whenever it was engaged. General Partridge did not concur. He maintained that Marine aircraft should be available to him if needed elsewhere in an emergency. He did consent, however, to permit 1st MAW armed reconnaissance sorties to check in with DEVAS-TATE BAKER [Marine Tactical Air Control Squadron (MTACS) 2] for any CAS requests.

This conference did much to clear up the situation. On 5 March no less than 48 Marine sorties reported to DEVASTATE BAKER, though there was little need for them in mopping-up operations. And during the next two weeks an average of 40 sorties a day was maintained.

From statistics which support the claims, during the Inchon-Seoul Operations in the fall of 1950, the average time from a request to planes over the target was 15 minutes. By May and June of 1951 it took 80 minutes—with approximately 35 minutes of the time required to process the request through JOC. In fact, only 65 to 70 percent of the sorties requested were ever received by Marine ground forces.

Again, complaints by Generals Shepherd and Harris to General Partridge were to no avail, as was a complaint to General Ridgway on 24 May. Partridge, however, maintained that he assigned the 1st Marine Air Wing and used it just as any other unit of the Fifth Air Force. He missed the point that close air support was either too little or too late or not at all.

A partial solution to the problem resolved when new commanders met and agreed on a plan to cut down delays. Major General Frank Everest replaced Partridge, commanding the

Fifth Air Force, and Major General Thomas Cushman replaced Harris, commanding the 1st Marine Air Wing. These commanders simply moved the Marine Aircraft Group-12 (MAG-12) up to K-46 at Hoengsong, 40 miles from the front and a 10 minute flight. Additionally, a four-plane alert for use by the 1st Marine Division was established as well as permission for DEVASTATE BAKER to put in an alerting call directly to the field. Only one problem remained, the Marines still had to make requests for close air support to JOC.

The system worked as described in *U.S.Marine Operations in Korea,* Vol. IV:

> There was, for instance, the occasion when OYs [fixed-wing observation planes] discovered an enemy regiment near the 1st Marine Division right flank. DEVASTATE BAKER called the 1st MAW direct on 31 May for 16 fighters as soon as possible. Wing called JOC for approval to launch the flight and put in a call to K-46 to alert the planes. In just 48 minutes after the initial call from DEVASTATE BAKER, 16 pilots had jumped into their flight gear at K-46, had been briefed, and were airborne on what proved to be a timely strike with excellent results.

> A new tactic of night support was introduced late in May when Marine R4D transports were out-fitted to operate as flare planes. Not only did these unarmed aircraft light up targets along the front lines for the VMF(N)-513 night fighters; they were also on call for use by the 1st Marine Division. Later, on 12 June, the Navy provided the 1st MAW with PB4Y-2 Privateers for the nightly illumination missions.

This document indicates that night illumination was

implemented in May. But on the night of 24 April a transport plane of this type dropped parachute flares during the Chinese spring offensive.

***

After a year of war in Korea our government's tactic was to negotiate with the communists because of U.S. opponents in Congress and the general public. "Don't push up the peninsula again. Let's just get this over with and get the boys home," cried the malcontents.

Unfortunately, because of our media, the Chinese knew of the disgruntled portion of our population. Consequently, they prolonged the negotiations for a cease fire in Korea in hopes of getting a better deal. The Chinese imagined that this outcry represented the majority of the United States public and the Chinese representatives stalled negotiations. This defeatist attitude of some of our citizens not only caused a questionable negotiation, but a war that lasted two years longer while these negotiations continued. Tragically, many, many more young men were killed or wounded.

We, the United States, had lost sight of one of the primary principles of war: wage absolute unlimited war in which victory depends on the total annihilation of the enemy.*

Ernest Hemingway stated this concept of waging war in a different manner, "... there are worse things than war; and all of them come with defeat. The more you hate war, the more you know that once you are forced into it, for whatever

---

*Unlimited victory had been our principle in every war we had ever fought until Korea and Vietnam. Slowly beginning in the 1950s and building in the 1960s and 1970s, the strident, vehement voices of the pacifists, communists, socialists, liberals and their sympathizers forced the military to discard this basic tenet of war. The outcome in Korea was undesirable, the outcome in Vietnam, pathetic.

reason it may be, you have to win it...."

This principle of waging war to the fullest to ensure victory evolved from the concepts of Prussian General Karl von Clausewitz. He systematized the revolutionary changes in warfare that had taken place in his lifetime and compiled them in his famous book *On War* published in 1833. The tenets of General von Clausewitz are as meaningful today as they were when he wrote them.

To paraphrase Von Clausewitz: War is part of the intercourse of the human race. It is a conflict of great interests which is settled by bloodshed. War is the province of physical exertion and suffering, where a certain strength of body and mind is required; and with these qualifications, man is at once a proper instrument for war.

***

One such proper instrument of war was Gene Burnett, who disembarked from the USNS Randall in Pusan, but did not take the train north like most of us. Much to his disappointment, he was not ordered to a rifle company on line. He traveled north by truck to a small sea coast town, Pohang-Dong, which was about half way up the eastern side of the South Korean controlled part of the peninsula. During World War II a Japanese air base had been located in the vicinity and this had subsequently become a Marine air base, K-3.

The 1st Amphibian Truck Company was headquartered at the "port" of Pohang where extreme tidal action required freighters and tankers to anchor a mile off-shore for unloading cargo. Utilized as cargo carriers the DUKWs (Dual Utility Kargo, Water) ferried supplies to the beach. This was Gene's first duty assignment as well as his introduction to DUKWs, but soon he would become a driver of one of these strange contraptions.

Later in his tour, Gene's DUKW unit was moved north from Pohang in support of the Korean Marines (KMC) and attached to the 7th Motor Transport Battalion. Subsequently, the entire Amphibian Truck Company would be attached to the 7th.

"Shorty," his driver/instructor, took him in tow and taught him all the fundamentals in short order. It seemed that since landing at Inchon, "Shorty" had tried to transfer to the 5th Marines, obviously without success. Apparently, he had been promised the transfer as soon as he trained a new driver. It took him only three weeks.

Gene remembers a side note to this three week encounter with "Shorty." As Gene left the train in Los Angeles on his return home from Korea, he met "Shorty," who had just been released from the Naval hospital. "Shorty" explained that he had been wounded about four weeks after leaving Pohang and joining the 5th Marines. In fact, he swore that Gene had been the driver of the DUKW that had ferried him across a river. But since "Shorty" was so badly wounded at the time, he could not get Gene's attention.

Nevertheless, "Shorty" taught Gene Burnett the basics of a DUKW* and Gene recalls that description as a six wheel drive with a high/low range transmission and a two man crew. This amphibian was about seven feet high, eight feet wide, 31 feet long, and weighed 11,000 pounds unloaded. Its

---

*Each tire could be individually inflated or deflated from inside the cab at the discretion of the driver depending on the terrain. A compressor control on the instrument panel provided this facility. Additionally, while in the water, four bilge pumps could be activated from the cab. On land, however, hand valves emptied the bilges.

Upon entering the water, the propeller was engaged from inside, and for most water travel, full throttle was required. If more speed was desired, all six wheels were left in drive. (*Continued on next page*)

payload was 2 1/2 tons (5000 pounds).

In Korea, DUKWs had varied uses. The two principal purposes, however, were: (1) off-loading cargo from ships— gasoline, bombs, ammo, supplies—and (2) ferrying troops across rivers, lakes and reservoirs.

Although well trained by "Shorty" during his three week training session in the intricately interesting care and tending of "ducks," Gene retained his morose attitude. He wanted to go to a line company. He didn't care which one or where they were. The routine of off-loading cargo ships was pure misery. How could the personnel assignment people not realize the obvious? He was a fighting marine! Not a keeper of "ducks." Likewise, following "Shorty's" example, he immediately put in for transfer—to no avail. The Marines needed a "duck" keeper. (See Figure 7)

"Smiley" Burnett, normally happy and carefree turned somber and slightly sinister. His morbid side appears in this episode:

> On one occasion upon being assigned the duty to off-load cargo, he had to ferry 40 to 50 Korean stevedores out to a ship in the harbor. These stevedores

---

Two storage hatches were located forward and aft for such gear as tarps and life jackets. In the rear deck was located the spare wheel, and in a well, the winch, which was used with a bi-pod to off-load cargo from other vehicles. Nevertheless, a more common use was to winch the DUKW out when stuck. A shovel and a hand bilge pump were carried on the front deck. Also located here was the engine compartment.

First utilized in World War II, the DUKW carried 105mm howitzers and the gun crew, as well as a supply of artillery shells to the beach, usually in the third or fourth wave. Each platoon had one vehicle with an "A" frame to off-load the guns. After performing this primary mission, the DUKWs were then used to carry ammo and rations in to the beach and wounded out from the beach.

unloaded the cargo into the platoon of DUKWs that ferried the cargo to shore. Before allowing the passengers to board, his assistant driver purposely moved aft and opened the petcock to a rear bilge.

When loaded with the Koreans, they entered the water and naturally the water started to fill the bilge. Of course, from the cab of the DUKW, cheerful "Smiley" could activate each one or all four bilge pumps. And as they moved out toward the ship, this he did.

Making a show of allowing his assistant to take over the controls when about half way between the shore and the ship—the point of no return—he sauntered back to the rear cargo boards. With the official bravado of a sea captain, he ordered the stevedores, who were sitting there, off the cargo boards and raised the boards gingerly.

Somberly and for a period of time, he stood peering into the bilge containing the rapidly rushing water. At least he stood there long enough to attract the attention of the gooks around him. In amazement, they, too, saw the rushing water in the bilge and beheld his grave visage. Slowly he closed the bilge boards, then opened the life jacket compartment and removed two life vests.

In a production rivaling Hollywood, "Smiley" returned to his assistant and both donned the vests. Shortly after, the strident cacophony of the panicked passengers drowned out the roar of DUKWs engines.

Fortunately Gene became "Smiley" for real when his platoon was transferred north to support the troops—it seems Marines as well as other troops couldn't swim rivers well. He not only supported the Marines, but also the Greeks, Turks, KMC, and the U.S.Army.

In fact, he supported the Army 7th Signal group and ferried men, equipment and supplies across the rivers. Conversely, in a way, the 7th Signal supported him. Such luck as being attached to the Army was almost beyond his comprehension because he met a supply sergeant. Even being generous one might catagorize Marine supply sergeants as stingy. But Gene's new friend, the Army supply sergeant, was in a different league. Gene asked for two flashlight batteries, he got two boxes. He needed socks, he got six pairs. In due course Gene supplied every man in his platoon with an air mattress and much more equipment. It was Christmas all over again.

His luck continued. One day while on a mission with six Army radiomen and their equipment, Burnett approached a bridge guarded by an Army MP.

"No tracked vehicles can go on this bridge, Corporal." he stated flatly.

Being a wise-ass Marine, Gene's retort was, "If you'll notice, this vehicle has no tracks."

The Army MP looked at the six wheels for a while and, then, said, "Well, anyway, the limit is 2 1/2 tons."

"Oh, that's OK." Gene answered. "This thing only weighs around 12,000 pounds."

"In that case, go ahead." The Army MP was satisfied.

Halfway across the bridge, the Army Sergeant-in-charge of the radiomen came to his senses.

"Jesus, man, this thing weighs almost 6 tons!"

Calmly Gene reassured him, "Yeh, but if the bridge gives way, we'll float when we hit the river."

As all good things come to an end, Gene Burnett's Army tour ended and he moved on to support the KMC. It was during this tour that he was assigned an assistant driver who had been a Greyhound bus driver in civilian life. During the assistant's early training, he and Gene were washing out rice, mud and blood from the bilges. Gene had just ferried a group of Korean Marine wounded across a river and vestiges of these gutsy fighters remained.

As the work continued, Gene became convinced that he should impress this new driver with a certain fact. He had heard it from the old salts; he had no doubt about it; he knew it must be true. The bilge pumps were so superb that they could discharge any amount of incoming water. Thus, he would awe this student and show him that the DUKW was almost unsinkable.

It was a new DUKW that had been exchanged just before he had joined the KMC that he and his assistant were cleaning. As they finished, Gene went through the launch procedures. Then off into the river they went with all four DUKW bilges open.

Almost at once he realized that a great mistake had been made. Whoever told him about the bilge pumps had overstated their capacity. He lost control of the vehicle and the engine died. He yelled at his assistant to grab the hand bilge pump, although that would have been like bailing out the ocean with a bucket. His student did not move. He was petrified.

Fortunately, the river was only six feet deep, but they sank to the bottom.

Gene was furious and ask his pupil why he didn't grab the pump. He said that he couldn't swim and forgot where the pump was stored. (This is strange. Supposedly, we could not graduate from bootcamp without passing a swimming test. It was possible, however, for reserve marines to be activated without bootcamp.)

After the vehicle was retrieved, the maintenance sergeant took Gene before the platoon leader and suggested that a court martial might be in order.

The lieutenant asked if Gene had an excuse and Gene repeated what he had been told about the bilge pumps. Because of that the platoon leader felt it was an honest mistake and the issue was dropped. In deference to the maintenance sergeant, however, Gene's promotion to sergeant was put on hold.

With the following "sea stories," Gene remembers highlights of his Korean tour:

We were called out very early one morning to make a "rush" ammo run to the KMCs. We drove south for about two hours to an ammo dump and loaded up with mortar ammo. Most of the guys were loading very light, but the lieutenant told me to load all that I could. So I stood the boxes on end and then pyramided them on top. My load was about three times everyone else. Because I was overweight and would have to set the pace, I led the convoy. It was not until later that I thought what could happen if I had (1) hit a road mine or (2) had been hit by an artillery shell in the load. I would have made a fast trip home.

The lieutenant wrote a letter of commendation for another driver and me regarding this trip.

When we arrived at the KMC base, they sent a request back to have all the vehicles (DUKWs) stay at the KMC location for an impending river crossing. So since we only had what we were wearing, we sent back one driver to pick up our gear.

The rest of us began ferrying the river. We started our "ammo over/wounded or dead back" river runs. We were supplied with an English speaking KMC for part of our crew. Realizing that this whole situation might become a bit hairy, I decided it would be nice to have a little heavier weapon on board than a carbine. At first, I was thinking maybe a BAR might do. However, my KMC crewman, CPL Buc Jun Do rounded us up a light machinegun along with a ground tri-pod. So my driver and I rigged up a holder. And we were the envy of the platoon. That started everyone to attempt to find extra weapons.

During this stint with the KMC, one day I was called to pick up passengers to ferry across the river. Lo and behold, there was a general, a colonel, two majors and a sergeant, body guard. After crossing, I was told to wait for them as they would reconnoiter for two or three hours and would be back.

Shortly after they left, some wounded came down a trail and a corpsman ask me if I could get them across the river. I said, "Sure. Load 'em up."

When across, the corpsmen ask if I could take them to the aid station because one of the wounded was in a bad way and might not make it. We had to follow some pretty rough country to get to the aid station some two miles back. On the way the corpsman told me that there were going to be quite a few wounded coming down the trail soon. So when we reached the aid station, I made a request for more vehicles to go back with me.

We would load up each group of wounded as they came down the trail and take them to the aid station across the river and two miles back. I decided that there was plenty of time before the general's party returned. But on one of my return trips as I rounded a corner, I spotted them just sitting there waiting on the opposite bank. So I plowed into the river and in my haste to get across the river, I got stuck on a large underwater rock. No matter how hard I worked, I could not get off that large rock. Another vehicle came along side to try to help, but I told him to go get the general's party. And he did.

On their way back across, they passed by me and the general said, "I understand you are doing yeoman duty with the wounded, Corporal. I salute you."

And he did. Here, all the time I thought you needed a Congressional Medal of Honor to rate a salute from a general, when all you need to do is get a DUKW stuck.

Speaking of getting a DUKW stuck, it's not easy! But when you did you were in for a difficult time. Usually, you had to "dead man" yourself out. That is, hopefully, find a tree near by and winch yourself out. More than likely you'll have to go out 30 feet to the front, thread your winch cable through the vehicle and attach your anchor putting it into a hole that is four to six feet deep and covering it up. Then using low range drive and the winch, you "dead man" yourself out. This method usually takes three or four tries to get out.

In fact, getting stuck worked like this for me one time.

During the rainy season, I had driven off the road and became stuck. We were just beginning to get unstuck when down the road comes three Army tanks. The lead tank stops and offers to pull me out.

I said, "It will take all three tanks to do it."

"Just hook on the cable," he replies.

So, I hooked the cable up and away he goes. The crack of the cable parting sounded like a rifle shot. Once again, he tries with the same result. Finally he tells me, "Let's try it your way."

It didn't take three, but it did take two.

I had a lot of fun when attached to the Army. Once we were on the East Coast practicing landings, when a request came from the Army to help unload 50 gallon drums of gasoline from a Merchant Marine ship. The Army had been using LCI's [Landing Craft, Infantry] to unload the ship, but due to bad weather, they were behind schedule. So they requested our DUKWs to help out. We worked around the clock, LCIs off loading on one side of the ship and DUKWs on the other.

One night in particularly rough weather, our Platoon Sergeant wanted us to get oriented on the future work schedule, so he and a number of us drivers went out to the ship in one DUKW. When we approached the ship, we could see that it was well lighted as usual (strong flood lights over the side). There were, however, no spring lines over the side. (A spring line is a series of lines put over the side to hook on to the DUKW in order for it to stay in place with the assistance of the engine on fast idle—a method to stabilize the craft.)

No one could be seen on deck, and there was only a "Jacob's Ladder" over the side. But no gangway. Nevertheless, the sergeant felt "someone" should go aboard to check out the schedule. That "someone" was "Smiley" Burnett.

Since we had left the beach, the swells had grown considerably, but I wasn't concerned. I didn't feel there would be any problem. Consequently the driver approached the "Jacob's Ladder," two guys grabbed it and I started up. After about three steps, I had second thoughts. I looked down to tell the guys, but I discovered the DUKW had moved away. (No spring lines!) Therefore, like life, I continued up this ladder to success, taking one step at a time—but try that on a rolling, pitching "Jacob's Ladder."

But I made it. I spent about fifteen minutes getting a decision on the schedule and back to the ladder I go.

As the DUKW started to come along side and I start down the ladder, I discovered that the sea had worsened extremely during my time aboard the ship. The DUKW would reach the ladder, the guys would grab it and try to maintain some stability, but the swells would carry the DUKW away. And here I am about half way down the ladder, hanging on for dear life.

So back up to the rail I climbed and waited until the DUKW could start another run and down I would go again. After about the fourth try the guys were telling me to just jump. No way! I may look dumb. But I'm not that dumb.

I was getting worried, however, as well as cold and weak, when a voice above cries out, "Get back on this ship!"

Any voice talking to me from above, I listen to. And I came back on board. When I did I found

myself standing in front of a gentleman who introduced himself as the first mate—his name, believe it
or not, was Kidd.

"They call me, Captain Kidd," he says. "The
Captain has been watching you for the last twenty
minutes. He says you are to stay aboard for the
night."

After I yell to the crew below about what's going
on, Kidd took me to the galley for coffee.

The cook asked me, "Are you hungry?"

"Sure," I replied.

"What do you want?" he asked.

"What can I have?" I asked.

"Any damn thing you want, " he said.

"Eggs?"

"Sure. How about some ham, potatoes and
toast?"

I thought I had died and gone to heaven!

After this meal, one of the crew took me to the
fantail of the ship and into a compartment with about
twelve bunks. He gives me a blanket and tells me to
make myself at home.

I picked out an upper bunk and dozed off.
Sometime later some of the Army "off loading"
crew came in. I heard one of them ask the rest,
"Who is that?"

"Must be the marine, who came on board,
tonight," says mystery voice number 1.

Someone with a deep Mexican-accented voice
says, "Watch thees."

He walks up to my bunk, shakes me, and says,
"Hey, Amigo, you in my bunk."

I made no reply, took off the blanket, picked up

my parka and found another bunk on the other side. I climbed aboard, rolled up the parka for a pillow, covered up with the blanket and had all intentions of going back to sleep.

"Are you happy, Lopez?' someone asked.

"Not yet," he said. "Watch thees."

"Now you in my buddy's bunk, Jarhead!" He tells me as he shakes me again.

Now several points should be made: (1) soldiers should never taunt marines and (2) personal weapons were allowed in Korea; most every marine had one. My personal weapon was a Police Special .38 cal. which I had concealed under my field jacket in a shoulder holster.

At the same time as I rolled over to face Lopez, I reached for my pistol and swung it around an inch from his nose.

His eyes widened and he says, quickly, "But you can keep it!" And he makes a fast retreat.

"Now are you happy, Lopez?" Mystery voice number 2 asked.

"That fucker has a gun," Lopez replies, "and he pulled it."

"Well, go tell him he can't do that." Mystery voice number 3 is not satisfied.

"Go to hell. As far as I'm concerned, he can sleep where ever he wants to." Lopez didn't want another encounter.

The duration of the storm was three days, but it was heaven on board. Whatever I wanted to eat, whenever. And, as I remember I made $50 playing poker with my new found Army buddies. Except for Lopez. He continued to give me a wide berth.

The Army NCO in charge and I became friendly. One day we were eating lunch when the first mate came to us and mentioned that almost all their silverware was missing—there were about 40 Korean stevedores on board and the cook was feeding them. The sergeant told an English-speaking Korean to line up all Koreans in the passageway.

The sergeant asked the first man about the silverware through the interpreter. He denied having any. Then we searched him and found three pieces. Quickly, the sergeant backhanded the Korean pretty hard and jerked him forward down the passageway.

The same scenario occurred with the next man. Wham! Jerk! After the third man experienced the same results, there was a crash of silverware hitting the deck all the way down the passageway.

Needless to say, the first mate was impressed. I think we received a steak treat that night.

On the morning after the storm, a LCI tied up to the ship and a cargo net was put over the side. And an Army major aboard the LCI called out and said, "I understand there is a marine on board, who we are to take ashore."

I report to him, then start down the cargo net. Cold weather thermal boots—that's what I was wearing— were not made for climbing cargo nets. About half way down, I lost my footing and slid the rest of the way down on my back, landing on my feet on the deck of the LCI.

The major looked at me with disdain and said, "You damn marines always have to do everything with a flair, don't you!"

***

Clausewitz defined another tenet which purported: War is the province of danger, and therefore courage above all things is the first quality of a warrior.

John Camacho, a man with this kind of courage, speaks about patrols:

> After many, many patrols I even lead the way because one lieutenant was new. In fact, as radioman, I was assigned to different squads and platoons throughout Charlie (C/1/1) company—especially when we crossed a mined area. (See Figure 8)
>
> Sometimes we left our lines at dark. The worst was when someone tripped a flare before we even got into no-man's land. But at daybreak, on our return, it was great to see those dirty grimy faces of our guys when we got to our lines.
>
> During the winter we dressed in white camouflage and patrolled to an outpost in front of our lines. A sniper with an "03" [a 1903 Springfield, .30 caliber, bolt action rifle] searched for targets while we formed a perimeter defense around him. As we left our lines to go to the outpost, we always greeted "Charlie," a very frozen gook right beside the trail.

Having quickly become one of the old-timers in Charlie Co.(C/1/1), John Camacho was interviewed about his combat experiences by a Marine Corps correspondent. This interview was taped for Armed Forces Radio and John received a copy which, he says, was heavily edited because Chinese and American tactics in the field were discussed.

> Correspondent: This is Marine Corps Radio Correspondent Al Rapechi in Korea recording a special interview with Corporal John G. Camacho of

Sacramento, California.

Correspondent: How about your home address there?

Camacho: My folks live at 2114 "X" Street.

Correspondent: Do you go to school there?

Camacho: Well, I went to school in a different county, Yolo County. It's right next to Sacramento County. I went to Woodland High School. When we moved to Sacramento, I continued school for four years at Woodland High School then went into the Marine Corps.

Correspondent: Well, what do you do when you go on combat patrol?

Camacho: Well, for the combat patrol, they usually pick a squad from a platoon and brief them on the area they are going into and what to expect. Sometimes, the squad leader is told to make contact with the enemy, see if there are any enemy stragglers or snipers. Anything like that.

Correspondent: Well, you actually get into enemy territory, then. Right?

Camacho: Oh, yes, sir. Definitely.

Correspondent: What happens when you run into some of these North Koreans or Chinese and they start firing on you? Then, what happens?

Camacho: Well, mostly the combat patrol squad is not up there to actually have a "go to town" firefight. They just estimate where the enemy are positioned and then come back and make the report to the company commander which is then relayed on to the regiment and division. They more or less put that up in the operations report, I guess, to see what's at the front.

Correspondent: You go on these patrols at night, too, huh?

Camacho: Yes, there's a commando party with a radio operator. But, the operator is not necessary when four or five men go out about 100 yards in front of the lines at an outpost. Then, there has been occasions when the squad patrol has been sent out either early in the morning before daylight and they wait out there as an ambush party. If they make contact, they report in. They return to their area at daylight and make the report.

Correspondent: What's the enemy doing if they walk into this ambush?

Camacho: Well, this ambush patrol is more or less set up to catch the enemy off guard. I mean the enemy may try to send a couple of men out for probing attacks. There was an incident about two months ago where one patrol went out and actually surprised the enemy; went up on a ridge and made contact with the enemy. It got back safely but that sort of patrol was more or less our kind of probing attack. Well, it caught the enemy off guard and caught their location and position. We called in artillery on them and it was a successful patrol with only one casualty.

Correspondent: What's your greatest danger when you're on these patrols? Small arms fire or what?

Camacho: Well, the danger, which has happened to a lot of patrols, is if the area you are walking into is mined. You don't know what you're running into. You're more or less in a questioning state of mind. I mean everything is apt to come as a surprise to you. I mean you don't know exactly what is going on except that you know that you are going into an area of danger.

Correspondent: What do you think about as you are going along? You're going through these areas which may be mined or may not be mined and you never know whether you're next step is going to be on a land mine or not. What goes through your mind?

Camacho: Well, it's hard to explain. You more or less got your mind on what you are going to do, get it done and get back. Actually, you are always on the alert. I guess, you don't think about much except what you are going to do.

Correspondent: Thank you very much. You have just heard a special interview with Corporal John G. Camacho. This is Marine Radio Correspondent Al Rapechi recording from Korea.

***

Another Clausewitz tenet is a fitting response: War is the province of uncertainty. Three-fourths of those things upon which action in war must be calculated, are hidden more or less in the clouds of uncertainty.

***

Jim Swartzwelder (Forrest) began his tour of duty in Korea as a BARman.* Later, he became a squad leader. (See Prologue)

---

* The Browning Automatic Rifle (BAR), M1918A2, Cal. .30, air-cooled, gas-operated, magazine-fed, shoulder weapon with tripod, was a

All of us in the Sixth Draft who disembarked from the USNS Randall experienced differing experiences in this "fog of war." So did Jim. (See Figure 9) The following are his reminiscences:

I guess my story started quite a little bit before Korea. In fact, when the Second World War ended, I was 15 years old. Between the time I was 15 and 19, I heard all kinds of war stories about what had happened during the war. As in most instances, you only remember the good things. So the things I heard about were fun and sounded exciting. And I was sorry that I had missed it.

When I graduated from high school, I went to work for a firm where my uncle was employed. He was a Marine Corps veteran of the Second World War and was also in the reserves. So I continued to hear more exciting things about the Marines.

---

relatively light, maneuverable weapon of great firepower. The BAR weighed approximately 20 pounds with a magazine capacity of 20 rounds. The effective range was 500 yards with a normal cyclic rate of 550 rounds per minute.

The basic Marine combat unit was the fire team, built around a BAR. Each fire team, composed of the BARman, assistant BARman, rifleman and lead by the fire team leader, supplied each rifle squad with three of these weapons along with the accompanying three fire teams. Each rifle platoon consisted of three squads and nine BARs.

Because of its great firepower, the BAR was the most vital weapon of the platoon and every man had to know that weapon as well as his own M1 rifle. The basic philosophy was that any member of the platoon could take over as a BARman, if necessary.

An interesting point is that the .30 caliber ammunition used in Korea could be utilized by the M1 rifle, the BAR and the light and heavy machineguns. The ammunition for the carbine, a shorter .30 caliber round, and the .45 caliber pistol, of course, were not interchangeable.

When I had worked for about a year and a half, the Korean War began. When it started I thought to myself, "Well, here's my opportunity to join and see what all these stories have been about."

It started June 25, 1950, and the original talk at that time was, "Well, it's only going to be a month or so. It's not going to be a big thing."

So I thought, "I certainly don't want to join if it's not going to be there whenever I'm ready to go." So I hung around until the end of August and by then I thought, "Well, maybe it might last long enough for me to be there." That's when I decided to join the Corps and went to bootcamp on September 5.

I think we've pretty well shared things that happened in bootcamp. But when I left San Diego aboard ship, I really didn't pay a lot of attention to the voyage. [Note: In an earlier chapter was Jim's description of drinking liquor and being sick for much of the voyage.] I do remember arriving in Pusan and boarding a train that was pulled by a pot-bellied steam engine. The cars were very much like box cars except they had wooden seats, and in the middle, was a woodburning stove. I remember that first day we went from Pusan up to Taegu and spent the night. I'm not sure exactly where we did spend the night, but I think it was in a large building. We just bunked on the floor. The next day we boarded six-by trucks and went to Wonju.

When we pulled into Wonju, it was practical- ly decimated. The civilians were all enclosed in a large barbed wire area and the buildings were just pretty much demolished. I was very surprised when I went back to Wonju in 1990 or 1991 and saw how much had changed. And how much of the main city obviously had been left standing. There was just a part of the city that I didn't see, but there were enough old buildings that made me know that it was not quite as destroyed as I thought it had been when I arrived in 1951.

We spent the night in Wonju. The next morning, we got up, got aboard trucks again and went approximately five or six miles directly north of Wonju. We stopped along the road and they started parceling out the replacements. A fellow from Fox Co., 2nd Battalion, 7th Marines (F/2/7) was there to get his replacements. He took eight or nine of us and said, "Follow me." Of course all he was carrying was a carbine and we had full packs on our backs.

We forded a small creek and started up the mountain to this very high, distant peak. As we climbed the mountain, we began to think, "Do we really need all this stuff?" And as we headed up the mountain, as you looked back you could see various items of clothing that were being discarded because the load was too heavy to carry. After being on the ship for such a long time, we certainly weren't in very good physical shape, regardless of exercises.

Of course, the leader was saying, "Come on! Come on! Let's go! Let's go!"

As we neared our positions at the top, we began to run into dead bodies. That's where I saw my first dead gook. And as we got up to the positions, it was evident that they had been attacked within the previous 24 to 48 hours because there were a number of bodies lying about. You could tell that they weren't very old. [see Map 2 above Hoengsong]

When we arrived, we were assigned temporary foxhole buddies for that night. I dug in with a guy named Warneke. And as it got dark, you could hear the North Koreans or Chinese, whichever they were. You could hear noises down in the valley. You could hear voices and you could hear unfamiliar things happening.

So we were on 50% watch.* I stood my first hour and then I awakened Warneke. I told him, "Warneke, it's your turn." Then, I rested my head.

He started shaking me. "I hear them. They're right down below. I hear them."

So I sat up and listened for awhile. I didn't hear anything. And I said, "You know, I can't hear a thing. I don't think so." I went back to sleep.

Then he awakened me and said, "OK, your turn."

So I sat up for another hour and listened. I stood the watch and then awakened Warneke.

No sooner had I lain down and again he's shaking me, saying, "Hey, they're coming up. I can hear them. They're right down there."

This went on for three or four watches. Finally, about midnight, he awakened me one last time and I told him, "Warneke, the next time you awaken me, it better be for my watch and not to tell me about what

---

*This was different from my 50% watch, meaning half the night for half the watch, then the other half of the squad took over. Jim stood an hour on watch then an hour off. "After a tough day," he maintains, "we found it impossible to stay awake if we split the night in half."

you hear. If you awaken me again, there better be
somebody looking in this hole or you and I are going
to go to war."

Then he started standing his watch and letting me
sleep when I was supposed to.

The next morning, we were assigned to our
respective squads. I went into a squad with George
Munson as squad leader. From Long Island, New
York, George was quite a character. Any time that we
got our rations, he would sit down and eat all of
them. Then when he got hungry, he would go
scrounge from anybody that was "scroungeable."
You know, there was always "Beef and Noodles"
or "Chicken and Vegetables" or "Corned Beef Hash"
or something out of the C-rations that somebody
didn't want and he would eat that.

So at times after he had sat down and had eaten
his rations, I would say to him, "George, what are
you going to do for more chow?"

And he'd always say, "Well, the good Lord's
going to provide." It always seemed that He did.
George always had enough to eat, but he never carried any grub.

We stayed on top of that mountain all that day
and got oriented. The next morning, bright and
early, the platoon leader, Second Lieutenant Robert
Buckman, a very bright guy also from New York,
hollered, "Get up. Roll up your gear. We're getting
ready to move out."

So we got up and rolled up our gear, leaving
behind what we didn't want to carry, and started single file down the mountain. On that day as we went
northward, we just went from peak to peak, nothing

exciting happened.

On the second day when we got up and moved out, we moved toward the east across the road that was between Wonju and Hoengsong. We started up the mountains to the east and we could hear shelling; we could hear firing. We got fairly near the top of this mountain to the east of where we had started; and as we worked our way up this ridgeline, we could hear machinegun fire off to the side of the ridge-line. So we crouched down there and soon the word came, "OK, move out." We were going up to our left towards the peak, where there were bunkers, a machinegun, and it was alive with gooks. So we burst over the top of the ridgeline and headed that way. No sooner had we gotten over the top than Buckman took a round in the chest. It killed him.

Then Donald Barclay, our platoon sergeant took over and led us. We chased the goonies out of the bunkers and disabled the machinegun, securing the top of the hill. That was where I learned one of my very first lessons regarding the way the Koreans fought.

As the gooks went down the other side of the hill, many people were shooting at them. We didn't really take cover as we should have. We were very much out in the open, shooting at these goonies. Then an incoming round landed right on top of the hill. That taught me that any time the enemy occu-pied a position, they had it zeroed in with mortars from another position. If you chased them off, it wasn't any time at all until you could expect incom-ing rounds. So if you got up on top of a hill, you bet-ter protect yourself and get in a hole because it wouldn't be long before rounds would be incoming.

I had been with the platoon just a few days when that happened. We lost Buckman and a couple of other fellows whom I didn't know and had really quite a number of wounded. But we secured the top of that hill. Then for the next four or five days we just moved forward, ending up on the side of a mountain overlooking Hongchon in the valley below. Later we went into a reserve area down in Hongchon. (See Map 4)

We were in reserve there for about a week and got replacements for the casualties we had lost. We got a fellow in named Malcolm Schaffer from either Phoenix or Flagstaff, Arizona, I'm not quite sure which. He wore a khaki, heavy wool, Marine Corps issue shirt with a US flag sewn across the back. It was a flag that his brother had carried during the Second World War while in the Navy. He wore this shirt the whole time he was there which turned out not to be very long.

But we left the reserve and went up by truck, as I recall, probably 15 miles and got off of the trucks and headed northwest up toward this range of mountains. As we got to the rice paddies at the base of the mountains, we started drawing fire. Schaffer was running across the paddy right in front of me, when somebody on top of the hill had seen his American flag. They had picked him out as the one they wanted to shoot. So as we ran there were spurts of water and dirt jumping all around him. But we made it across and we went up the mountain.

As we got within 100 yards of the top, the firing

stopped and we pushed on up to the top. The enemy had scuttled down the other side. And as we looked down the other side to the west, probable 800 to 1000 yards, in a valley there was a dirt road heading west with heavy brush along the left side of it and a small stream running to the right side.

As the Marines gathered on top of the mountain, carrying machineguns, BARs, M1s, carbines and .45s, all kinds of weapons, we looked down and saw eight or ten men running down this road. So everybody started shooting at them with all these weapons.

These gooks would dive into the brush on the left side of the road; then they would come out and high port it down the road. They would go as fast as they could with all these Marine characters, roaring with laughter, shooting at them.

The gooks would run until either they tired or they felt it was time to duck under cover. They were jumping out of the brush and running down the road in just a volley of fire. Everybody thought that it was grand fun, kind of like a shooting gallery; but at that distance I don't think we hit any of them.

We pushed on, continuing forward for I don't remember how many days, until we ended up in a position quite a ways north of Hongchon. We ended up on this prominent point where you could look down into this rather large city, probably Hwachon, off to our left front. It was in enemy hands. Off to the right front, down the valley probably 600 yards away, rose another large mountain.

We sat up there on top of our mountain and dug in. That night the goonies came up all along the

line. They came up to our positions and we shot a
bunch of them. We could also hear shooting to the
east and west in front of us. About 2 o'clock, they
stopped their attack and were gone. We killed quite
a large number of them; they were all lying out in
front of us.

At first light, while bunking with George
Munson, I was startled by a loud "ka-pow." Of
course, it awakened me. George was sitting on the
edge of the foxhole and he said to me, "You want to
shoot a gook?"

And I said, "George, what are you doing?"

He said, "I've been watching them. They're
going up that mountain (the one to our right front)
and they're working up a trail through the brush
along a parallel trail that runs over the saddle at the
ridgeline. When they get up fairly near the top,
there's no brush to hide under and they have to run
over the top in the open."

It was probably 80 to 100 yards that they had to
run up the exposed trail to get to the top and over the
ridgeline. As an added targeting incentive, the
goonies were in their white uniforms.

George watched a couple of them and decided,
"Well, the next one that comes out, I'm going to
shoot him." So he sat there, shooting at them, as
these goonies ran across the mountain saddle.

At 10:30 or 11:00 o'clock that morning, we got
the word, "Come on, we're going back. We're moving out."

To the west and our left flank, a ROK outfit [the
6th ROK Division] had broken ranks and had been
overrun. The plan was for us to pull back so that the

Chinese would not cut us off at the rear. [This was the beginning of the Chinese Spring Offensive. See Map 4 for 2nd Battalion, 7th Marines (2/7)]

So we started walking. We went back down the hill, down into the valley and started walking down this dirt road at a pretty good clip. We walked all the rest of the day and all night. The next morning, the Chinese were firing on our flank. We finally set up positions 20 miles back at what was called the BLUE Line. [The BLUE Line was most probably the officially designated NO NAME Line] We established our positions on the BLUE Line on high ground, of course. And we stayed there a week.

Then the word came down, "OK, we're going to execute a 'mousetrap operation.'"*

We found out that when the gooks broke through the ROKs, the Chinese had taken off just as hard as they could go to the south. They wanted to make as deep an incursion as possible, then try to roll up the flanks. The theory behind "mousetrap" was a simple ambush, taking this Chinese tactic of fast incursion into consideration. We were to go back up the road a mile or two and form a loose defense line from the ridgeline down across the road and up the ridge-line on the other side. We would wait for a probing attack in force and then peel open, letting them go through just like they had broken through us. We'd let them charge right through us.

Down the road about a mile, we had our tanks

---

*Jim remembered this as "Operation Mousetrap." Many times, official nomenclature differed from what we called out. Most likely, this was the Morae Kagae Pass situation of 16-17 May 1951. The blocking or ambushing unit was 3rd Battalion, 7th Marines (3/7).

waiting with their cannons and machineguns. Actually, there was quite a force [a battalion, 3/7, a platoon of tanks and a Weapons Company platoon] awaiting the Chinese.

So one night I was on this high ridge line to the east of the road when the gooks came in. I could hear the firing in the valley along the road and, sure enough, our guys peeled aside. The gook force, thinking they had broken through, took off down the road to the south as hard as they could go.

The next afternoon, we pulled back down the road to where the ambush had been set up. There were mounds of enemy dead. Some of them lying in a line just where they had been wiped out; for example, like a mortar man carrying the tube, another guy carrying the base plate and four or five ammo carriers with mortar rounds all lying in a line—killed in an instant as they came down this road as hard as they could go. They thought they had enveloped our rear but in reality they were coming right into this ambush. [82 prisoners, 112 counted dead]

Not long after, it was getting into summer and there was not an awful lot happening. We'd get up on top of a mountain and dig in. We'd look over on the other mountain and see the gooks filling sand bags, building bunkers and fortifying their positions. After we were there for 2, 3, 4 weeks, our command would say, "OK, we're moving out."

And our job would be to go over and roust out the gooks off of that other mountain that you'd just watched them fortify. It always seemed to me it would have been a hell of a lot easier to go on over and kick them off in the first place. But that was the political end of the war, I guess.

About this time, I remember there was a guy named Robert Pitt, whose dad had mailed him a pistol in a box of oatmeal. His dad sent it that way because it was against the law to send weapons through the mail. But Pitt got this Colt pistol and ammunition. Since we found that it was much easier to stand watch with a pistol, Pitt used it to stand watch.

On one occasion another guy, Andrew Sanchez of Firebaugh, California, was going back down the mountain to battalion; and because he didn't want to carry his rifle, he asked Pitt if he could borrow the pistol. Pitt said that he could. So Sanchez went down the mountain with Pitt's prized pistol.

Sanchez ended up getting shot. I don't know just how that happened, but he ended up taking Pitt's pistol with him. And Pitt was fit to be tied.

From September until we went into reserve in December at a place called Camp Stark, I think, not a whole lot happened. I do remember that I got a sniper's rifle—an 03 that had a 12 power scope.* Later, they took that back and gave me an M1 with a scope.

Since we were in such stable positions in reserve, Pitt and I used to sneak off and go back to the rear to try to shoot pheasants with the sniper rifle. In fact, we returned to the outfit one day after bagging a

---

*At the beginning of the conflict, Marine snipers were supplied this World War I set up. An 03 was a 1903 Springfield .30 caliber, bolt action, single shot rifle. The consensus at the time was that it was more accurate than the Gerand M1.

pheasant. And Pitt told our first sergeant, Pianezza—
we called him, "Pizza Pie Pianezza."—"Hey, we got
one!"

Old Pianezza said, "That's good." Of course, he
was thinking that we had shot a gook with the sniper
rifle. He said, "Where is he?"

Pitt said, "We brought him back to camp."

Pianezza asked, "Well, what are you going to
do with him?"

Pitt says, "We're going to eat him."

Old Pizza Pie Pianezza was aghast that we were
going to eat this gook! But all we really did was
cook the pheasant.

Clausewitz even had a tenet for old Pizza Pie: ...the actor
in war constantly finds things different from his expecta-
tions; and this can not fail to have an influence on his plans....

***

John Ontiveros, member of our bootcamp platoon I-65
from Houston, Texas, was delayed in his journey to Korea by
the chance illness of his father. He was not in the Sixth
Draft, but arrived with a later draft. In his own terse fashion
John provides his perspective:

We left the states in April 1951 aboard the USS
Minafee; our Draft commanded by LT Eddie
LeBaron, later to become quarterback of the Dallas
Cowboys.

We arrived in Pusan Harbor, Korea on May 5, in
the morning. We disembarked, met the Red Cross
and had coffee and doughnuts. The doughnuts
looked like they came over in a sea bag. We visited
with other units that were there, mainly the Canadian

Princess Patricia's Light Infantry, and departed that evening for the BLUE Line [See Map 4 for 1/7 and NO NAME Line], where I joined my unit as a BARman—1st Fire Team, 1st Squad, 1st Platoon, Able Co., 1st Battalion, 7th Marines.

On the sixth, before I could wake up, before I could get up, a short round from our artillery came into some tanks parked behind our lines. One tanker was wounded and all hell broke loose. That's how my first day began. Also, on the morning of May 6, I ran into Philip Gutterrez and Henry (Ham) Hamilton of my old bootcamp platoon. They told me about that running fight they had on the QUANTICO and KANSAS Lines all the way back to the BLUE Line [NO NAME Line and refers to the Chinese Spring Offensive, Map 4.]

The next morning we jumped off in the attack. We moved on a forced march all the way to Chunchon. In the evening we reached our objective, the ridgeline south of Chunchon, and set up our lines. The following day we made our first patrol into Chunchon. We went in to pick up a squad that had been dropped off to spend the night in the town. Nothing happened.

A few days later we made our second patrol into Chunchon, this to be an armored patrol. We rode on tanks into town and one of the tanks hit a land mine. Gutterrez was riding on that lead tank when it hit the mine and I saw him blown off. It shook him up but nothing more serious happened.

We went across to the northern part of town, came to a divided road and took the right road around some small mountains, when we started taking incoming fire. It was the first time I had been under fire so I didn't know what the hell was going on. So one of the guys from the squad told me to get off the tank we were riding and I did. We had just crossed a small bridge when the Chinese started dropping in mortar fire. They were trying to knock out the bridge to trap the tanks and our company. So all of a sudden, we got the word to move out. We withdrew back to the fork in the road and this time we took the left branch.

Down this road were two small hills. My platoon was to take the first hill and then provide covering fire for the second platoon as it took the other hill. The third platoon was left in reserve. We got to the top of our hill and laid down covering fire on the other hill. Of course, by the time the second platoon got up on that hill no one was there. The trenches were empty. So we came back down off the hills, boarded our tanks and came back to our lines. We set up operations there for several days waiting for Operation Mousetrap. [John remembers this being called "mousetrap" the same as did Jim Swartzwelder. The Marine Corps called it the Morae Kagae Pass situation of 16-17 May 1951.]

Several days later the Chinese broke through our left flank and all hell broke loose a few miles behind our lines. The idea was to let them hit our MLR (Main Line of Resistance)—which they did— and catch them in a valley by some tankers and somebody else. [3rd Battalion, 7th Marines, a tank platoon and a heavy weapons platoon]

By six o'clock the next morning we're pulling out of Chunchon, headed back to the MLR. We went through the valley where they had caught the Chinese. There were hundreds of bodies laying around.

About the 18th or 19th of May, we went on the offensive until the 29th. Our battalion was constantly on the move until then—when I got hit.

Charlie Company had taken the lead then Baker Company. Able Company was last. We had fire fights all along the way, but we finally made it to a ridge at night, we set up and Baker had the front. About 2 o'clock in the morning they got hit and hit hard. No one was allowed to go to their rescue because the ridge was too narrow. So we had to wait until morning. Then we pulled through Baker and moved up to the top of the ridge.

We got to the ridge and got ready for the attack. We had the high ground and waited for support—artillery and air. We couldn't get any, so the "Old Man" [Company Commander] decided to go at it without air or artillery support. Just before we attacked, word came that we were getting some air support. So we were ordered to hold up.

I went up to the line and I saw the company commander, Captain Smith, looking down on the terrain below. All of a sudden, a sniper shot him right through the chest. He fell back and rolled over a couple of times. The Corpsman got to him and opened his jacket where he had been hit. I thought he had died, but later I saw him at the Aid station.

I came back to the reverse slope and was sitting down waiting for the word to move out when we got the air support we were waiting for. It was from the South African Air Force with P51 Mustangs—

and they were good. Of course, at other times we had
our own Marine Corsairs supporting us in the
attack—and they were damned good at this.

After Captain Smith got hit, we started getting
incoming mortar fire. There were trees close by and
we were getting tree bursts. Shrapnel was scattering
all over the place, but it didn't last long.

I had the air panel to spread out to show the air
support where we were and I was supposed to lead
the attack when we moved out. It wasn't long before
I saw Gutterrez coming by. He had been hit. He had
shrapnel on his face and arms. And all he could say
was that he was going home. [Henry (Ham) Hamilton
was hit also.]

So the next thing I know I felt a blast on my
arm. I thought it was just a blast from the mortar fire.
But when I reached down to pick up the BAR, I saw
blood coming out of my jacket. And I realized I
had been hit in the right arm muscle. I don't have to
tell you I cursed every Chinaman in the world. I
got mad as hell.

The Corpsman ran over and started opening my
jacket. I said, "What are you doing?"

He says, "You got hit in the chest!"

I said, "No." But that's when I realized that the
shrapnel had gone through the front of my jacket at
an angle and caught my right arm muscle.

He patched me up. But after that I was so mad
I got the BAR, went back up on line and began really chopping up the real estate because I was so pissed
off. I didn't hit a damned thing.

Then the Corpsman sent me off the hill with
some other marines down to the Aid station, where

we arrived late that evening. That's where I saw
Captain Smith lying on a stretcher. He said that he
was all right.

So from the Aid station they took us by train to
Pusan to the hospital ship, The Haven. [I left the hospital ship, The Haven, on 20 May. This must have
been about 10 or 11 days later.] I got hit on the 29th
of May around noon, went to The Haven for about a
week and then got sent to Japan to the Yokuska
Naval Hospital. I didn't think I was hit that bad but
it took about three months to get back to my company.

While aboard the hospital ship, I ran into some
Puerto Ricans from the 65th Army regiment. Hell,
I didn't even know that there were Puerto Ricans
fighting in Korea.

After my release from the hospital, I went for
retraining at Otsu, an Army camp that had been
turned over to the Marines and was used to retrain
marines returning to Korea. I rejoined my company
sometime in late September and by this time, all my
squad was gone. So I joined up with the First squad
again but with all new members.

A few days after I returned, we went on a raid. I
will never forget it because I was frightened to death.
Somehow or another, we got behind their lines. And
I will never forget coming onto these Chinese all
sitting around a campfire with a guitar singing what
sounded like cowboy songs. It was really weird,
out of this world.

The lieutenant must have choked up [became
immobile from shock] because he waited for a long
time. But finally he gave the order to open fire and

we did. All hell broke loose. Then as soon as they were all killed, I was running for my life along with everybody else, getting back to our lines. I didn't stop shaking for about two days because we had been in dangerous enemy territory.

Another thing. On the way back I heard some shots and asked someone what it was. They said that it was our sniper behind us, who was covering the return to our lines. He came in about an hour after we did.

We went into regimental reserve where the rest of the squad I had joined left. So I wound up as the squad leader. I only had nine men in the squad, [should have been 12] about half regular and half reserve marines. One of the reserves was a corporal, but they made me the acting squad leader [should have been a sergeant] and I was a PFC [See Figure 9]

When my new squad went back on line, we set up on the left flank of a river. My section of the MLR was about 60 yards from the river bed straight up. The problem here was that we had to use ropes to get up and down because it was so steep. I checked out the terrain and set up the fire teams. I thought I had done a good job. But I failed to go down to the river bed and check the terrain, looking up. I never thought about that—which almost got me killed.

The next few days it was cold. It was below zero. I had two man bunkers and I had the first bunker. I placed my rifle grenadier [grenade launcher] at the very top bunker. He was a young Indian kid named Vincent St.Cyr from Oklahoma. I didn't expect anybody to come through the river bed because the weather was so damned cold.

One morning about 2:30, I woke up and checked on my man that was on watch. And he was having a hard time staying awake. I told him to go ahead and knock off and I would stay the rest of the watch. A few minutes later I heard the crunching of the snow and here the Chinese came.

I woke up the grenadier in the bunker and got myself into position on top of the bunker. So I saw them coming and passed the word that the signal to open fire would be that I would drop two hand grenades down to the river at the same time. I waited until they got right below me.

There were about 16 of them in the patrol. I think they were heading for the battalion CP because it was a few hundred yards past my position on the river bed. I dropped the two hand grenades and the fight was on.

After I fired a couple of clips, dropped a few grenades, I realized I was the only one firing. So I started hollering, "What the hell is going on."

My squad told me they couldn't see the enemy. That's when I realized I had made a mistake. When you look at the river from the top, you could not see that the wall of the river was concave. At the top I was the only one who could look down on the Chinese and they were looking directly up at me. So I tried to spot for the men so they could fire, but they still said they couldn't see anything. It was a hell of a fight with red and green tracers.

So I finally ordered the grenadier to drop two rapid grenades in the river bed in case they tried to make a run for it. He did so and I had them pinned.

And it was one good fight. Until the lieutenant in
charge of the 60-mm mortar section decided to get
into the act. The only thing wrong was that he did-
n't know what the hell he was shooting at. By the
third round, he almost blew me off the top of the
bunker. And I called him everything but a child of
God.

***

John Ontiveros' actions were awarded the BRONZE
STAR MEDAL:

UNITED STATES MARINE CORPS
HEADQUARTERS
1ST MARINE DIVISION (REINF) FMF
c/o FLEET POST OFFICE
SAN FRANCISCO, CALIFORNIA
In the name of the President of the United States, the
Commanding General, 1st Marine Division (Reinf) FMF,
takes pleasure in awarding the BRONZE STAR MEDAL to

CORPORAL JOHN C. ONTIVEROS
UNITED STATES MARINE CORPS
for service as set forth in the following
CITATION:
"For meritorious achievement in connection with operations against the enemy in KOREA while serving with a
Marine infantry company from 7 May 1951 to 30 March
1952. Serving as a fire team leader, Corporal ONTIVEROS
displayed outstanding courage, initiative and devotion to
duty. On one occasion when seriously wounded during an

attack on heavily defended enemy positions, he refused evacuation and continued to designate targets and direct the advance of his fire team until forced to be evacuated. On 17 January 1952 when his company came under a savage attack by a reinforced enemy squad, he left the cover of his bunker, exposing himself with complete disregard for personal safety to intense enemy fire. This action, causing many enemy casualties, assisted in the final repulsing of the attack. Corporal ONTIVEROS' heroism and fortitude throughout were in keeping with the highest traditions of the United States Naval Service."

Corporal ONTIVEROS is authorized to wear the Combat "V".

/s/　J. T. SELDON
Major General, U. S. Marine Corps
Commanding

Copy

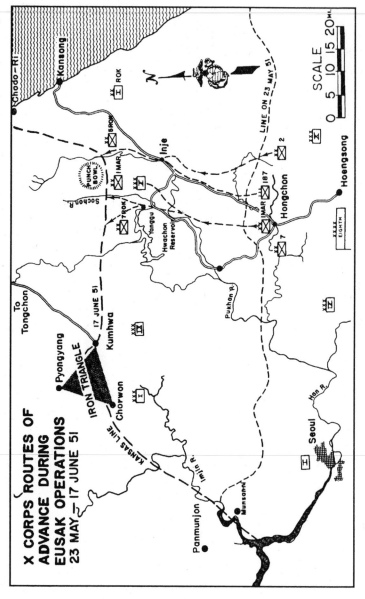

MAP 6

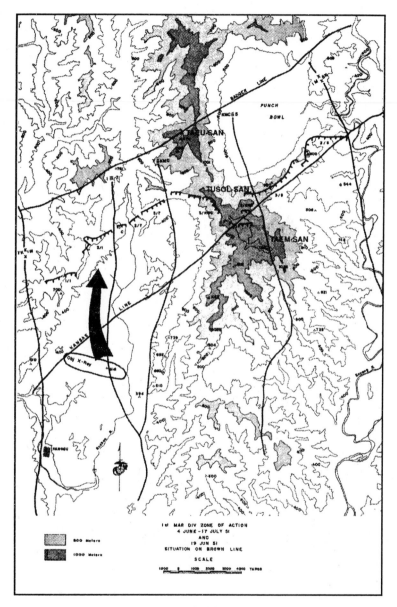

1st MAR DIV ZONE OF ACTION
4 JUNE - 17 JULY 51
AND
19 JUN 51
SITUATION ON BROWN LINE

SCALE

1000   0   1000   2000   3000   4000 YARDS

MAP 7

CHAPTER NINE

THE DRAGON'S PUNCHBOWL

In May, a limited drive north to keep the Chinese off balance centered around the Punchbowl, a circular valley surrounded by high mountains used by the communists as a staging area. The 1st Marine Division was sent to capture Yanggu on the eastern end of the Hwachon Reservoir and to the west of the Punchbowl. Airborne units and the Army 2nd Division were to take Inje and, on the east coast, Kansong. These movements were intended to surround and cut off tens of thousands of Chinese south of the Inje-Kansong road. (See Map 6)

The Chinese, in fact, were in swift withdrawal to avoid the trap. They were in flight to the rear, a departure from the fight-to-death of the past. No longer a single soldier surrendering here and there, but remnants of platoons and companies, even battalions. In May the communist casualties included 17,000 counted dead as well as 10,000 prisoners. The situation had become a rout until the Chinese ordered the North Koreans to "hold until death" to allow the PLA to regroup.

And "hold until death" they tried. John Camacho remembers the terrain littered with North Korean bodies:

> During this drive as we approached the jump-off

area, our trucks crossed a river and we were shocked to see the enemy dead lining the bottom, their faces and bodies distorted by the rushing water. The trucks bumped along, not on a rough road, but over the hip-bones and body parts stewn on the road.

The enemy tried to hide their dead, but they never had enough time—thus, their casualties were buried along the roads and trails, visible as we moved along the way.

Charlie Company occupied one hill where we jumped into ready made foxholes only to find enemy bodies buried on the bottom. We thought the bottom of the foxholes were strangely soft, but soon, with the blood oozing through, we knew what was there.

From the hill, we saw enemy wounded down in the valley—still alive and flailing their arms about. A major came up and borrowed a rifle to see if he could nail some of the wounded gooks.

I walked up the trail and sat down at the hill top. Then my friend just ahead of me told me to get up and walk slowly towards him—I had sat on a broken trip wire connected to a 'bouncing Betty' mine which was six inches from my side. And so goes the life of a marine....

***

The 5th Marines began their drive on 23 May and encountered strong enemy resistance, the die-hard North Koreans. The Marines steadily advanced and by the last of May had taken Yanggu, adjacent to the Hwachon Reservoir. (See Map 6, also lower left quadrant of Map 7)

By the first of June, all three Marine regiments were in

line: the 1st on the left, the KMCs in the center, the 5th on the right and the 7th in reserve. The Korean Marines (KMCs) in the center were just south of the Punchbowl, the Marine objective. But to get there they had to vanquish a dragon.

Their plight is best described by *U.S. Marine Operations in Korea,* Vol. IV:

> From the air, the ground in front of the KMCs resembled a monstrous prehistoric lizard, rearing up on hind legs. The 1st Battalion was to ascend the tail and the 2nd the hind legs. The two would meet at the rump, Hill 1122. From this position the backbone ran northeast to the shoulders, Hill 1218. Still farther northeast, along the neck, was the key terrain feature—Taeam-san, the head of the imagined reptile. [See mid-map below Punchbowl, Map 7]
>
> The 1st and 2nd Battalions ran immediately into the opposition of an estimated NKPA regiment. In an effort to outflank the enemy, the 3rd Battalion swung over to the east and attacked up the ridge forming the forelegs. Seizure of the shoulders (Hill 1218) would render enemy positions along the back, rump, hind legs, and tail untenable. Major General Choe Am Lin, commanding the 12th NKPA Division, was quick to recognize the tactical worth of this height and exact a stiff price for it.
>
> That the KMCs could expect little mercy from their fellow countrymen was demonstrated when the bodies of ten men reported missing were found. All had been shot in the back of the head.

The battle continued for six days until a surprise night attack by the KMCs led to the fall of Taeam-san. In this steadfast operation, the KMC had suffered 500 casualties.

The 7th Marines fought along an extended ridge that ran northeast of Yanggu and offered access to the southern rim of the Punchbowl. As ordered, the North Koreans, rather than the Chinese, were manning bunkers all around the Punchbowl and appeared to be in force in this area. The 7th Marines had fought several counterattacks when the 3rd Battalion (3/1) of the 1st Marines relieved them on 2 June.

Early on that morning, the 3rd Battalion (3/1) commander was making a reconnaissance when his group was hit by mortar fire. The barrage killed one officer and wounded two forward observers, four company commanders, the battalion operations officer, and 32 enlisted men. The stunned battalion was stopped in their attack for one full day until they could reorganize.

Ross was not wounded; but this decimation of the battalion seemed to provide a new resolve to his platoon. Shortly after, his company set up three machineguns to cover a defile that ended at their ridge. A few nights later, the North Koreans counterattacked up toward the ridgeline and the three machineguns slaughtered them. The next morning, Ross counted scores of bodies that the North Koreans had not had time to carry away before light.

***

Ross tells the story:

> We had set up the defense on a hill across from the gooks. Our positions were about 500 yards apart. And we marines were on the front side of our ridge in three big machinegun bunkers, facing the gooks. And our bunkers could cover any assault with no problem.
>
> We had been there for several days during which

they had been mortaring us heavily. And we had taken casualties. One mortar even hit right in the foxhole with our sergeant just after he had made his rounds.

Finally one night, about midnight, we heard the horns and bugles blowing. So we knew the gooks were coming. Our three machinegun bunkers were side by side with lots of ammo. And we covered our fire lanes solidly. We were ready.

The gooks came wave after wave and it was like a "turkey shoot"—must have killed over 200, although the next morning, we found only 30 or 40 bodies. We sure made up for their mortar barrages!

***

The 1st Marines continued the attack to the ridges north of the Hwachon Reservoir. The advance was especially difficult but by 20 June the new line was secure. The objectives taken. After two months of fighting, the 1st Marine Division had reached the Punchbowl. (See Maps 6 and 7)

In May and the first half of June, the "Dog" Company Commander (CO of D/2/1) was 1st Lieutenant Alexander L. Michaux. His Executive Officer was 1st Lieutenant Jay J. Thomas; his 1st Platoon Leader, 2nd Lieutenant Robert Dickey; his 2nd Platoon Leader, 2nd Lieutenant Stanley Olson. The other officers were Heck, Westervelt, Culpepper and Champion.

Moving up to Hill 516 (in meters, over 1600 feet) in June required the normal single file movement of "Dog" company (D/2/1) along the ridgeline trails. Evidence of battles both past and recent emerged along the path. From the valley to the rice paddy to the hummock and hill, climbing

higher to the ridgeline on ancient paths, we sought the enemy.
We encountered light resistance as we attacked toward Hill
516: on the first day mortars as we crossed the paddies, on the
second day mortars again which hit a machinegun squad.
The third day, we began our assault on the Hill. (See Objective
X-Ray, Hill 516, Map 7)

During our first day on line after reserve, we relieved
units of the 7th Marines and took their positions. To make the
replacement we crossed an open rice paddy pounded by mortar fire and found foxholes on a hillside.

In the late afternoon of that day I needed to make a head
call. Seeking privacy I picked my way down the hill to a
point secluded by vegetation from our foxholes above. This
point, I discovered, must have held some military advantage in the recent past. Remnants of battle lay about—spent
rounds here, holes from mortar explosions there. Vestiges of
troops littered the ground—C-ration cans, a dried-blood
stained dungaree jacket. But, most importantly, in the debris
I found a carbine with a 30 round "banana" clip.

All ammo carriers wanted a carbine because it weighed
less than six pounds whereas the M1 rifle weighed almost 10
pounds. Although the range for the carbine was less than
half that of the M1, the movement of a lever changed the carbine from a semi-automatic rifle to a fully automatic submachinegun. Moreover, although the caliber was .30, the
rounds were shorter than the .30 caliber round used for the
M1, BAR and machinegun; thus, a lighter bandolier to carry.
No doubt about it, this was my lucky day.

Organizationally, the carbine was the designated weapon
assigned to the machinegun ammo carriers. In combat, however, the replacement drafts armed with M1 rifles filled the
line companies' open billets. Indeed, most ammo carriers carried M1 rifles. Therefore, only by accident or by receiving

the carbine of a veteran going home could a new man get the weapon that he rated. The fact remained, and understandably so, that reduction of weight was uppermost in ammo carriers' minds, recognizing that two cans of ammunition weighed almost 40 pounds. With that thought dominant I felt that I had found gold in those hills.

But how to dispose of an M1 while on a hill during an operation? An armory was unavailable. The supply sergeant was way to the rear. Although the Corps rammed the value of our assigned weapon into our heads, I took the liberty of field stripping this US government property and throwing the parts as far as I could throw them down the hill in every direction.

What a lucky day!

On the second day, a grove of dense trees shadowed the morning sunlight as we trudged the inclined path up to the top of one ridge. Perhaps for a moment the shadows shielded the snake-like entrenchment adjacent to the path. But suddenly, like a spotlight, a beam of sunlight streaked through the trees, revealing a startling display of the dead.

Dusty and small, as only the dead can look, the North Korean bodies lay askew in the trench along the trail. And the smell of the dead was upon us as we quickened our pace.

We moved out through the trees into the bright sun, leaving the mauled, dark bloodied things behind. But in those few moments passing by the trench, each of us felt an implicit assurance of our own immortality—a superiority over those dead and death. We would not remember the darker side again until later, if only in our dreams.

Breath from those bodies had left sometime before. The North Koreans were not recently killed, only now had they begun to decompose.

The North Koreans always removed their dead and wounded from the battle unless that was not possible. Obviously this squad of ten or 12 soldiers was not retrieved, leaving one imminent conclusion. This unit had been left to "fight and die" in order to deter the Eighth Army and allow remnants of the NKPA to escape north in October 1950 after the Inchon landing. The nights and days must have been cold enough to prevent deterioration. With the snows the bodies lay blanketed until spring.

But with the warm spring sun the natural process began.

Nothing in the world is more quiet or still than a dead man. Friend or foe, a man dies and stiffens into a smaller than life-like replica of himself, a wooden dummy. We glanced with furtive curiosity and moved on.

High on a ridgeline that afternoon, we stopped for some reason.

Holding to the high ground along the ridgeline trails prevented ambush except from the front. Thus in single file our company meandered along the paths to the north with a fire team at point, leading the way. The pace, however, was uncertain and varied. At one time fast, covering ground, tiring without rest. At another slow, halting and sporadic, spawning uncertainty. In fact, many events dictated our progress at any given time.

A plugging of a gap in the line, a necessary tie-in with another unit along the line, or a replacement of a unit on the line might cause a hurried pace. A sporadic march, however, might be the outcome of the company or platoon leader being lost or map disoriented, the point men suspecting enemy ahead and probing for ambush, an observation plane suspecting enemy ahead, or even headquarters changing plans.

Other less obvious restrictions on the pace are countless.

For example, fording a stream and then climbing a slick trail up a slope more than 45 degrees—a difficult, slow traverse, at best—causing the majority of the column to stop. Consequently the troops must patiently wait their turn.

High on a ridgeline that afternoon, we stopped for whatever reason. The warm June afternoon sun cast the shadow of our pinnacle down the east side of the slope over a rocky stream, some 300 to 400 feet below. This freshet, the Sochon River, followed the contours of our mountain, flowing at the edge of a valley for almost a half mile before curving out of sight around the mountain. Beside the stream, paralleling its meanders, a path bordered by a thicket of trees became the scene that lulled us as we dropped to the ground and took a break. The trees on our ridgeline shielded us from the sun and provided shade as we rested.

Having relaxed for a time, the squad leader of our machinegun squad was the first to see a group of gooks moving north along the path by the stream. Immediately he ordered the machinegun to be placed to direct fire on them. And they did make a perfect target, the path providing a long gauntlet before running out of our sight.

This was the scenario when, for the first time, I was allowed to fire the machinegun in combat. After the gun was set up, Andy, the squad leader, let me fire on the gooks as they ducked for cover in the trees. Or they ran as fast as they could on the path then dove for cover again. This continued down their gauntlet to the concealing bend of the stream.

As an ammo carrier, this was my time of glory—my place in the sun.

Later in the afternoon, we set up on another hill and gook mortars salvoed a direct hit on the other machinegun squad of our section.

Later as the hometown correspondent, I described these bloody days in the following dispatch of June 7, 1951:

From where I'm sitting on this mountain, I can see the Hwachon Reservoir. We're dug in with bunkers and barbed wire. Maybe this will be the line we are going to put all across Korea. Anyway, we're heavily fortified and are supposed to stay here about two weeks. Then, to reserve in Mason, I hope.

Ross is over across the valley with the 3rd Battalion. On the other side of them, next to the reservoir, is a 600 yard gap in the lines. We hope the Chinks don't find out. However, we seem to be fighting "diehard" North Koreans, now. Overhead, some Marine planes are running an airstrike on a hill 300 yards away. They are coming directly over us. It's hard to write with bombs and strafing that close.

I think the gooks have some grudge against machinegunners. There aren't many old faces left. In fact, we hardly have enough machinegunners to go around. The other day, we had only 9 in our section and we're supposed to have 17. We hadn't been that short since last winter when the company withdrew from the Chosin Reservoir. But, some replacements have come in, now.

I've just about decided not to make any friends over here. They just don't last. This morning, a patrol got hit, so twelve of us were sent up the mountain to help bring down the wounded. The first one was "Little Jake." He was a funny little guy. Always in a good mood. He had his guts blown out. They had to apply a large bandage to hold in his insides. I don't know if he will live or not. The next one was

"Harby" Harbison. We have been buddies ever since
I got here. And, we were looking forward to going
on liberty together in Mason. He got hit in the groin
and thigh. The thigh bullet may have broken his
leg. Another bullet creased his scalp.

I helped to carry him all the way down on a
stretcher. It seemed like a mile down and it felt like
it took hours. The path was unsparingly rugged.
And, he suffered, terribly. I kept giving him cigarettes. Hopefully, he'll probably be back in the states
in two weeks.

It just doesn't pay to have friends, or you have to
have iron nerves when they get killed or wounded.

When I came back from the hospital ship, we
were in reserve for two days. Then "Dog" was
thrown on line. We knew what was coming. We had
to take this ridge so we could form the line we now
are set up on. But, it was supposed to be really
rough going. The first day we relieved the 7th
Marines and took over their positions after crossing
an open rice paddy with mortars dropping in on us.

We set up on a hill the next day and mortars got
a direct hit on the other machinegun in our section.
Three more machinegunners gone.

The day after, we moved out in the attack. [on
Hill 516] I was in the assault platoon and we moved
up the trail. We had walked along the ridgeline for
a long time before we surprised some gooks. They
really cut loose on us and I jumped behind a little
knoll. Then, began a terrific firefight. Our machinegun was rushed back to where I was and the gunners
said that our section leader had been hit (another

machinegunner gone).

I was right by the gun when our squad leader lurched around and started slipping down the hill. At first, I thought he had just slipped; but then I saw his face. I knew he had been hit. It wasn't bad, just a flesh wound to his back but the corpsman took him back down the hill (another machinegunner gone). My gunners [Krauss and McGrath] couldn't decide on where to place the gun. They started to move it up and then brought it back. They couldn't decide where to put it. That's when we really needed the squad leader. All this time I'm jumping about trying to follow the gun so my ammo would be ready.

As I followed the gun back the second time, my ammo strap broke and my two cans of ammo went down the hill.* So I had to go get them. I didn't think I was ever going to get back up to the gun. The hill was almost straight up and sandy. I slid all over the place. Finally, after a struggle, I made it back up to the trail and got into the action.

This was really a firefight.** But, it was a lot of

---

* Ammo straps might be a canvas strap with hooks on each end which retained the handles of the ammo cans or a strap tied to them, but in either case, the ammo strap reached around the marine's neck so he could carry the ammo cans on each side.

** This firefight was typical of a new North Korean tactic employed in conjunction with their "fight and die" order. We followed a trail single file which led up to a saddle, crossing over a transverse crescent-shaped ridge. Positioned along this ridge, the die-hard Koreans had waited for us to advance into their crossfire.

U.S.Marine Operations in Korea, Vol. IV describes this positioning:

"During the heyday of the battleship, every midshipman dreamed of some glorious future day when he would be on the bridge, directing the naval maneuver known as crossing the T. In other words, his ships would be in a line of battle, firing converging

fun. We laughed at our 2nd platoon leader. [2nd LT
Stanley Olson] When the company commander
[1st LT Alexander Michaux] told him to hurry up and
take those positions, he yelled back on the radio that
we were doing the best we could, "Damn it!" He's
about the best platoon leader I've seen. You would-
n't think he was an officer. He kids everybody. (Did
you know that the marine platoon leader leads his
men into battle? In the Army, the sergeant does.)

Well, the guys would yell at the gooks and the
gooks would yell back, sometimes. I was firing my
carbine that I just got. I saw movement up on the
ridgeline above and fired away. Just like a shooting
gallery. We called in an air strike and a Corsair
practically landed on the tree tops 25 or 30 yards
away, dropping the napalm on the gooks. That's
what a Marine pilot can do. Finally, one of the

---

broadsides on an enemy approaching column. Obviously, the
enemy would be at a disadvantage until he executed a 90 degree
turn under fire to bring his battered ships into line to deliver
broadsides of their own.

"It was a mountain warfare variation of crossing the T that
the Korean Reds were using against the Marines. Whenever possible, the enemy made a stand on a hill flanked by transverse
ridgelines. He emplaced hidden machine guns or mortars on
these ridgelines to pour converging fire into attackers limited by
terrain to a single approach. It meant that the Marines had to
advance through this crossfire before they could get in position for the final assault on the enemy's position.

"There were two tactical antidotes. One was well directed
close air support. The other was the support of tanks advancing
parallel to enemy-held ridgelines and scorching them with the
direct fire of 90-mm rifles and 50 caliber machine guns."

The antidote for "Dog" Company in this firefight was close air support.

BARmen took a squad and rushed the hill.

You know, no one wears a helmet in this platoon, so we call this guy "The Pirate" because he wears a red bandanna on his head. And he looks like a pirate. You would expect him to pull out a sword, any time. And he's crazy. He banzais hills all the time. Charges up the slope firing his BAR.

This charge led by "The Pirate" finished the last gook resistance and we followed up the hill. I went over to where I had been shooting and found a dead North Korean in a foxhole and I took his two epaulets which show his rank. He was a major. Although he was the one I was shooting at, I don't know whether I hit him or others of us did. Someone sure had! In fact, all the gooks on the hill were dead. We had five wounded. That's a pretty good average.

We went down to the valley and set up for the night. It got dark and began to rain, again. It rained for 3 days. I just lay down in the mud. I was soaked to the skin.

But, now, it's bright and beautiful.

***

In late May the 9th Draft of replacements arrived, one of which was PFC Phillip Andre Lierse, who became another ammo carrier. We now had three in our squad: Andrews, Phillip and me. The firefight in which I took the Korean major's two epaulets was the first combat that Phillip had seen. Fate had dealt him losing cards. He never should have seen combat.

It seems that it is difficult for some people to cope with life. Each of life's experiences seem new to them and they do not connect one experience with another in a maturation process. They seem to be eternal neophytes. And their naivete is appalling.

Phillip was one of these unfortunates.

From Gates Mills, Ohio and born June 27, 1931, he almost lived to be twenty. He might have lived longer had he not been a marine. Unfortunately for him, he had joined a reserve unit and had never gone through bootcamp. Not having been toughened to meet the enemy in battle, Phillip had floated into this situation by applying for active status from reserve. He had simply wanted to move out of his mother's and her husband's house, to be somewhat independent. But this thrust for independence cost his life.

Phillip was not equipped mentally or emotionally for war.

After his first firefight, "Dog" Company (D/2/1) set up a stationary line for almost a week along a ridgeline. We dug in two to a hole as we usually did but this time there was a difference. Andrews sacked in with the new replacement squad leader and I was stuck with Phillip. I was angry about this but Andrews said there was nothing he could do. The new squad leader had asked Andy (Andrews) to dig in with him.

By default, I became the instructor/mentor. I had to show Phillip how to dig a foxhole. How wide and how deep. During our digging, he told me about himself and that after he had left home, his mother's husband had found a new job in Tennessee. Shortly, they would be moving there. He seemed perturbed about that.

Other things worried him or caused a quandary. He asked questions like a child.

"Andy, why did the Lieutenant shoot that prisoner?" Phillip's face was open and questioning.

"That's about all he could do, I guess." My answer was not good enough and I knew it. We didn't really talk about the fact that we rarely took prisoners. But my answer had been the truth. After a pause to rethink, I tried again.

"Phillip, there just wasn't much he could do. The prisoner was shot in the groin by a .50 caliber from that strafing Corsair. He didn't have any gonads left. He was bleeding badly. We had no one to take him back to the aid station, way down the hill a mile or so. So the lieutenant really had no choice but to shoot him and get him out of his misery."

After Phillip's first firefight we had moved up the hill past the gook positions. On top of the hill we had found a North Korean soldier who had been terribly wounded when our planes had strafed the ridgeline.

We were close to him as our long line stopped for a while and someone, showing compassion, gave him a cigarette and lit it for him. The prisoner nodded his head many, many times to show his appreciation. It had been a kind act.

As we moved out again, the lieutenant walked back behind the prisoner. And as the North Korean soldier smoked the cigarette, the lieutenant quietly placed the barrel of his .45 caliber pistol close to the back of the prisoner's head and pulled the trigger.

At another time, Phillip asked inanely, "Why isn't 'The Pirate' afraid to die?"

"The Pirate" was our company "wild man," if not our hero. He wore his bright red bandanna on his head, knotted at the four corners. Since he had torn off the sleeves of his dungaree jacket, his muscular arms were bare. And firing his Browning Automatic Rifle (BAR) while shouting, "Suck a hotchy, you fuckin' gooks!", he led many charges up the hills. Just his looks and his primal scream for oral sex may have frightened some of the gooks to death. None the less, he had to be given credit for changing our fortune in many seemingly loosing firefights.

"Phillip, I have no idea what makes that wild-assed marine tick."

I certainly didn't know why "The Pirate" took so many chances. It was as if he thought he was invincible. I was thankful, however, that he thought it was necessary. Definitely he had gotten us out of more than one bad predicament. And I tried to explain that to Phillip.

We received mail. Over the next few days Phillip seemed extremely agitated over his. Then again preoccupied, he kept mumbling, "What am I going to do?" "What am I going to do?"

Consequently, his agitation and flightiness grated on me until one night they finally brought me to a breaking point as I lay dozing, almost asleep. A night that Phillip had first watch.

Suddenly jumping out of the hole, he ran a few feet and fired off two rounds into the blackness, then jumped back into the hole. The resounding shots caused me to almost jump out of my skin. Terrified, I abruptly charged up out of my dream. For a fleeting moment, I thought that my time had come and the gooks finally had gotten to me.

Realizing what had happened, I choked, "What in hell do you think you're doing?" I was in shock.

"Why, firing for effect. I thought I heard a noise."

To say I was astonished would be an understatement. "Damn it, Phillip don't you ever do that again. Now, shut up, listen to me good, and you might live longer."

"I don't know where you learned about 'fire for effect,' but it sure as hell doesn't mean what you just did. 'Fire for effect' means covering fire. Like a rifle squad or a machine-gun firing to keep the enemies' head down. It's primarily to keep the enemy off balance while you attack or put some other movement into action. In other words, you fire for an effect on the enemy. He knows where you are and you know where he is. Now, that statement is important. Do you get it!"

"Damn it, Phillip, that was so stupid." I caught my breath as my heart calmed down. "But at times like now the gooks may not know where we are. So that's why they send out patrols at night to find out where we are. You just jumped up and said, 'Look, here. Here we are!' The flash from your rifle can be seen a long way off. The sound of your shooting can be heard a long way off."

"So, now, remember this, Phillip. DO NOT ATTRACT ATTENTION! DO NOT FIRE FOR EFFECT LIKE THAT, EVER AGAIN!"

Obviously, we would have to be extra alert this night.

How could he be so dumb? Just as soon as we got off this ridgeline, I vowed to get back with Andrews to dig in. This Phillip character was not only dangerous to himself but others around him.

During the last days we were together he became more morose and then confided in me. "Andy, what am I going to do? My mother and her husband have gone to some little town in Tennessee. I don't have any home to go home to. I don't have any place to stay in Ohio if I go back to see my friends. And besides how am I ever going to find where my mother lives in Tennessee. I have never been to that town. I don't even know how to get there. But if I did, I don't know how to find the street that they live on."

I tried to tell him that he worried about it to much. That it would work out. That it was not a big problem. But to no avail.

Phillip Andre Lierse, within weeks of his twentieth birthday, continued to worry.

***

The kill ratio for the Marines for the month of May was a surprising nine-to-one, nine wounded marines to every marine killed. The casualty lists revealed losses for the 1st Marine Division as 75 KIA, 8 DOW and 731 wounded. In June, the ratio rose to an astonishing 15 to one. Various explanations were offered: cool professionalism, not taking needless risks, perhaps, even good luck. The comparatively low death rate might be credited in part to the alertness of Marine officers adapting to changing situations.

The new commander of the 1st Marines, Colonel Wilburt S. Brown, was such an officer. Amusingly, he took advantage of the enemy who believed their own propaganda accusing Americans of crimes against humanity. Upon taking command, he had insisted upon colored smoke shells for signaling. At the same time he also became aware through POW interrogations that NKPA prisoners were terrified of what they believed to be the use of frightful new poisonous gases. By this ruse, sending volleys of green, red and yellow smoke into the communist lines, Colonel Brown had a devastating effect on their soldiers. Unfortunately the supply ran out and was not renewed under Brown's command.

Another such officer, Major David W. McFarland of Marine Observation Squadron-6 also exploited enemy ignorance. He noticed the presence of observation planes (OY) would silence the enemy, even on night missions.

His explanation was simple: "The aerial observer was often unable to determine the location of the enemy artillery even though he could see it firing, because he would be unable to locate map coordinates in the dark—that is, relating them to the ground. Fortunately, this fact was unknown to the enemy. From their observation of the OYs in the daytime, they found that the safest thing to do was whenever an

OY was overhead was to take cover. This they continued to do at night."

***

The following letter only lists the casualties for my squad in taking Bunker Hill, the next battle. It did not mention the casualties the squad had suffered during the night before the attack on Bunker Hill.

June 14, 1951

Dear Folks,

Just a line to let you know that I'm OK. On the 10th of June, "Dog" Co. just about got annihilated. We "banzaied" a hill. We heard it was the heaviest fighting done so far in the Korean War. Our company is supposed to get a unit citation. Those who are left are in reserve, recuperating. I've written to you before right after my experiences, but this one you'll have to wait for. I'm a little shaky.

A mortar hit next to me. It got everyone in my squad but me. The squad had 6 wounded and 1 dead. I didn't get a scratch. A miracle, don't you think? So, now, I just want to rest.

Love,

Burton

On June 16, 1951, six days after the Bunker Hill battle and two days after writing the above letter, I had recuperated enough to describe the events of June 9-10 when "Dog" Company (D/2/1) assaulted the "die hard" North Koreans. (See Map 7, 2/1 above arrow)

In my last letter I said that I could see the Hwachon reservoir; we had set up a fortified line and dug in. But, we jumped off in the attack, again, to clear gook artillery and mortars out ahead of the line for about ten miles. Well, on June 10, Dog Company just about got annihilated. But, I'm OK and we're back again close to the Hwachon Reservoir.

The rainy season is here so we spent some miserable nights trying to keep dry during the first few days. And, our company didn't hit any resistance. The night of the 9th, we were dead tired. We had been going up and down the mountain trails all day. We didn't get to dig in until dark and then it began to rain.

Our platoon had to extend down a ridge, across a road, then across rice paddies to tie in with some tanks. There were three ammo carriers, now. And, I had dug in with a new replacement [Phillip] for awhile. But, that night I thought I would dig in with my friend, Andy [Andrews]. There was some mix up and those two guys dug in together which left me with the new squad leader.

Those guys, the other two ammo carriers, dug their hole by the road. Then, the gunners [Krauss and McGrath] dug their machinegun hole, next. The squad leader and I were dug in out in the paddy on the other side of the gun. We were on 50% watch and I had first watch. The squad leader had the second. We set up the shelter halves on poles to protect us from the rain and so that we had an opening to fire into the rice paddy to the front.

About 12:30 that night we got hit. Many times, the gooks will send out probing units to see where we are. I think there were three or four of them. They came down the road and made contact with [Phillip] the new replacement, the guy I had been digging in with. He made a fatal mistake.

He said, "Halt. Who goes there?" He didn't fire and ask questions, later.

The gooks ripped him with a burp gun. Then they ran to the hole and shot Andy, the other ammo carrier. Fortunately, the new guy fell into the hole on top of Andy and his body took most of the fire. Andy was only shot in the leg.

The gunners in the next hole grabbed the gun and whirled it around to face the road; but the gooks heard them and fired into their hole, wounding [Krauss] the gunner.

I guess I had been asleep. So, with a start, I jerked my carbine around toward the road and I caught the tent pole. The shelter halves fell over us as the squad leader was jumping awake. As we threw it off our heads, I got just a glimpse of the gooks in the light of a flare that someone had thrown.

The next day we moved out into the attack with four of us, the squad leader, the gunner, the assistant gunner and me. The gunner said he wasn't wounded bad enough to be sent back. Today, we had to take the biggest hill, yet, in this attack. We called it Bunker Hill because the gooks had bunkers all over it.

But, before we started up, we got replacements. We were so undermanned that they sent us 1st Marine Division Headquarters cooks, drivers and clerks for ammo carriers. They are marines, but they just didn't have the experience.

My platoon was the reserve platoon that day. So, the gooks had a long time to zero in on the trails by the time we got there and we caught mortar fire all the way. The lead platoons took some of the lower ridges by "banzaing" them. The battle became really hot. The gooks were throwing everything at us. Some of our guys were running up and throwing hand grenades into the bunkers. We saw a platoon sergeant race down the hill to a machinegun, pick it up, throw the belt over his shoulder, and charge up the hill firing at a bunker like John Wayne. Unbelievable! The gun weighs 30 pounds. You just don't fire it from the hip. But he did. [Probably S/SGT Frank A. Derrico, WIA 6-10-51, also WIA 11-28-51]

Although we were taking ridges, we were having many casualties.

We were up running from one defile to the next and dropping down when we heard mortars. A directive had come out to wear helmets and I was glad to be wearing one. But, they were heavy and uncomfortable. So, I wore a dungaree cap underneath the helmet to keep it from bouncing on my head and to soften the pressure of the headband. This was particularly necessary when running and dropping to the ground, suddenly.

As we started this attack, this Division Headquarters clerk, who had been assigned to us as an ammo carrier, began to complain about being there. He complained about being shoved in the line when he should have been back at Division Headquarters. As we got higher up the ridgeline, he lost his helmet and it rolled away down to the bottom of the hill no telling where. Now, he was scared as we all were. But, he made a display.

He whimpered that the gooks would see his blond hair and he wanted my dungaree cap to hide his hair. I was appalled. That cap was how I kept my helmet on. But, he said his hair shone in the sun and the gooks might see the shine. He pleaded with me for my cap. So, finally, I gave it to him. Now, my helmet bounced all over my head, even down over my eyes. I was completely disgusted.

Late in the afternoon, we still had to take the top most ridge. We were pinned down and there was no movement up the mountain. We were in desperate shape. Our machinegun section of two machineguns and some 14 men with the replacements were pinned down in a defile or a gully. No one was operating the guns. We were all packed in like sardines in the bottom of this ditch, when the gooks finally got us zeroed in. They dropped in 12 mortars in and around our platoon in groups of four.

It is an awful feeling to hear the "swoosh" and wait for the explosion. You can tell how close they are by the sound; and, I knew the last four were right on our section in the gully. The first two weren't so bad; they bracketed the gully. We were all dry mouthed, a little sick with apprehension, cowering there; running, however, is not what Marines do.

We were all lying on one bank. The third came right in behind us on the other bank. It seemed that the fourth one would never come, but I knew it would. I knew this one was it because they came in a pattern. I lay there and prayed. I've never been so scared in my life. Fear is terrible when you realize the next minute you may be ripped apart with shrapnel.

Your stomach is tied in knots. You want to run. But you don't.

Then, it hit. It was so close I thought it had blown me up. I seemed to float above our gully and there were bright lights above. I was free. Now, think about this. I had no worries. I thought I was dead and my only sorrow was for you [my family] because you wouldn't see me anymore. I was happy because I had no worries. All my worries were gone! I think perhaps death may have been revealed, if just for a moment.

I guess the explosion picked me up and threw me down. And, then I came back to reality and heard the cries of the Division Headquarters clerk next to me. He started screaming. I looked at him. He was hit in the head and hands, one finger missing at the second joint. (Later, he died.) And, the cap I had worn from my first day in combat, the cap I had loaned him, was a bloody mess. All I felt was disgust because he had ruined my cap.

The mortar had hit at the edge of the gully just above my head. My pack was riddled with shrapnel. I looked up the line of our machinegun section and every member of my squad was wounded. I looked down the line of our section and every member of the other squad was wounded. All the machinegun section wounded as well as all the new replacements. I was the only one who did not have a scratch.

Since I was the only survivor left, I took the gun and ran up the hill. I jumped in an artillery hole and waited for orders.

It was almost dark when we reformed and made our final assault. We got to the top of the hill at midnight. At the beginning of the drive the company had three machinegun sections, consisting of six guns and perhaps 40 or 45 men with reinforcements. We got to the top of the hill with two machineguns and 12 surviving machinegunners. I don't know how many casualties Dog Company had.

When we got to the top we found a gook bunker large enough for four of us. But, we had to roll a dead gook out of it first. He was stiff and he rolled down the hill with a kerplop, kerplop, kerplop. We were too tired to roll another one down. He lay by the hole until morning. That's when we discovered we had been lying in pools of blood all night.

Well, the scuttlebutt is that we're going into reserve, soon.

In the afternoon of that fateful assault on Bunker Hill, our company commander, LT Alexander Michaux, wounded in the foot, was evacuated. Over 40 years later, he maintains that "Dog" Company (D/2/1) experienced casualties of 55%. Such a percentage is astounding, but bears out my contention in both letters that we were almost annihilated.

Historically, the battle is described in *U.S. Marine Operations in Korea,* Vol. IV:

On the left flank, the 1st Marines devoted several days to consolidating its position and sending out reconnaissance patrols in preparation for an attack on the ridge just north of the Hwachon Reservoir. From this height the Communists could look down the throats of Colonel Brown's troops. [Brown was Regimental Commander, 1st Marines]

From 6 to 8 June, Lieutenant Colonel Hire's 3rd Battalion led the attack against moderate but gathering resistance. A gain of 1,500 yards was made on the right flank by 2/1, commanded by Major Clarence J. Mabry after the evacuation of Lieutenant Colonel McClellan, wounded on the 5th. [Major Mabry commanded the 2nd Battalion, 1st Marines including "Dog," "Easy,"and "Fox" Companies] On the left, Lieutenant Colonel Robley E. West's 1/1 held fast as the 5th ROK Regiment, 7th ROK Division, X Corps, passed through on its way to a new zone of action to the west.

Early on the 9th, as 2/1 was preparing to launch its attack, an intense artillery and mortar barrage fell upon the lines, followed by the assault of an estimated NKPA company. The Korean Reds were beaten off with heavy losses. And though the enemy fire continued, 2/1 jumped off on schedule, fighting for every inch of ground. Colonel Brown committed 1/1 on the left. It was an all-day fight for both battalions. After taking one ridge in the morning, it was used as a springboard for an assault on the next objective. The weapons of the regimental Anti-Tank Company built up a base of fire that enabled this ridge to be secured by 1600.

The pressure, which had been building up for several days, reached a new high on 10 June. Late that morning Colonel Brown met General Almond and the Division G-3, Colonel Richard G. Weede, at a conference. By 1100 the entire 2nd Battalion of the 1st Marines [and "Dog" Company] was committed. On the left, Lieutenant Colonel West had to hold up the 1st Battalion until 1330, when the ROKs completed the occupation of the high ground dominating the route of advance.

For several hours it appeared that the Marines had met their match this time. A tenacious enemy defended log bunkers expertly, refusing to give ground until evicted by grenade and bayonet attacks. At every opportunity the Communists counterattacked. So effective was their resistance that at dusk the two Marine battalions were still short of their objectives in spite of casualties draining the strength of both units.

Colonel Joseph L. Winecoff, commanding officer of the 11th Marines, remained on the telephone for hours with Colonel Brown. He gave all possible artillery support, not only of his own regiment but also nearby Corps units. By nightfall, with the attacking battalions still held up, the atmosphere was tense in the regimental forward CP. Lieutenant Colonel Adelman, commanding the supporting artillery battalion, 2/11, helped to coordinate air strikes and artillery with Lieutenant Colonel Donald M. Schmuck, executive officer of the 1st Marines, and the air liaison officers.

"Everything I had ever hoped to see in years of teaching such co-ordination of fires seemed to come true that night," commented Colonel Brown at a later date. "I stayed in my regular CP until I was sure all I could do through Winecoff was done, and then went forward to see the finale. It was a glorious spectacle, that last bayonet assault. In the last analysis 2/1 [including "Dog" Company] had to take its objective with the bayonet and hand grenades, crawling up the side of a mountain to get at the enemy. It was bloody work, the hardest fighting I have ever seen."

This was no small tribute, coming from a veteran officer whose combat service included three major wars, not to mention Nicaragua and China. It was nearly midnight before Mabry's battalion [and "Dog" Company] took its final objective. Casualties for the day's attack were 14 KIA and 114 WIA exclusive of slightly wounded, who were neither counted nor evacuated. West's battalion, which seized Hill 802, overlooking the Soyang River, had won its all-day fight at the cost of 9 KIA and 97 WIA.'

The 1st Marines had outfought and outgamed a tough enemy. Never again, after the 10th, was the NKPA resistance quite as determined....

This official Marine Corps account lacks the trauma of my individual experience. My remembrance of that fateful June battle is more explosive in nature:

The mortars came, wounding everyone in the gully except me. In reaction I had grabbed the gun, run up the hill and dived into a shell hole. I suppose I did this to get the gun and myself out of harm's way. I was in deep shock.

An explosion strong enough to blow the body off the ground is terribly shocking. Even more so was the contemplation that I had experienced an out-of-body trauma. The experience was not so much a vocal response—putting into words—but rather a feeling that an ultimate truth had been revealed: that for a fleeting period, a small fragment of eternal knowledge had appeared, or a curtain had been pulled aside so that I might peer into the future.

In this state, I sat in the shell hole that afternoon, machine-gun at my side and waited for orders. None came for hours. My chain of command was broken. My section was immobilized. My place in the fighting unit was gone. I was the only one left.

My mind was numb. I became an observer of events such as the Staff Sergeant charging up the hill with a machinegun, shooting from the hip. Moreover, I noticed the warm rain as it dampened the sandy soil around me. And I peered at the wet grains of sand that clung to my hand. Oblivious of the crackling of rifle and machinegun fire, ignorant of the thump of mortars, I pondered the grains of sand to distinguish the past. My mind turned inward.

This was no small hill we attempted to conquer. This was a mountain almost 2,000 feet high, yet ancient paths trailed around and over it. We had followed a path until we had taken cover in that fateful gully. So to what had these grains of sand been privy over the eons of time? Was this the first battle fought on this sandy mountain side? Or was this an archaic battle ground? Had the various Korean tribes fought here? Had the Chinese? Or the Japanese?

Perhaps, I had suffered some small concussion that afternoon because my mind left the realm of action. Dusk was upon us as I heard the order to move out and my mind again engaged. And I came back to action and the business at hand—to climb the mountain and attack in the gloom.

***

After the trauma of Bunker Hill, boredom was a blessing and I wrote of it on June 28, 1951.

> For the past eight days, we have been on line. We set up a new line like we did once before. [See 2/1, Map 7]
>
> We built bunkers and are dug in. We just sit around all day. And, all night for that matter. We had 4 1/2 hour watches at night. Artillery and mortars

come in on us ever so often. But, it isn't bad. There
is a stream down from us where we can get water and
wash up. We live on the reverse side of the hill and
have our bunkers on the forward slope. This is a
pretty easy life, but it's boring. I've been asleep all
day, just about.

We still hear that we are going into reserve, the
whole Division. Also, I guess there's supposed to be
a peace conference in the UN. But, I guess we'll just
have to wait to see how things work out.

I saw Ross about two weeks ago. There really
isn't much to tell.

After the Battle of Bunker Hill in mid-June, a major
change of officers and commands took place. The Company
Commander became 1st Lieutenant Jay J. Thomas. His
Executive Officer was 2nd Lieutenant Stanley Olson; his
1st Platoon Leader, 2nd Lieutenant Robert Heck; his 2nd
Platoon Leader, 2nd Lieutenant Pierce Power; his 3rd Platoon
Leader, 2nd Lieutenant John Gearhart. The Machinegun
Platoon Leader was 2nd Lieutenant Ernest Brydon and the
Mortar & Rocket Section Leader, 2nd Lieutenant Arthur
Woodruff.

"Dog" Company habituated this line of bunkers mentioned in my letter until after the 4th of July before going into
reserve along with the rest of the 1st Marine Division. Three
events occurred during this time that provide some insight into
the vagaries of combat.

The first event concerns sounds and psyche.

Marines soon learn the sounds of war. By sound the
combat veteran learns how close a bullet or shell is coming.
The pitch varies as well as the length of time the sound is
heard. The older veterans said that you didn't hear the one

that has your name on it. More specifically, the higher and shorter the sound or no sound, the closer; the lower the pitch and the longer the sound is heard, the farther away.

At the end of every day when we set up on line, our artillery would zero in for the night. They set coordinates so that they could hit specified areas during the dark hours. Each evening before dusk, our supporting artillery, the 11th Marines, registered their weapons to make sure that their shells hit in the desired place. In this way, should we be attacked at night, they could automatically support us.

Positioned around our ridgeline, bunkers extended down to the valley on the left side of my bunker as well as more up the ridgeline to my right. One evening before dark I sat at the entrance of my bunker cleaning my carbine.

I had field stripped it to clean the various parts. With parts lying in my lap, I heard the first boom of artillery and the freight train sound high overhead as the shell raced down range. The gunners always started far out, then walked the rounds in toward our lines to insure close support at night. This continued for several more rounds. Suddenly, a short horrible sound I knew too well screeched toward me in an instant. I dove into the bunker, carbine parts flying. With a horrible roar, the short round smashed the second bunker from mine around the ridge line some 25 feet away.

Dust billowed around me as I came up coughing. I knew accidents did happen. We had experienced a 4.2 mortar short round when we first set up in this position. But this near miss by friendly fire made its mark on my psyche.

Perhaps I had not thought very much about my unique existence. This short round gave me pause to contemplate and the seeds of anxiety began to grow.

My buddies were gone. One night, I sacked in with someone other than the two guys with whom I had been sacking in, and one was killed, the other, wounded. Those in my squad, even the reinforced squad, were all wounded and one killed. I was the only survivor.

Some of the wounded came back. Krauss and McGrath did. And those who came back earned their "Purple Hearts." Other wounded earned theirs, but did not come back, like "Little Jake" and "Harby." Still others, like Phillip, earned theirs posthumously.

The germinating idea flowered into a monstrous anxiety. I was positive that I would earn a "Purple Heart," that I would be wounded. How badly would I be wounded? Or would the award be made posthumously? After that time, both questions were never quieted in my mind.

Fortunately, no one was in the bunker that was hit. And I found all the parts to my carbine.

The second event concerned a patrol.

At first, life was easy on this line of bunkers, but later we made one probing patrol, or rather, a patrol to locate the enemy. Actually that is not correct. We went out on a patrol so the enemy could locate us.

Marines are taught to be warriors. Heroes who charge straight forward in combat, taking the day. It is not foolhardy to charge enemy bunkers with bayonets and grenades. It is not madness to charge bunkers firing a machinegun from the hip, John Wayne fashion. It is not absurd to "banzai" a hill, firing a BAR and shouting obscenities.

These acts are usually accomplished spontaneously without orders. But orders have led to the acts. Generally, the order of Marine officers and non-commissioned officers are studied and reasonable. At least once in June 1951, an order was stupid and inane.

After more than a week of inactivity, early one calm morning the 2nd Platoon saddled up for a patrol. On this gorgeous warm, spring morning with no cloud in the sky, the birds' songs saluted us as we strode out on the high ridgeline trail. It was a morning to glory in being alive.

We headed on a northeast path, the troops not knowing exactly what the plan or what our orders were. And for not quite an hour the platoon continued on our plodding course. On this day, I distinctly remember forging a stream, then climbing a steep slippery path which slowed our platoon to a stop.

As the sun heated us in the mid-morning, we stopped along the ridgeline path and gazed down a gradually inclined grassy slope which, after some 300 or 400 yards, bordered a small mountain stream. Although the path had meandered through forested areas, the path and the ridgeline, here, were devoid of vegetation except the grass. This immediate line of march was absolutely open, providing no cover whatsoever.

Surprisingly, the order came to take a break, but spread out—not along the safer reverse side of the ridge but on the open forward slope. Somewhat confused, the platoon deployed itself over the face of the mountain, dropped their packs and relaxed. Some even took naps over the next hour or two. Others opened cans of C-rations.

Across from us, another mountain sloped up steeply from the stream. That mountain side was quite different from ours. It was heavily wooded, a perfect place for gook snipers as well as artillery or mortar spotters to hide.

Not long into our lazy, restful morning, the troops became restless and edgy. They had realized why we were there. To attract gook fire! We were there, exposed on this open slope, to entice the enemy to reveal his position. We were there so the enemy would fire on us with his mortars and artillery. We were there to draw him out. But how many casualties was this order going to bring?

Upon the realization that we were like tethered goats secured to lure a wild animal to come in for the kill, I became ill. My head began to pound and I became sick to my stomach.

I was furious. How could these officers put us in such a potentially dangerous situation? Who had decided that our lives were so valueless? So expendable? What a dumb, stupid thing to do!

The blame for giving that mindless order falls on one or both the company commander and/or the new 2nd platoon leader who had just assumed his command. Coming less than a month after "Dog" Company had suffered 55% casualties, this misuse of troops was appalling. In retrospect, however, this may have been simply the mistake of a new platoon leader.

Whether it was our fate, good luck or the will of a higher power I do not know, but apparently no gooks were hiding on the opposite mountain that day. After a period of time without incident, we saddled up and moved out.

The return trip to our lines occurred in the early afternoon. The day had become hot and we sweated under our heavy helmets.

Not only the contemplation of the troops on the event that had recently taken place, but also the exertion of the march held back conversation. A silent group snaked down the trail.

Their concern may have been much the same as an abused child has for his parent. A child is so vulnerable. Likewise vulnerable are the troops under the command of an officer. They respect him and his orders. In return, they should expect honorable treatment. With troubled thoughts, we continued on our way.

The third event concerned girls.

Whether it was our fate, good luck or the will of a higher power I do not know, but a sudden bend in the path revealed a scene to uplift our hearts and make us push aside our dark feelings. For in a small niche between the mountain side and the path stood a papa-san and his two daughters, heads bowed shyly, waiting for us to pass by.

Papa-san wore bloomerlike trousers; the girls wore high waisted long white full skirts. On this hot June day, all three wore traditional open white vests above the waist. The girls were in their late 'teens, fully filled out with mature breasts openly revealed. Almost never did we find civilians on the front lines, certainly, never old men and young girls. Probably they were seeking shelter to the rear and had come from some farm secluded in these mountains.

For them this was proper attire at that time and place. Not so in the lifestyle of marines. In those days, even burlesque strippers ended their act with pasties and G-string. No topless bars existed. Public nudity was not accepted in the 1950s.

This platoon of marines stared, open mouthed, as they passed by. Not a sound or cat-call. These guys were just too shocked to make any audible sound. Thus, after our harrowing experience on the mountain side, we returned to the bunkers, happy to a man.

The *U.S. Marine Operations in Korea,* Vol. IV summarizes the advances during the spring of 1951:

> Thus ended two months of continual hard fighting for the 1st Marine Division, beginning on 22 April with the great CCF offensive. Few and far between were the interludes of rest for troops which saw both defensive and offensive action. After stopping the enemy's two drives, they launched a month-long counterstroke that had the enemy hardpressed at

times for survival. Only the ruthless sacrifice of NKPA troops in defensive operations enabled the Chinese Reds to recover from the blows dealt them in late May and early June.

The cost in Marine casualties had been high. Throughout the entire month the 1st Marines alone suffered 67 KIA and 1,044 WIA, most of them being reported during the first 2 weeks. This was a higher total than the regiment incurred during the Chosin Reservoir operation. Reflecting on the caliber of these men, their regimental commander had this to say:

"They were war-wise when I got command; I contributed nothing to their training because they were in battle when I joined them and I left them when they came out of the lines for a rest. They used cover, maneuvered beautifully, used their own and supporting arms intelligently, were patient and not foolhardy; but when it came to the point where they had to rely on themselves with bayonet, hand-grenade and sheer guts, they could and did do that too. I have long ago given up telling people what I saw them do on many occasions. Nobody believes me, nor would I believe anyone else telling the same story of other troops."

Colonel Brown, of course, paid this tribute to the troops of his regiment. But it is safe to say that any commanding officer of the 1st Marine Division would have felt that these sentiments applied equally to his own men. All the combat Marines of the 60-day battle had shown themselves to be worthy heirs of the traditions of Belleau Wood, Guadalcanal, Iwo Jima, and the Chosin Reservoir.

CHAPTER TEN

SUMMER SUN
AND TRUCE TALKS

My anxiety burgeoned. Daily my fear grew. It expanded into a great cloud surrounding me like the monstrous worry of Phillip Andre Lierse. Indeed, it was the medal that dominated my thoughts. How would I get the "Purple Heart?" In only three ways could I perceive the possibility of "getting" it: a slight wound requiring only a short recovery time; a serious wound requiring hospitalization; or posthumously. I knew that I was going to be wounded. But how?

On the morning of the Fourth of July 1951, I had the last watch.

The order had been passed the night before that there would be no unauthorized activity—no celebration, no firing of rifles, no throwing of grenades. A quiet Fourth was to be observed.

On the morning of the Fourth of July, I stood the last two hours in the cold before morning and pondered some futile attempt to block my fate. But as the faint light of dawn revealed our lines, my quandary changed to a resolve to action. I was going to cast aside my anxiety and commit an offense. I was going to break the order and have some fun. I was going to celebrate the Fourth of July.

On this morning as the dawn brightened, I looked down

upon a unit of the Reconnaissance Company, Headquarters Battalion, 1st Marine Division—otherwise, cordially termed "hotdogs" or "cowboys" or "thoseassholes." This Recon outfit was stretched across the valley below. "Dog" Company (D/2/1) manned a line of bunkers from just above the valley up the ridgeline to the top of the hill and continued along other ridges to another 2nd battalion (2/1) company. Likewise, across the valley a company of 3rd Battalion (3/1) manned bunkers up and across the ridgeline of that hill. The Recon outfit, however, strung itself across the valley and tied in with our battalions on the hills. After our intense battles and heavy casualties of May and June, the Recon Company was re-cast as infantry and manned the line.

It is difficult to describe Recon. Of course, from the infantrymen's point of view, we thought they were expected to reconnoiter. We expected them to explore, to survey and to scout—in other words, search out the gooks for us. In our view, however, the only apparent reality we saw were guys charging up a road in a Jeep, slamming on the breaks, stopping in a cloud of dust, and maybe asking us some idiotic question. Their reputation and our experience indicated that Recon guys were a "shaky" group. Seemingly not disciplined in relation to us, they would fire at anything, at any time. But, oh, how they got the glory. (My apologies to Recon. Our envy and rivalry are evident.)

Only on rare occasions does fate provide an opportunity for the worm to turn. Rarely is the downtrodden allowed retribution.

On 4 July 1951, my opportunity was revealed in a flash as I saw the whole Recon outfit displayed below me.

Just at the break of dawn, as most of the Marines slept in bunkers along the ridgelines and Recon slept in their foxholes in the valley, I distinguished my flare canister from my grenades. Actually, it was shaped like a can, whereas the grenade shape was quite identifiable—"pineapple-like" in miniature. I picked up the flare canister, pulled the pin and threw it.

I possessed super human power that morning. My physical strength was beyond my belief. Even John Wayne could not have done better.

The canister arced over the trees. Farther and farther, it arced out over the valley. It flew through that morning air as if it had wings. For an instant it was a bird losing its bonds with earth.

Incredibly it landed almost 50 feet in front and at the mid-point of the Recon line. It exploded and lit the valley with strobe-like detail.

"Shaky" Recon fired down the valley for twenty minutes. Not just rifles, either. Light and heavy machineguns as well as BARs. The night crackled in a fusillade. Every marine along the line was awakened to this apparent major dawn attack.

Through the din, I chuckled. I laughed uproariously. I celebrated the Fourth of July.

Following this exuberance, my attitude as well as my physical well-being improved. With no more patrols carrying heavy ammo cans and with casual time for changing socks regularly, my feet healed for the first time since joining "Dog" Company. Finally I became healthy and whole again.

***

My high spirits were evident in my next letter of July 9, 1951.

We've been in battalion reserve for three days,

now. Movies, showers, and hot chow. Really fine!
I've just been enjoying myself instead of writing
like I should.

Supposedly, we would go back up on line in
four days; but since the division is going into 10th
Corps reserve on the 15th of July, that would put us
on line for only two days. So, I don't think we'll go
back for such a short time.

When we were relieved the other day, we had to
walk five miles to get aboard trucks. It was really a
beautiful day—white tufts of clouds in an azure blue
sky, various shades of green in the vegetation around
us. Just like being in technicolor.

As we came down off the mountain onto some
small rolling hills, it struck me that I really felt good,
again. There ahead of me was that never-ending line
of canvas-covered helmets. Over the rise ahead,
they walked and disappeared. We imagined the war
might be over for us. Truce talks were beginning.
Peace was in sight.

These were Marines, walking over these never-
ending hills, and, more than anyone else, they are the
men who have made peace possible. My pack
became lighter; I straightened up. Perhaps, it was
pride; but, it seemed more than that—a feeling without definition. Something far deeper than pride. So,
I held my head high and marched down the trail.

Further along, an interesting incident occurred
which shows that courage and fear go hand in hand
The gooks must have spotted us. Their observers
with field glasses must have seen our line trailing
down the valley—although several miles from the
front line. And, we received a barrage of artillery

fire.

For some reason, my instincts weren't exact. Perhaps, I hadn't expected fire in what I thought to be a safe defile. When the barrage hit, I fell to my knees. I couldn't think what to do. I was shocked and surprised. The platoon sergeant in the rear of our column was shouting, "Keep moving! Keep your interval!" [to keep a proper distance separating the troops, so artillery incapacitates the fewest number]

That was what told me what to do. I started yelling, "Move out! Keep the interval!" Over and over, I yelled. I surprised myself. Me, a PFC, giving orders. But, I was scared; and the faster we moved out, the faster I would get away from there. It was a small incident, but this is why people do things under stress they never would have done in calmer moments. I believe most of the heroes of this war or any war were not really heroes but just scared little people who had to do something.

Beginning my fifth month in Korea, I'm getting to be quite an old veteran. But, I believe I've learned more in the past month than I ever learned before. I know sounds, now. Bullets, mortars, and artillery. I know what to do for each sound. Seems like everything has a different bang and you get to know the sounds. I also know it pays to be careful and alert. Because two men in our squad were careless, they are dead.* That has taught me a lesson.

Relief of the Marines was completed by the 2nd Infantry

---

*My reference to the two careless dead marines regarded Phillip Lierse and the Headquarters clerk. The one shouted, "Who goes there?" The other carelessly lost his helmet.

Division on 15 July, and by the 17th all units were on their way to X Corps reserve. This was the second time since the landing of the 1st Provisional Marine Brigade on 2 August 1950 that the Marines had been away from the firing line for more than a few days.

On July 26, 1951, I told my folks about life in reserve.

> I guess the rainy season is really here. We are set up in division reserve above Hungchon. We are in a big tent but it leaks like a sieve. We spend most of our time trying to stop leaks and keep dry.
>
> Our schedule runs here until the 26th of August. Unless something drastic happens, we'll be in reserve for another month.
>
> We have reveille at 6 am, then calisthenics and police call when not raining; then we have chow from 7 to 8 am. Classes are held on just about everything from tactics to gun drill until noon. From 1:30 to 2:30, we have more classes. Then we're off the rest of the afternoon.
>
> There is a big river where we can go swimming. It has nice clear water. Over by where Ross is set up, they have dammed up a tributary of the river and made a really nice swimming hole. I see Ross quite often, now. In fact, the gooks do all our washing in the river for cigarettes and candy. So, I can take my clothes over there and get them washed while I visit Ross.
>
> Just not much more to tell except we have USO shows and movies that are really fine.

One USO show in particular was "really fine." I'll never forget it.

On a beautiful, vibrant afternoon, I managed to work

my way up close to the stage of a Betty Hutton show. I no longer remember the other performers because Betty Hutton grabbed my fancy and I became oblivious to all the rest. The object of my tunnel vision was more specific than the whole of Betty. It centered on her thighs. She simply had the largest thighs that I had ever seen. Not fat by any means, she was a dancer with muscular legs. To say her torso was gorgeous was an absolute understatement. I remained open-mouthed, sexually aroused, transfixed throughout her performance.

***

The verdant flood plain bounded by opposing green hills was a half a mile wide. This particular spot on the flood plain, some ten miles north of Hongchon and some 40 miles north of Wonju, had been chosen for Division reserve not only because this valley provided enough flat area for the Division's encampment but also provided an adequate water supply for showers as well as for drinking and cooking. Neither was it close to a town (Hongchon being reduced to rubble), which might attract the attention of the relaxing marines. We had to have special permission to travel to Wonju.

Curving down the valley from the northeast, the blue-green river meandered; but at the north end of the camp it cut into the lush greenery of the western hillside in a wide and deep swath. On the opposite side of the river was a broad, white, sandy beach. It was the ol' swimmin' hole about which all young lads dream.

Ross and I would meet there many times during the summer of 1951. We would give our dirty clothes to gook washers, then strip to our skivvies and go for a swim. Afterward, we would sit or lie on our dungarees and exchange scuttlebutt until our underwear had dried.

On any summer afternoon when not on maneuvers, most of the camp went swimming also, and got their clothes washed at the same time. Half of the swimmers were nude and the particular incongruity of this time and place was the naked Puritan ethic grounded American standing nonchalant beside the Korean washer woman and haggling over the price of the laundry. Such are the effects of war.

That afternoon was hot. The water was cool. The conversation light-hearted. It was like being back home again.

"Ross, do you see that Indian, over there?" Chief * was a curiosity to me. Was he really reliving ancient times? Perhaps, instead of his dungarees, he should have worn a loin cloth and carried a bow and arrows. He was close to no one. Didn't really have friends. A loner from another time, another place? He was not the noble savage. He was a savage adversary.

Chief was on his second tour of duty. He had actually requested to stay in Korea in a line organization. He loved war. He adored combat. He was a professional killer who loved his job. This was the only place he could legitimately ply his trade.

"Yeah." Ross, had spotted Chief going into the water.

"Well, this guy carries a .30-06 with a snooper scope. He's our scout.

"He doesn't do much until we set up. Then he goes out at night alone and hunts for the gooks' lines. Of course,

---

*Many "Dog" Company members will remember our scout Technical Sergeant Augustine Oberg. As late as the Korean War, a few scouts still carried the 1903 bolt-action Springfield .30-06, the soldier's weapon of World War I, circa 1914-1918. Chief's old weapon had a modern infrared snooper scope attached, which provided him with eyes in the dark. In addition he carried a very sharp six inch knife.

that's why he's our scout. He finds out where the gooks are. However, if he kills one he takes a little souvenir. Chief cuts off an ear. He has them strung on a string and keeps the bunch in a bag. He tries to add an ear every time he goes out. And he'll show them to you if you ask.

"You know, I read somewhere that the Indians mutilated the bodies of their enemies in the belief that the dead men's spirits would then be identically crippled in the afterlife. I really wonder if Chief is heeding the call of his ancestors?"

"Yeah." Ross chuckled. "We had a guy—got rotated about a month ago—he collected little fingers. Just cut 'em right off at the second joint. Said it was easy."

"Now, what do you suppose he did with 'em when he went home? Can you see him sayin', 'Hey, Mom, look what I brought back from Korea.'" Ross laughed.

He was always funny because he chuckled when he talked or laughed outright when something was even mildly funny. This hearty characteristic generally infected the listener until everyone was laughing.

Ross returned to the dangerous business of scouting.

"Al, you know, that goin' out at night is scary. That's when those gooks are tryin' to find our lines. They stay hidden during the day 'cause their afraid of our planes. But at night, those little devils are out and about.

"Why, you know, I learned a lot pretty fast. You remember we went up north from Pusan on the train and then they let us off at night and we pitched our tents in a field?"

"Yeah, it was snowing." I remembered how cold it was.

"Well. you remember we got separated the next day and I went up to the 5th Marines. They were set up in the ol' perimeter defense, you know, but the next day we jumped off in the attack and when I heard some of those big guns goin', you know, I dived down along this rice paddy. Well, this big

Greek sergeant comes along and says, 'Hey, those are our guns firin'.'"

Ross laughed uproariously at his joke and continued.

"Well, I felt like a fool, but that was my first experience with those big guns firing.

"Why, I learned pretty quick what was a bad sound and which was ours. You know, you learn fast how close bullets and mortars and big shells are comin'. It got my attention real fast on my first day when I saw our Lieutenant lyin' on the ground, shot—as to what could happen. Of course, Lieutenants are a dime a dozen since they're at the head of the column and we went through a lot of them. But it's only after seein' do you get the full effect.

"After that little incident with our big guns, I ran on up the ridgeline maybe two or three hundred yards and dirt started kickin' up around the bottom of my feet and I figured right fast that I should be on the side of that damn hill. Yeah, I learned to get on the other side of the ridgeline to keep out of their fire and not make a target on the skyline. Now that was a fun little deal.

"Another thing I learned was these reserves just couldn't cut it. Goin' up to the top of the hill, the gun has to have ammo. And all the way up the hill, these ammo carriers are droppin' like flies. When it boiled down to it, we had reserves scattered everywhere. They weren't in too good a shape, I found out. So, consequently, the regulars could get ammo to the gun and reserves couldn't. So I found myself comin' from last ammo carrier to first ammo carrier, right away.

"It really tells you a lot about the Marine Corps reserves. They just aren't ready. You know, to climb these hills they aren't in shape at all.

"And I learned pretty fast that you don't go out at night and you don't make a light or sound. Especially, you don't attract the attention of those little gook fellers. So, no thanks. I don't want to be a scout or cut off ears."

Ross chuckled. It came from the back of his throat and gurgled out. His typical laugh had no duplicate that I had heard.

But he didn't laugh when I asked, "You haven't been wounded, yet, have you? I haven't, either. Ross, do you ever wonder how you're going to get it?"

"I just hope it's not posthumously," he said quite seriously.

"Oh, I've got another story that's hard to believe." This seemed appropriate for me to tell and change the subject on this hot afternoon.

"We had this guy we called 'The Pirate' in Dog Company. And he was a BARman. Unbelievable guy. Just say 'go' and he would charge hills. He would banzai the gooks firing that BAR with the trigger held back with no let up.

"So he wore a red bandana on his head. You know, tied at the four corners so it fit snug to his head. He looked meaner than hell. And he'd scream at the gooks. Well, I wouldn't be surprised if some of them died of fright.

"This guy became the hero of Dog Company. Man, they had him up for Silver Star medals and I don't know what else.

"Well, you'd never guess what happened. He was due to rotate next week. Old Pirate wasn't going back to the line. So, last week he went down to Wonju and went to a whorehouse. The place was so rickety the roof fell in on him and the girl and killed them both.

"Can you imagine? This guy goes through combat, constantly exposing himself to fire. He should have been killed I don't know how many times. But he gets killed in a whorehouse, just before he is due to go home."

Ross thought this to be highly amusing and through his laughter he could barely get out, "Yeah, but he died in the saddle with his boots on."

He sang a few bars of Gene Autry's "Back In The Saddle, Again."

Done with that, Ross said, seriously, "Say, Al, tell me what else is new."

I told another strange story. Again about whores.

"Do you remember when we were set up in X Corps reserve in April?" I asked.

Ross nodded.

"Remember that gook house down by the river that had a line of guys going in the front door and others coming out the back?"

"Yeah," Ross chuckled, "horniest bunch of guys I ever saw. I think that whole tank company that was set up over across the river on that bluff came down there and lined up for a half a mile."

I agreed, "Right, there were two gook girls in there and they took on maybe more than a hundred guys in one day. I never went down there, though, because I was too chicken. I was afraid of VD."

"Well, yeah," Ross added, "you've got to go to the Corpsman to get a rubber and that's a hassle. So half those guys didn't use a rubber. But what does this have to do with anything? Did you get syph or clap or somethin'."

"No. No. I said I didn't go. I found out about a guy who was running the girls. He was taking the money. The guy was a pimp."

"No shit," Ross was incredulous. No chuckle, but curious.

I explained what the clerk from Headquarters had told me during the assault on Bunker Hill where he had been a replacement ammo carrier, behind me in our machinegun squad:

> Since we had been so desperately reduced in manpower, the 1st Marine Division truck drivers, cooks, and clerks had been sent up to the lines to augment our decimated companies. They were thrown into combat and most were terrified. This clerk was no different.
>
> In the early morning of that day, trucks arrived bringing the neophytes. Since none of us had been informed, we made no move to investigate these new arrivals. My first sighting of the clerk was when he walked up to the squad and ask if this was Dog Company machineguns. He checked in with the squad leader and came over.
>
> He did not seem very friendly and let me know that his being sent up to the lines was the dumbest thing "they" could have done. Then he told me that he was a clerk at division headquarters. But aside from this assignment, he was in business and making money. And when he got back home he would have a bundle. He made me feel like I was some kind of dunce for being in a line company.
>
> The clerk maintained that he had started his business by finding several gook girls, camp followers, who would exchange sex for the food and protection that he could give. Offering free sex to the cooks from division mess, he was supplied with food for the girls. With the same arrangement with the truck drivers, he had transportation to reserve areas when troops came off line for rest and relaxation. That explains the house that Ross and I had seen in April.

Three dollars, Script money, was the price and the clerk was racking in the profit. It was all profit. No money went to the girls. They received only food and a place to sleep.

US troops in Korea had only Script but this could be converted to money orders and sent home. If his story were true, the guy was building a bank account.

I told Ross about how he boasted of his good fortune before we jumped off into the attack on the lower slopes of that steep battle ground. As we moved along the trail to higher ground, gooks dropped mortars close to us. He became fearful and cursed his bad luck and the officers who put him in this situation. On still higher ground, he was distraught. Almost whining.

But when his helmet bounced off his head and careened down the mountain out of sight, the clerk became a tearful coward. He demanded my utility cap so that the gooks would not see the shine of his blond hair. I was disgusted with his actions and gave him the cap in hopes it would quiet him.

Finally, as we were bunched together in the gully and the mortars rained in on us, it was the screams of the clerk that brought me back to reality from the concussion of the exploding mortars.

His hands were bloody. His face was bloody. And the cap I had worn from my first day in combat was a bloody mess. I remember acutely that his little finger on his left hand was missing at the second joint.

I looked at him and my only emotion was a feeling of disgust and loss for my cap. He died and his nearest companion felt nothing but repulsion.

Ross understood.

That was enough conversation for then. We went swimming again.

***

My letters did not always divulge all the details. Of course, I had revealed more information of the "clerk story" to Ross than I could ever tell my folks. But my letter of August 13, 1951, concerned a new importance that I had acquired in "Dog' Company and provided the details of how this came about. At least, in my opinion.

I must apologize for not writing sooner. We've been in reserve for some time, now, and it looks like we will be for another month. We're set up about ten miles north of Hongchon in a beautiful valley beside a river. We can go swimming every day and I see Ross all the time. We even took pictures on the sand by the river the other day. We keep our gear and sleep in big pyramidal tents. We have hot chow and a PX set up, too. We even have ball diamonds and hot showers. Last but not least, we have great USO shows and movies.

Yesterday was Sunday, so some of us went to Wonju, which is 40 miles south of where we are. We stayed there all day and went through the market places. They stink like you wouldn't believe. Most of the smell comes from their cooking. Well, the only thing I bought was a Korean Papa-san pipe about a yard long. I don't know how I will ever get it home.

I came off the lines as 1st ammo carrier and

expected to make assistant gunner when the old guys left. Well, my chances for advancement were nil when the 10th draft came in with a bunch of Reserve corporals and sergeants. In all the companies I've ever seen, they promote the old men; but, they gave all the good jobs to these guys who have no combat experience. To top it off, instead of assistant gunner, I became 2nd ammo carrier, again, because I was still a PFC.

I had to think hard when the order came that anyone that had come over in the sixth draft could transfer to the rear echelon (motor pool, supply, MPs, etc.). But, I decided to stay in a line outfit. I guess I just like that old machine gun.

The very next day my luck changed. The machinegun platoon commander [LT Ernest Brydon] transferred me to machinegun platoon runner, which is one of the best jobs in the company. When we're on line, I stay with our lieutenant in headquarters company. In the attack, headquarters is last. No more ammo can carrying. I carry my carbine (I, also, have a .45 in a shoulder holster) and my walkie-talkie, the little hand-held radio. We call our platoon leader [LT Brydon], "mouse." He's a short guy with a loud voice, a mighty "mouse." He's really a character.

Since our platoon is split up and each section (3 sections to a machinegun platoon) goes with their respective rifle platoon (3 rifle platoons to a company), I have no real assignment on line except to stay at headquarters. Even when our platoon is in reserve and our machinegun platoon sets up, together, I don't do much. Just pass the word from the lieutenant. Whatever orders he has.

In a rifle platoon, the runner is always with the platoon leader. He has his walkie-talkie and relays the platoon leader's orders or makes calls on the walkie-talkie for the platoon leader. But, a machine-gun platoon leader stays at the C.P. (Command Post), and his runner is more or less just a figure-head. In other words, I have really got it easy, now. I've really got it knocked!

The other day, I was walking up the company street with the lieutenant and he said, "Well, I put you up for another stripe." He said the battalion is full right now, but as soon as the next draft goes home, there should be openings.

When we go on maneuvers, I'm always with headquarters so I know what's going on. Makes me feel like a wheel. Now, all the officers in the company know me. The other day on maneuvers, I was off trying to find a platoon that had gone too far, and I ran into the company exec. officer [LT Stanley Olson]. He said, "Hey, Andy, what's the scoop?" So, I told him. I'm more or less the 2nd company runner, so I know the C.O. [LT George Benskin] pretty well, also. The other day, the C.O. needed someone to observe Fox company when they jumped off in the attack during maneuvers so we could raise our covering fire. He sent me. Seems like all of a sudden I've really come up in the world.

In hindsight, LT Brydon did not have many options. And I suppose I represented a problem. What to do with a PFC that was an "old" veteran, although somewhat tarnished—I seemed to have continuous foot problems. As assistant gunner, I would exchange 40 pounds of ammo for 30 pounds of machinegun. Not much trade-off there. It still was a load to carry, particularly with potentially bad feet. Also the continuity of personnel had to be considered. The squad needed someone dependable. Were my feet dependable? Luckily, the reserve sergeants and corporals came with the 10th draft and settled that question.

Although to my knowledge a machinegun platoon runner had not existed before, Brydon rated one. In the past we had been undermanned; but now we had replenished our manpower with the new draft. So the "mouse" made a smart decision that made me happy.

In August, the command of "Dog" Company, 2nd Battalion, 1st Marines, 1st Marine Division, FMF, (D/2/1) changed. 1st Lieutenant George H. Benskin became the Commanding Officer. 2nd Lieutenant Stanley Olson remained the Executive Officer. 2nd Lieutenant Pierce Power moved to the 1st platoon. 2nd Lieutenant Arthur Anthony became platoon leader of 2nd platoon. Remaining at their posts were 3rd platoon leader, 2nd Lieutenant John Gearhart; machinegun platoon leader, 2nd Lieutenant Ernest Brydon; and mortar and rocket section leader, 2nd Lieutenant Arthur Woodruff.

Most of our days were devoted to training along with occasional maneuvers. But we found time for play.

Each man received a ration of two beers per day. Of course, the ration was distributed only in reserve, off the line. Naturally, the ration built up as the units remained in combat. When we were in reserve, however, command made the determination that "Each man in Dog Company gets two six-packs," or whatever the amount might be.

It seems that I always drank my entire ration immediately, then became sick with diarrhea for several days after. Not being an expansive drinker, John Camacho traded his beer ration for C-ration fruit. I believe I traded for more beer with those non-beer drinkers like John. And, as I remember, it was always Pabst Blue Ribbon, never Schlitz, the most popular and expensive brand at the time.

On the other hand, the officers received a ration of whiskey, a fifth bottle for some period of time similar to our daily ration of beer. The brand most distributed was Four Roses.

Obviously, the message seemed to be that a Marine officer could handle liquor better than the enlisted man. Nevertheless, after a rousing officer's party one night, it was either LT Anthony's or LT Gearhart's inert body we found lying in the company street the next morning. Fortunately he recovered.

My drinking beer during a similar enlisted party unfortunately led to a quite different circumstance.

Although we could find washerwomen at the river to launder our clothes, we still maintained our personal gear, our bedding, and the tent interior and surroundings. Consequently, to acquire a houseboy to perform all these tasks was the coup most envied.

I acquired Kim quite by chance or so I thought. He had been in our camp since we had set up and seemed to be of local origin. I had seen him working for other tents. And although he seemed to change tents quite frequently, I thought nothing of it.

I had found a servant. In return for food, he would launder my clothes, sweep the tent, freshen my bedding and be my general flunky. This 14 year old that looked ten just shuffled up to me and asked if he could be my houseboy. I was overjoyed. He carried few personal things, but he had a makeshift bed—a cast off sleeping bag—and flopped it out next to

mine in the tent. Our pyramidal tents accommodated six
men, their gear and their air mattresses on which were placed
blanket-weight summer sleeping bags. Kim fitted easily
into the space between my bunkmate and me.

For a week I enjoyed his servitude. He was a conscien-
tious and tireless worker. I was amazed at his industriousness
as well as at my good fortune. Then I went on a beer party.

Early the next morning, reviving from my almost
comatose state of drunken stupor, I slowly realized I was
being sexually manipulated. The sensation was first difficult
to comprehend—like coming out of a dream. It did not stop,
however, and I awoke to find Kim's hand in the fly of my
dungarees. This was an uninvited experience. This was a vio-
lation that I abhorred.

Now I understood why he had been kicked out of the
other tents. I knocked his arm away. Throwing him into the
aisle of the tent, I tossed his belongings after him, yelling,
"Get out!"

This was behavior we did not tolerate. Others awoke and
asked what happened. My only explanation was, "That little queer Kim tried to jack me off." My bunkmates understood. It was not discussed again.

It was a simple matter of morals. Marines of the Korean
War era just did not tolerate homosexual acts. The subject
was closed.

***

Mao Zedong's forces had lost face by the failure of their
Spring Offensive. Moreover, they had been badly mauled
during the UN counteroffensive. Pretension of high morale
of the communist forces could no longer be maintained when
the troops were laying down their arms without a fight. Nor
could Chinese charges of low UN morale be supported when

the fighting spirit of the Eighth Army was apparent every day at the front.

By the end of June 1951, the communists held even less territory than they had occupied when they began their onslaught the year before—2,100 square miles less. In the first year more than a million communist troops had been killed or wounded, or lived comfortably in UN prison camps. Communist equipment lost included 391 aircraft, 1000 pieces of artillery, thousands of machineguns, automatic rifles and mortars. Industrial North Korea lay in ruins; cities, factories and power plants were rubble.

The communists needed a break in the fighting to recuperate and re-build their forces. Their tacticians and strategists let it be known through several channels that they would be interested in truce talks. And American public opinion, searching for the remote possibility for a cease fire, pressured Washington to negotiate. UN military leaders in Korea saw through the communist ploy and were skeptical, believing that the truce talks would just prolong the war. Of course, this would be the case.

The truce talks would cause the UN forces to lose their momentum in attacking north. In fact, they would slow the pace and grow stale while the communists would rest, regroup, and resupply. Negotiation with the enemy to gain time to re-group was old tactic for the Chinese. They had used this crafty trick with success during the civil war with the Nationalist Chinese.

Moreover, craft and guile abounded in the Chinese camp. The UN suggested that the truce team meet on the Danish hospital ship Jutlandia, neutral ground, since the Danes had no combat forces in Korea. The communists insisted that site of the talks be Kaesong. The UN Command conceded.

The ruse was soon evident: Kaesong lay in the path of

the Eighth Army advance; it would, therefore, be immune to attack when talks began. It was the ancient Korean capital in no man's land, but the communists soon managed to include it within their lines.

As the UN delegates drove to Kaesong, they were requested to display white flags on their vehicles for identification. The communist photographers, placed strategically, photographed the obviously beaten UN representatives coming to plead for terms, displaying the white flag of surrender. Countless pictures of a surrendering enemy were distributed to Asia's illiterate millions. Other photographs showed unarmed UN delegates being mustered about Kaesong by burp gun carrying communist guards.

The symbolism at these talks was not overlooked. Oriental custom dictates that at the peace table the victors face south and the losers face north. Obviously, the UN delegates were seated facing north. At the conference table, Admiral C. Turner Joy, Senior Delegate and Chief of the UN Command delegation at the truce talks, was singled out as a recipient of more communist badgering.

U.S. Marine Operations in Korea, Vol. IV, describes the situation:

> Some of the propaganda schemes bordered on the ridiculous. "At the first meeting of the delegates," Admiral Joy related, "I seated myself at the conference table and almost sank out of sight. The Communists had provided a chair for me which was considerably shorter than a standard chair. Across the table, the senior Communist delegate, General Nam Il, protruded a good foot above my cagily diminished stature. This had been accomplished by providing stumpy Nam Il with a chair about four

inches higher than usual. Chain-smoking Nam Il puffed his cigarette in obvious satisfaction as he glowered down on me, an obviously torpedoed admiral. This condition of affairs was promptly rectified when I changed my foreshortened chair for a normal one, but not before Communist photographers had exposed reels of film."

In the war of propaganda, the communists mauled the Americans and their UN allies almost as badly as the Marines and Eighth Army had recently mauled the communists during the spring battles.

Again, *U.S. Marine Operations in Korea,* Vol. IV, explains:

> ... Kaesong was actually a second UN front.
>
> After the preliminaries had been settled—most of them to Communist satisfaction—the UN delegation, headed by Admiral Joy, held the first meeting on 10 July 1951 with his opposite number, NKPA Major General Nam Il, and the Communist truce team. This was the first of the talks that were to drag on for two dreary years.
>
> Nam Il, a Korean native of Manchuria, born in 1911, had been educated in Russia and had served with the Soviet army in World War II. His career in Korea began when he arrived as a captain with Soviet occupation troops in 1945. Rising to power rapidly, he took a prominent part in the creation of a Soviet puppet state in North Korea.
>
> An atmosphere of sullen hatred surrounded the UN delegates at Kaesong. The CCF sentinel posted at the entrance to the conference room wore a gaudy medal which he boasted had been awarded to him

"for killing forty Americans." When Admiral Joy
tried to send a report to General Ridgway, the mes-
senger was turned back by armed Communist guards.
These are samples of the indignities heaped upon
the UN truce team. After several UN delegates were
threatened by guards with burp guns, Joy protested
to Nam Il, "demanding prompt elimination of such
crudities."

In order to give their battered armies more time
for recuperation, the Communist delegates met every
issue with delaying tactics. They proved themselves
to be masters of the ancient art of dragging a red
herring across the trail. Going back on their word did
not embarrass them in the least if they found it to
their advantage to renege.

The truce negotiations were bound to have an
immediate effect on military operations. In the
United States it seemed a pity to newspaper readers
that American young men should have to die in battle at a time when headlines were hinting at the possibility of peace. Mothers wrote to their congress-
men, requesting a halt in Korean operations.

General Van Fleet minced no words after his
retirement when he commented on the effect of the
truce talks on strategy:

"Instead of getting directives for offensive action,
we found our activities more and more proscribed as
time went on. Even in the matter of straightening out
our lines for greater protection, or capturing hills
when Reds were looking down our throats, we were
limited by orders from the Far East Command in
Japan, presumably acting on directives from
Washington."

It was the opinion of Admiral Joy that more UN casualties were suffered as a consequence of the truce talks than would have resulted from an offensive taking full advantage of Red China's military weaknesses in June 1951.

"As soon as armistice discussions began," he wrote, "United Nations Command ground forces slackened their offensive preparations. Instead, offensive pressure by all arms should have been increased to the maximum during the armistice talks.... I feel certain that the casualties the United Nations Command endured during the two long years of negotiations far exceed any that might have been expected from an offensive in the summer of 1951."

Apparently by August 1951, the communist forces had had enough time to recuperate and the Reds walked out on the truce talks after falsely charging that UN planes had violated Kaesong neutrality by dropping napalm in the area on 22 August. No credible evidence was produced.

Left on the table unresolved were the two opposing positions.

The communists had concentrated their efforts and demands for the 38th parallel to be the line of demarcation— as it had been before their attack in June 1950—once a truce was signed.

The UN insisted on the line (DMZ) to be 20 miles in depth, following the present battle line. In return it would halt air and naval activity beyond the northern border of the line.

Eventually the talks would resume and move a few miles east to Panmunjon, where they continue to the present. Today tourists still visit the Panmunjom site.

On 26 August, all Marine units received a Division warning that offensive operations would be initiated in the immediate future. The 5th Marines, 7th Marines, and KMCs were alerted to move up to areas south and west of the Punchbowl on 27 August. The 1st Marines was to remain in Division reserve.

***

In Division reserve, rest and relaxation continued. John Camacho remembers his summer:

> The respite from action during the August reserve was really good for me. I spent my 19th birthday on some training-maneuver outpost, watching fireflies for the first time.
>
> We had boxing matches and I was in two of them. The first one was easy, a snap: the second, a disaster—my squad leader, Martin Rivas, gave me a perfect boxing lesson. He had been involved in "Golden Gloves" competition in Texas. Unfortunately, later, he lost his foot to a mine.
>
> I had dysentery the rest of the time: strangely, I could only eat apples. Following this, I got a nasty cold which I managed to "sweat out." Finally, I was cured and ready to return to the lines at the end of our rest period.

The reserve provided not only time for rest and training, but also the opportunity to hold memorial services for the marines who had died in battle during the previous months. Each regiment held services: the Seventh Marines' service, "IN MEMORIAM," typified the honoring of the dead on 12 August 1951.

The memorial service dedication read, "For the men of

the Seventh Marines who gave their lives serving their country and all mankind in Korea during the period of 1 January 1951 to 1 August 1951."

The ceremonies began with "America The Beautiful"; both the regimental commander, Col. H. Nickerson, Jr. as well as Maj. Gen. G.C. Thomas, Commanding General, 1st Marine Division, offered remarks. Separate chaplains provided the invocation, memorial prayer and benediction. "My Country 'Tis Of Thee" preceded the benediction. In slow cadence, "Taps" followed and closed the memorial service.

Although we continued reserve—rest and relaxation—our thoughts focused on the future. Eventually, we must return to the line.

Our letters reflected this uncertainty. Mine of August 27, 1951, did.

> Just a few more days and I'll have a year in the Corps and 24 months to go. I'm anxious to see where I'll spend my 21st birthday. It's hard to say where it might be. Of course, the last was in boot-camp. We are still in reserve although we might move out at any time and on to any front.
>
> I hear our letters are going to be censored, now. I guess they don't want us to tell how fouled up this war really is. Now, I might not be able to write where I am and what I am doing. Incidentally, you won't hear about the Marine Corps, anymore. If the Army makes a drive or does something, the news will tell what division did it; but, if it's the Marine Corps, it will just say the Eighth Army advanced in such a sector. Apparently, we got so much publicity, the army couldn't stand it any longer.
>
> [As is the case in war, this was scuttlebutt, rumor.

Censorship did not happen. Marine Corps publicity continued.]

The weather here must be just about like what your having back home. It's real quiet, and the crickets are chirping. If it wasn't for the mountains, I might imagine I was home.

We've been on a week of maneuvers. It was pretty rough training. And, we go back again next week.

From the looks of the rotation, I won't be home before Christmas. [Rumor, again. I arrived home in March of 1952.]

We are on a stand-by and don't know when we'll go back to the lines. I hope it's a long time yet.

The reserve as well as the relaxation and letters were growing short.

September 8, 1951

Dear Folks,

We're still on stand-by and might move out any time, but we've still got it pretty good, here. Sometimes we have USO shows and Army shows. They stink. I think they ought to send more shows with big names like Betty Hutton, for example. At least, they should get somebody who can put on a stage show, instead of amateurs. [Obviously, in ten weeks, I had become a critic of stage shows.]

I heard some scuttlebutt today, that a major in battalion says the 5th draft will be out of here in December. At the rate of rotation, now, that looks like he will be right. That means January for me. [Wrong. March]

I also hear that the 5th Marines, which aren't

on line now, will stay on line; while the 7th Marines and the 1st Marines, along with the 3rd Brigade, which is forming in the states, will make a landing. Of course, that will take two or three months, and we will probably stay right here until we go back to train for the landing. But, it's all just rumor. [It certainly was. The 5th Marines were on line as were the 7th. No landing contemplated.]

That's about all there is here.

Love,

Burton

The last two letters prove the point that rumors continuously bombard the combat marine. Very few of them had any real substance. At times, however, rumors did fuel the spirit.

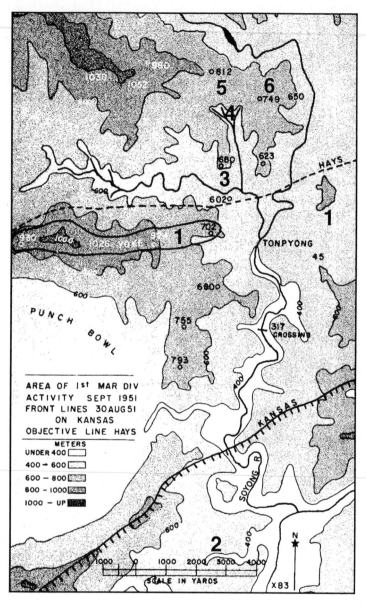

AREA OF 1st MAR DIV
ACTIVITY SEPT 1951
FRONT LINES 30 AUG 51
ON KANSAS
OBJECTIVE LINE HAYS

METERS
UNDER 400
400 → 600
600 – 800
800 – 1000
1000 – UP

PUNCH BOWL

TONPYONG

HAYS

317 CROSSING

KANSAS

SOYONG R.

N

SCALE IN YARDS
1000   0   1000   2000   3000   4000

X83

MAP 8

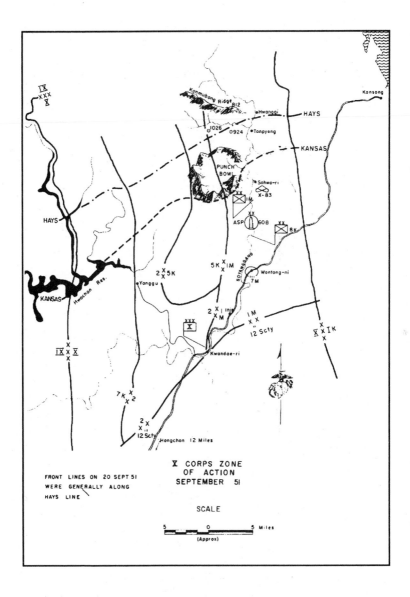

X CORPS ZONE
OF ACTION
SEPTEMBER 51

FRONT LINES ON 20 SEPT 51
WERE GENERALLY ALONG
HAYS LINE

SCALE

5 ___ 0 ___ 5 Miles
(Approx)

MAP 9

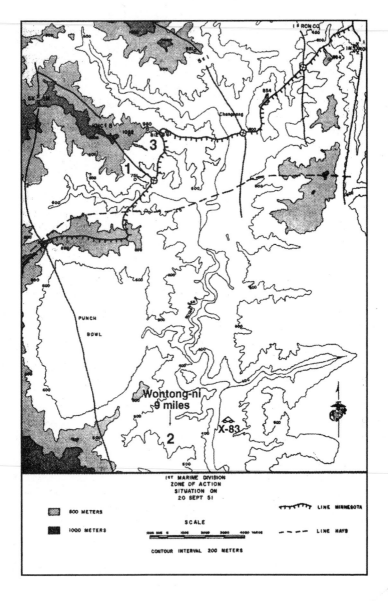

1ST MARINE DIVISION
ZONE OF ACTION
SITUATION ON
20 SEPT 51

☐ 800 METERS

■ 1000 METERS

SCALE

CONTOUR INTERVAL 200 METERS

LINE MINNESOTA

LINE HAYS

MAP 10

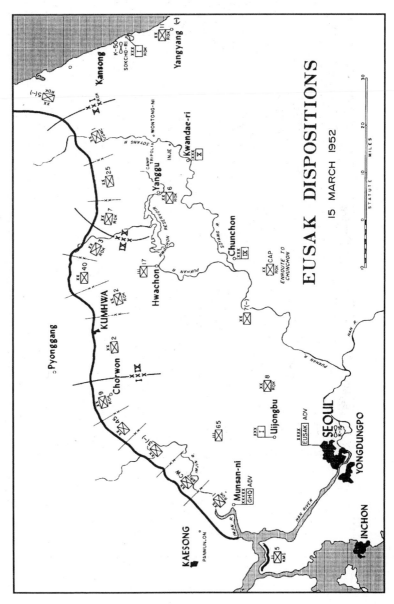

EUSAK DISPOSITIONS

15 MARCH 1952

STATUTE MILES

MAP 11

CHAPTER ELEVEN

HILL 749

"See, I got no yo-yo." These plaintive, nasal lyrics of a popular oriental love song, "China Night" floated into our minds through our western ears and found sanctuary. Whether our westernized version caused consternation among those who knew the language and the proper words, we did not know or care. To us, the singers' oriental twang sang of yo-yos not love, and we mimicked what we heard.

During the two months that the 1st Marines were in reserve from 6 July to 10 September, some of us began the return from the barbarity of war to normalcy and a more civilized way of life; others turned "gook" and sang "gook" songs. An observer might conclude that some of us were only absorbing more Korean culture.

My western ear heard a popular old Korean folk song, "Arirang," (substituting "Ah-de-dong.") phonetically:

"Ah-de-dong, Ah-de-dong, Ah-ra-re-Yo-oh-oh,

Ah-de-dong, Ko-ge-ro, No-mo-gan-da."

Similarly, using the Do-Re-Me scale, a somewhat passable tune can be rendered:

"Re-me-do, Fa-so-me, La-so-fa-me-re-me,

Re-me-do, Fa-me-re, Me-re-me-me"

Getting "gooky," we alternated these songs as we finished our training and prepared for the word we knew was coming.

As the time to go back to the line approached, our outward appearance of nonchalance concealed our apprehension. Our false bravado belied our fear as we awaited orders.

***

The 1st Marine Division came out of reserve and renewed the attack after the breakdown of the truce talks. The assault is described by *U.S. Operations in Korea,* Vol. IV:

> The new Marine zone of action, in the Punchbowl area, was as bleak and forbidding as any expanse of terrain in Korea. Dominating the Punchbowl from the north and blocking any movement out of it was YOKE Ridge, looking somewhat like an alligator on the map. Hill 930 represented the snout. Hill 1000 was the head, and the body extended eastward through Hills 1026 and 924.
>
> Two smaller hills, 702 and 602, spread off southeast and northeast respectively to the Soyang River and its unnamed tributary from the west. On either side of YOKE Ridge were numerous sharp and narrow ridges. Some of the hills were wooded with enough scrub pine to afford concealment for outposts and bunkers. Altogether, it was an area eminently suited to defense.
>
> The defenders were identified by Division G-2 as troops of the 6th Regiment, 2nd Division, II NKPA Corps. Apparently they did not lack supporting weapons, for 3/7 positions on Hill 680 were hit by an estimated 200 mortar and artillery rounds during daylight hours of the 30th.
>
> The 7th Marines and KMC Regiment, ordered to relieve U.S. and ROK Army units on the KANSAS

Line, started their march in a downpour on 27
August. The 5th Marines (less 1st Battalion) at Inje
had orders to follow the 7th up the narrow Soyang
valley.

The relief proceeded slowly. Two KMC battalions on the left of the 7th Marines took over the
zone formerly held by elements of the 2nd Infantry
Division and the 8th ROK Division. The cos-
mopolitan character of the Eighth Army was revealed
when 2/KMC relieved the French Battalion of the
2nd Infantry Division. Linguistic chaos was avert-
ed only by the best efforts of the exhausted inter-
preters.

A formidable hazard, land mines were a constant and
increasing menace to the assaulting troops—"friendly" mines
were encountered as well as enemy. Both sides had been busy
planting the mines during the summer months.

The two assault regiments, the 7th Marines and KMCs,
attacked the Corps Objective YOKE on the morning of the
30th. This was the ridgeline running from Hill 930 on the
west through Hills 1026 and 924 on the east. Objective 1, the
hill mass 1 1/2 miles northeast of Tonpyong, was occupied by
1/7. Objective 2, generally that part of YOKE Ridge east of
Hill 924, was seized by 3/7. The KMC was assigned
Objective 3, Hills 924 and 1026. By 3 September, these
objectives were taken. (See Nos. 1, Map 8)

Other Division missions on 31 August were:

a. 5th Marines- patrol along KANSAS Line; protect
defensive installations.

b. 1st Marines- remain in the rear in Hongchon area.

c. Division Recon Company- patrol Punchbowl and mop
up enemy.

d. Tank Battalion- remain ready to support assault regiments.

U.S. Marine Operations in Korea, Vol. IV indicates:

... At 1800 on 3 September, the 1st Marine Division was in full possession of the HAYS Line, dominating the entire northern rim of the Punchbowl....

On 4 September, with all objectives consolidated, 1st Marine Division units patrolled northward from defensive positions. Plans were being formed for the second phase of the Division attack—the advance to seize the next series of commanding ridgelines, 4,000 to 7,000 yards forward of the present MLR.

As evidence that the enemy had profited by the breathing spell during the Kaesong truce talks, it was estimated that NKPA artillery fire in the Punchbowl sector almost equalled the firepower provided by the organic Marine artillery and the guns of attached U.S. Army units. NKPA strength in mortars and machine guns also compared favorable with that of Marines.

***

Jim Swartzwelder (Forrest) remembers other events of this time as a member of "Fox" Company, 2/7.

> During the very first part of September, we [Fox] were up on top of this mountain. And we were catching quite a little bit of stuff [mortars and artillery] up on top of this hill. We had a young kid in our platoon from Oregon named Pete Mamerill, a Filipino kid. Pete and a new guy, a recent replacement, who had only been there for a couple of days along with a half dozen other guys were standing in this saddle of the ridgeline about 50 yards from my

foxhole. I guess from the other mountain across the valley, the gooks had been watching this. And when these guys clustered up in a bunch, the gooks shot an artillery round in and killed six of them including Pete Mamerill and the new guy.

I don't know, but it always seemed to me that the guy that was going to "get it" was the guy that had just gotten there and didn't have a whole lot of experience or the guy that was just getting ready to go home. I don't know why those times seemed to be the most particularly susceptible to getting killed, but they seemed to be.

Anyhow, I was in a foxhole with a kid nicknamed "Wags". I think he was from Indianapolis. And "Wags" had taken a machine pistol off of a gook officer the previous spring. But now things [obviously, the war and the possibility of becoming a casualty] were bothering him to quite an extent.

One afternoon he said to me, "When it gets dark tonight, I'm going to shoot myself."

I said, "Well, goddamnit, that seems kind of dumb to me."

"Nope," he says, "I'm going to shoot myself with that machine pistol that I have. Hey, it's an enemy weapon. I'll get out of here and I won't have to put up with this stuff, anymore."

I repeated, again, "Well, that seems kind of dumb."

He says, "Well, if I do, I'm going to holler at you and I want you to start shooting down the mountain like there's enemy down there."

So at around midnight, he awakened me and said, "I'm going to shoot myself."

I didn't want him to and said, "I wish you wouldn't. It's really dumb."

He says, "I'm going to."

So he wrapped a handkerchief around the barrel of this machine pistol, put the barrel in the palm of his hand and shot himself right through the center of his hand.

Well, I fired a couple of rounds down the mountain. And since everybody is antsy, pretty soon everybody thought that they saw things and a fire fight ensued. It certainly was one sided. After a minute or two, the firing stopped. Then I went to get the Corpsman. And he came down and gave "Wags' a shot of morphine.

On the next day, they took him down the mountain and that was the last I saw of him until I went home. I saw him again when I went down to Sokcho-Ri to come home on the USNS General Gordon with what was left of the sixth draft. "Wags" told me that he went down to the field hospital, where they took care of his hand. And it didn't hurt at all. The shot didn't break any bones, nothing serious. It healed and they sent him back to the regiment [7th Marine regimental Headquarters] as a clerk typist. While he was there, they received frequent mortar fire. He ended up with three more Purple Hearts!

***

Plans for the second phase assault, however, were delayed because of supply problems. Logistic shortages made it necessary to call a six-day halt and build up a reserve of artillery and mortar ammunition at the Ammunition Supply Depot (ASP) 60-B, which was about 7 miles behind the Marine artillery and 5 miles behind Airfield X-83 (VMO-6), but 48 miles from the supply point at Hongchon. (See Map 9) From this forward supply dump, trucks ferried ammunition and supplies up to battalions on line or as far forward as practicable.

U.S. Marine Operations in Korea, Vol. IV reveals these facts:

> Only human transport was available for supplying Marines on the firing line. X Corps started the month of September with 20,070 Korean Service Corps, the successor to CTC, and civilian contract laborers—the equivalent in numbers of a U.S. Army infantry division. Even so, 14 air drops were necessary during the month, only one of which went to a Marine unit. This took place on 1 September, when 20 Air Force cargo planes from Japan dropped ammunition and rations to the KMCs. A 90 percent recovery was reported.
>
> It generally took a full day in the 1st Marine Division zone during the first week of September for a cargodor [Korean civilian porter] to complete the trip from a battalion supply point to the front lines and return. This made it necessary to assign from 150 to 250 Korean laborers to each infantry battalion. And, as the Marines advanced farther into the rugged Korean highlands, the logistics problem increased.

During the six-day lull, enemy groups were spotted by air observation, moving southward into the Marine zone. In fact, Division G-2 had established through POW interrogation that the 2nd NKPA Division, II Corps had been relieved by the fresh 1st NKPA Division, III Corps. Patrols ran into brisk mortar fire when they approached too near enemy bunkers. And accurate 76-mm fire from well-hidden guns was received by the Marines throughout the lull.

Surprisingly, increased infiltration did occur. During the night of 4-5 September, the 5th Marines units on the KANSAS Line were assaulted, five miles to the rear of the 7th Marines deployed along the HAYS Line. Yet both the 7th Marines and Division Reconnaissance Company patrolled forward 2,000 yards the next day and encountered no enemy. (See Map 8)

New orders were issued on the morning of 9 September, which called for the 7th Marines to jump off at 0300 on the 11th and attack Objectives ABLE and BAKER, Hills 673 and 749, respectively, while maintaining contact with the 8th ROK on the right.

The 1st Marines were released from reserve near Hongchon and were to prepare to pass through the 7th Marines, after the 7th secured their objectives, and continue the attack to seize Objective CHARLIE, the ridgeline leading northwest from Hill 1052.

The 5th Marines were to leave one company on KANSAS Line while occupying positions along HAYS Line in rear of the 7th Marines. The KMC Regiment was to patrol on the Division left and exert pressure on enemy defenses south and southeast of Objective CHARLIE. The 11th Marines (artillery) were to move forward and support the 7th Marines (See No. 2, Map 8).

***

The "fog of war" conceals the battle—facts are elusive. Therefore, extensive quotes from the official Marine document, *U.S.Marine Operations in Korea,* Vol. IV, are contained in this chapter in order to compare discrepancies with facts.

The epic of the 7th Marines during 11-12 September is portrayed from the reference:

The area ahead of the 7th Marines was ideal for defense. From YOKE Ridge the assault troops had to descend into a narrow valley formed by a small tributary of the Soyang-gang, cross the stream, and climb Kanmubong Ridge on the other side. [See No. 3, Map 8 and Map 9] This formidable piece of terrain was dominated by three enemy positions, Hills 812, 980, and 1052. Thus the attack of the 7th Marines had as its primary purpose the securing of initial objectives on Kanmubong Ridge that would give access to the main NKPA defense line, some 4,000 yards north.

The 7th Marines was to seize the eastern tip (Objective ABLE) [See ridge to right of No. 3, Map 8, Hill 673, Objective ABLE, designated as Hill 623 on the map.] of this commanding terrain feature and "run the ridge" to hill 749, Objective BAKER [See No. 6, Map 8]. While Lieutenant Colonel Louis G. Griffin's 2/7 maintained its patrolling activities on the left, tied in with the KMCs. Lieutenant Colonel B. T. Kelly's 3/7 in the center and Lieutenant Colonel J. G. Kelly's 1/7 on the right were to attack.*

Again, from *U.S. Marine Operations in Korea,* Vol. IV:

As an intermediate regimental objective on the way to Kanmubong Ridge, the 680-meter hill

---

*During this operation, Nolen Sullivan of our bootcamp platoon I-65 was in "Able" Company, 1/7, but John Ontiveros had not yet returned to "Able" from the hospital; Phillip Meek was in "Easy" Company and Jim Swartzwelder (Forrest) was in "Fox" Company of 2/7.

directly north of B. T. Kelly's position on Hill
602 was assigned to his battalion. He ordered How
Company to move forward under cover of darkness
and be prepared to attack at dawn. Rain and poor vis-
ibility delayed the attempt until surprise was lost,
and after a fierce fire fight How Company was
stopped half-way up the southeast spur. [of Hill 680,
see No. 3, Map 8]

In order to relieve the pressure, the battalion
commander directed Item Company to attack on the
left up the southwest spur. [of Hill 680] This maneuver enabled How Company to inch forward under
heavy mortar and machine gun fire to a point with[in]
50 yards of the topographical crest. Item Company
became confused in the "fog of war" and finally
wound up on How's spur at 1245.

Twice the two companies made a combined
assault after artillery and mortar preparation and air
strikes with napalm, rocket, and strafing fire. Both
times the North Koreans swarmed out of their
bunkers to drive the Marines halfway back to the
original jump off line. It was anybody's fight when
the two battered companies dug in at dusk.

Across the valley to the east, J. G. Kelly's 1/7
had no better fortune in its attack on Hill 673. [to
right of No. 3, Map 8, Hill 623] Heavy enemy mortar and machine gun fire kept the assault troops
pinned down until they consolidated for the night.

With both attacking battalions in trouble, Colonel
Nickerson ordered 2/7 to advance up the narrow valley separating them. [Hill 680 and Hill 623 (673)
No. 4, Map 8] His plan called for the reserve battalion to move under cover of darkness around the

left flank of 1/7 and into a position behind the enemy before wheeling to the northeast to trap the North Koreans defending Hill 673.

The maneuver succeeded brilliantly. Griffin's troops were undetected as they filed northward during the night, making every effort to maintain silence. By daybreak on 12 September 2/7 had two platoons in position behind the enemy [on Hill 673] to lead the attack.

The assault exploded with complete surprise as 2/7 swept to the crest of Hill 673 against confused and ineffectual opposition. Griffin's battalion and 1/7 had the enemy between them, but the jaws of the trap could not close in time because of NKPA mine fields. Thus 1/7 continued to be held up on the forward approaches to Hill 673 by NKPA mortar and small-arms fire. Grenades were the most effective weapons as J.G. Kelly's men [1/7] slugged their way to the summit at 1415 while 2/7 was attacking Objective BAKER, Hill 749 [See No.6, Map 8]. [Jim Swartzwelder's (Forrest) story of this attack by 2/7 follows these references.]

On the other side of the valley, 3/7 had seized its initial objective.'[Hill 680] While How and Item Companies attacked up the southeast spur, where they had been stopped the day before, George Company launched a surprise assault up the southwest spur. This was the blow that broke the enemy's will to resist. George Company knocked out seven active enemy bunkers, one by one, thus taking the pressure off the troops on the other spur. At 1028 all three companies met on the summit.

The 2d Battalion, 7th Marines, radioed that

Objective BAKER had been secured at 1710 after a hard fight, but this report proved to be premature. Enough NKPA troops to give the Marines a good deal of trouble were still holding the wooded slopes of Hill 749, and it would take the attack of a fresh battalion to dislodge them. Along the ridgeline from Hill 673 to Hill 749, an undetermined number of enemy soldiers had been caught between 2/7 and 1/7, and events were to prove that they would resist as long as a man remained alive.

***

Nolen Sullivan of our bootcamp Platoon I-65 and member of "Able" Company, 1/7, remembers that, "My fireteam (only three of us left) took Hill 673 [Hill 623] from the left flank ridge. The rest of Company A got pinned down by incoming 76s and mortars." Nolen was wounded for the second time on 12 September.

As a member of "Fox" Company, 2/7, Jim Swartzwelder (Forrest) recalls the assault on Hill 749 [See No.6, Map 8]:

On September 12 or 13, I'm not sure of the date, we took off from the mountain and went down into the valley. [F/2/7 must have come off the ridgeline of Hill 673 (623) and headed toward Hill 749 on 12 September because 2/1 relieved them on the 13th.] Then we started up this draw heading up toward this higher mountain. [Hill 749]

At the time, I was squad leader. Right in front of me was one of the ammo carriers for the machinegun outfit, a guy named Jamie Marsh. They had told us to stay on the trail because each side was mined. So we were working our way up the trail, and as you go up, it's stop and go, stop and go, because it's so slow going up these steep trails.

Finally we stopped and Jamie turned around and sat down—right on top of a mine. It just blew him to pieces. It blew me off of the trail, down into a gully and a small stream, which ran down the draw. And it wounded me, also. Fortunately for me, certainly not Jamie, he took all the blast, which killed him. But enough blast and shrapnel escaped wounding me. Actually I think there were probably wounds from rocks as well as metal shrapnel. It tore me up but didn't really hurt me particularly.

About this time, the gooks started dropping in 121 mortars—I think that's what they were—just a smidgen larger than our 120's. The mortars dropped in the draw and wounded a couple more people.

Then down the draw came two guys carrying a stretcher. On the stretcher was a guy who had been shot through the leg.

He was exclaiming, "Oh Boy, a million dollar wound. I'm going home. Look, I'm shot in the leg."

About the time he finished this hoorah, the front guy carrying the stretcher stepped on a mine. It blew the stretcher bearers leg off and killed the guy with the million dollar wound.

It really got very hairy for awhile.

We made our way on up the mountain and ran into just lots of gook soldiers up on top. We had T.C. Smith who won a Silver Star up there. So did another guy named Schneider from Duluth, Minnesota. We had a lot of casualties. It was just quite an operation. [Hills 673 to 749.]

Of course, Jim received the Purple Heart.

***

In these hill battles all the 7th Marines exhibited that "valor was a common virtue." During the assault on Hill 680, the battered companies of 3/7 needed men like Second Lieutenant George Ramer of "Item" Company who led his men uphill through a wall of enemy fire that left most of them wounded. At the summit he organized a hasty defense with the few men he had left and faced an enemy counterattack. Unable to sustain the defense, he ordered his men off the hill, taking their dead and wounded. While individually providing covering fire to protect his men, he was killed by the enemy. LT Ramer was awarded the Medal of Honor, posthumously.

On Hill 673, a similar story unfolded. When 1/7 could make no progress, SGT Frederick W. Mausert III of "Baker" Company began his unquestioned heroism when he rescued two wounded men. Although hit in the head, he was able to retrieve the men and go on to lead a bayonet charge up the hill. He was knocked to the ground again when a bullet struck his helmet, but he recovered to knock out a bunkered machinegun. Alone he charged to the crest and destroyed other bunkers and machineguns before the enemy stopped his advance, mortally wounding him. SGT Mausert also was posthumously awarded the Medal of Honor.

***

As the 1st Marine Division renewed the attack in the Punchbowl area, close air support (CAS) became a mounting problem. The difficulty lay in the time-lag between the request for air support to the time planes arrived over target. Resulting in the heavy casualties of September, this lack of timely air support to the troops was singled out as the cause.

With the philosophy of interdictory air strikes first and close air support a far distant second, the U.S. Air Force which had operational control over the First Marine Aircraft Wing siphoned off the sorties as they saw fit.

The Fifth Air Force Commander, Major General Otto P. Weyland, maintained, "In a static situation close air support is an expensive substitute for artillery." This may sound enlightened, but the statement grossly lacks the intimate understanding of a ground commander.

Infantry commanders were aware that there was nothing static about the situation. Close air support was an inherent part of the Marine attack. Thus a better balance between interdiction air strikes and close ground support was absolutely necessary, because the lack of it cost men their lives.

Major General Gerald C. Thomas, Commanding General, First Marine Division, charged that as a consequence of this lack of CAS, many of the 1,621 casualties suffered by the Marines during September were due to inadequate close air support and that the division's tactical capabilities were strongly restricted.

Another problem for the division was logistics. One ridgeline after another had to be taken. The lines of supply grew longer and more treacherous. The Korean cargodors could not keep up with the consumption of the Marines. At least there were leveled dirt roads for trucks from Hongchon to ASP 60B, the forward supply dump (See Map 9). Ammunition and supplies could be trucked up from there to the 11th Marines near the KANSAS Line. But to haul supplies and ammo any further past the Punchbowl to the battalions and from the battalions to the men on line was mostly by cargodor. Obviously a remedy for this logistics problem was a necessity.

The answer had been coming since 1945, when the Corps began working on techniques and tactics in connection with the movement of assault troops by helicopters in amphibious operations. In fact, a Marine Helicopter Experimental Squadron 1 had been organized in 1947. Working with Sikorsky aircraft, Marines helped to design a helicopter which cruised at 60 knots loaded with six fully equipped combat Marines.

By September, Marine Transport Helicopter Squadron 161 was not only operational but also in Korea. By 13 September, 15 HRS-1 Sikorsky helicopters lifted a day's supplies to the 2nd Battalion, 1st Marines, who were relieving the 7th Marines. The choppers made history ferrying in 18,848 pounds of cargo and evacuating 74 casualties.*

***

September 10, 1951

Dear Folks,

We just got the word that we are moving out. [my italics] I don't know where but rumor says that we are going up around the Punchbowl. I guess we'll go up on trucks, tomorrow. This looks like it could be a big attack. And, I wonder where I'll be tomorrow on my 21st birthday. Just think, I have been in the Marine Corps over a year now. My last birthday was spent in Receiving Barracks of the Recruit Depot at San Diego. It's hard to say where I'll spend this one.

I spent most of yesterday, Sunday, with Ross. We took more pictures down at the river. The other

---

*This was designated Operation WINDMILL I, ferrying supplies in and lifting wounded out at the 2/1 CP. The first Marine assault by helicopter was Operation SUMMIT in which units of the Recon Company were transported to Hill 884 on 21 September. That was the first helicopter assault in history—a precursor of Viet Nam operations!

day, we were talking and I was telling Ross that of all
the old guys in our company who were left, only
two of us had not been wounded and didn't have a
Purple Heart. It's kind of funny, Ross has never
been wounded, either. He's one of only a few in
his company, too.

Well, I'm kind of glad that we're moving out.
This place was getting rather old.

Love,

Burton

***

The Operational Order on 9 September called for the
1st Marines to pass through the 7th Marines after the 7th
took its objectives and to continue the attack to seize
Objective CHARLIE, the ridgeline northwest from Hill 1052.
Events modified that objective to extricating 2/7 from a surrounding North Korean force.

Moreover, the date and time when the 1st Marines
relieved the 7th appears to be at odds depending on the
source. A few of these sources are compared in the following text: the official version, a military history and my recon-
struction.

U.S. Marine Operations in Korea, Vol. IV reports the
official version:

> The relief of the three battalions of the 7th
> Marines by their corresponding numbers of Colonel
> Thomas A. Wornham's 1st Marines took place dur-
> ing the night of 12-13 September. [The date is incor-
> rect.] By daybreak 3/1 and 1/1 had assumed respon-
> sibility for the zones [Hills 680 and 673] of 3/7 and
> 1/7, which were on their way to Division reserve at

Wontong-ni at the juncture of the Inje and Kansong roads. In the center, however, 2/1 could not complete the relief of 2/7. Not only was that battalion engaged most of the day with the enemy, but the units were separated—one company south of hill 749 being unable to join the other two companies on separate spurs northwest of that height. All three were under persistent NKPA mortar and 76mm fire.

The discrepancy, indicated above, should read, "...during the night of 11-12 September...." Being there on the night of my 21st birthday as a member of "Dog" Company, 2/1, I maintain this point.

The military history, *The Bloody Road to Panmunjom* by Edwin P. Hoyt describes the events more accurately:

On September 12 the 7th Marines were relieved in the line by the 1st Marines. By dawn [of the 12th] two battalions had changed over, and the 3rd and 1st battalions of the 7th marines [sic] were on their way to the reserve station at Wontong-ni. The 2nd Battalion of the 7th Marines, however, was stuck in the middle of North Korean positions, and one of its companies was separated from the other two. The 1st Marines [2/1] were to attack to get them out....

The following is my interpretation of the events surrounding the 1st Marines during 10-16 September 1951 in the battle for Hill 749 (See No. 6, Map 8):

Although Division orders had been prepared on 9 September returning the 1st Marines to the line, we members of "Dog" did not get the word until the morning of 10 September. Immediately, I wrote my parents that trucks

were going to take us "up around the Punchbowl...tomor-
row." The rest of the day rushed by with personal packing as
well as dismantling our bivouac of two months.

As is the custom of the Marine Corps, we were fed well
at the mess tent that evening—steaks, I believe. And the
next morning before jumping off in the attack, breakfast
included the traditional steak and eggs.

One does not forget the events of his 21st birthday. On
11 September, my birthday, we were loaded aboard trucks and
transported north to very near the Punchbowl, several thousand yards south of the ridgeline called Yoke. As precisely
as can be determined, the trucks took us via roads to an
assembly point just south of the 11th Marines (artillery).
The 11th was about two miles north of the Airfield X-83,
close to the KANSAS Line. (See No. 2, Map 8) Thus we
had traveled about 54 miles from our encampment near
Hongchon.

The 1st Marines ostensibly would relieve the 7th and
seize the ridgeline northwest of Hill 1052 (west of No. 5,
Map 8). Since it had required most of the day to load up and
to travel, in the late afternoon we disembarked from the
trucks behind the 11th Marine artillery, 155 howitzers, and our
2nd Battalion was reformed. Here we received orders to
move out into the attack. From research has come the apparent "line of battle." On the right, 1/1 would relieve 1/7 on
Hill 673 (623). In the center, 2/1 would attack up the valley
and extricate 2/7 around Hill 749. 3/1 would relieve 3/7 on
Hill 680 on the left.

We ate our "C" rations for the evening meal and around
1730 we began to move out north through the valley past
the 155 howitzers. We passed YOKE, the ridge running
perpendicularly west from the valley's west side. Several
thousand yards in back of YOKE rose a higher ridgeline,

also perpendicular to the valley, and our destination. (From No. 2 to No. 4, Map 8) Other higher ridgelines could be seen in the distance to the north.

Being September, days were growing shorter; the equinox was nearing. Perhaps an evening haze hung in the valley. Maybe the abrupt mountains to our immediate west, rising some 1000 feet above the valley floor brought shadow and dusk and darkness early that day. Or did the gooks have more pressing problems? The fact that we did not receive incoming fire while slowly moving up the Soyang valley that evening, indicates that we were extremely lucky as well as possibly benefiting from natural phenomenon.

It was dark, however, when we entered the valley between the two ridgelines of Hill 680 and Hill 673 (623). And we finally had made it to the bottom of the mountain on which were the 7th Marines. We were safe in that secluded pocket in the small valley, out of sight of the gooks. The 2/1 Command Post (CP) was established here (See No. 4, Map 8).

In this operation to relieve 2/7, "Dog" Company was the lead company for 2/1, with "Fox" Company next, then "Easy." Very slowly "Dog" started up the trail that led from the left fork of the small valley. No moonlight on this night. The only perception of silhouette or shadowy outline came from the night-glow perceived after the eyes become accustomed to the dark. The climb was managed in the blackness of that night. You could hardly see two guys in front of you.

The path led up a long gully and then onto a ridgeline heading north up toward Hill 1052. The trail eventually turned east along an intersecting east-west ridge which meandered across the mountain top to the battle for Hill 749 and the remnants of 2/7.

(See No. 5, Map 8)

At one point each man had to hand a trip wire to the

next man who had to then step over the wire, which was attached to a mine beside the trail. To be subject to the possible mistakes of others is nerve-wracking to say the least. Although only detectable in the dark from a few men away, the movement of stepping over the trip wire and then handing it to the next man can be a frightful experience. As one gets closer the fear mounts. "Will someone make a mistake and trigger the mine?" Fortunately, no one did.

About 2200 hours we made it to the east-west ridgeline, where we found some of the 7th Marines. Relieved, they happily moved out down the hill. "Dog" Company took over their foxholes for the night. Being in the Headquarters section of the company, I got to sack-in with four or five HQ guys—runners, radiomen, officers—in a large gook bunker. "Dog" Company had not encountered any appreciable opposition that night.

The ridgeline, facing north toward the gooks, that we set up on was intersected on the east by another north-south ridge which rose up to an even higher east-west ridge. That was the objective for the next morning. But for the rest of the night, our HQ group slept or took our turns at watch on the company radio.

The topography at the head of the valley between Hills 680 and 673 (623) where we started our climb was a drainage fan from which we took one of the creeks and gullies leading up to a ridgeline. From there its direction generally ran from southwest to northeast to Hill 749. Although zig-zagging from east to west then north to south, the ridge lay in a somewhat perpendicular line in relation to the tongues of land mass that jutted down from Hills 1052 and 812. (See No. 5, Map 8. Unfortunately this ridgeline is not shown on the map.)

On the morning of 12 September, "Dog" Company

advanced only up to the next ridge. We could not clear that upper ridgeline further to Hill 749 in order to get the 7th Marines out. Defending against the enemy hidden in the brush down the ridgeline or up on Hill 812 as well as those across the valley to the north, "Dog" Company stalled as we followed the meandering ridgeline trail leading east toward Hill 749 (See No. 6, Map 8).

The attempt lasted most of the day.

SGT George E. McGarity, a member of "Dog" Company and retired Detective Lieutenant with the Massachusetts State Police, also remembers that day:

> D/2/1 was ordered to attack the crest of Hill 749. [Actually, this was the ridgeline leading to Hill 749 as previously described.] LT Anthony, platoon leader of the 2nd platoon, was given the go-ahead. He ordered the 1st squad on the left and the 3rd squad on the right [each side of the ridgeline trail]. I can still hear LT Anthony's order to, "Fix Bayonets." My thought at the time was, "He's got to be kidding."
>
> The last time I had heard that was in Tent Camp 2 at Camp Pendleton while running through an obstacle course.
>
> The rest [of the day] is a blur of firing, smoke, explosions, screams, and for all too many, pain.
>
> The hill was secured and one half hearted attempt was made by the North Koreans to retake the position without success. At one point during our attack, I yelled to LT Anthony that we needed grenades badly, calling him, Lieutenant, in my excitement. Tony, as we referred to him, screamed back at me, "Don't call me, Lieutenant, damn it. Call me anything. Call me, Shithead." I guess we all know what we called

him after that!* Later that day, LT Anthony was
wounded and relieved, but returned several days
later. My first squad suffered one casualty, wounded.

LT Anthony's 2nd Platoon had secured a strip of
ridgeline that the company defended from our foxholes for the rest of the day on 12 September. We did
not reach 2/7 nor Hill 749.

From my bootcamp platoon, Steve Kerr from Texas and
my buddy, Ross were both members of "Item" Company, 3/1.
They came up the valley the evening of 11 September to
relieve 3/7 on the Hill 680 ridgeline.

Steve was fire team leader of the 2nd Platoon of "Item"
Company and led the company up the Soyang valley, where
they relieved 3/7 at dusk, beginning an assault under cover of
darkness.

He says at this point, Sergeant James Barney Southall told
him to lead his fireteam and the company in the attack against
bunkers on the hillside. Steve thought he had done enough
and he adamantly told Barney what he thought. With a few
choice words and phrases, Barney convinced Steve that he
had not yet done enough.

After this misunderstanding, Steve led the assault up the
hill and with grenades knocked out a bunker.

According to Steve Kerr, "The attack began at 1900 and
the crest of the hill, an altitude of 2000 feet, was our ultimate
goal. We encountered bitter resistance, involving heavy fire
and movement all the way up the hill. Midnight found the hill
secured, and in spite of the strong resistance, casualties were
not extremely heavy."

---

*Marine officers on line wore no insignia, whatsoever. Of course, they were
not saluted or addressed as officers. The gooks had an affinity for killing
them.

Then he added, "It was a miracle. The guys on that hill withstood ten Banzai attacks in the next three days." Steve was wounded on the third day.

He remembers that night and the next morning, vividly. Steve recalls that a new lieutenant took over command of the platoon while in reserve. He had been a marine during World War II and was not only Gung Ho but also "spit and polish." His seasoned troops figured him to be either a hero or a loud-mouthed coward. Unfortunately they did not find out. Steve says the officer was wounded during the morning in the assault and went to the rear. He did not last the first day.

This allowed Sergeant James Barney Southall to take command and lead the platoon, earning the Navy Cross. His story was presented in *Leatherneck* magazine in the September 1991 issue, "The Hill Battles." In error, they made him a member of the 7th Marines.

Steve Kerr relates that although he was a fireteam leader, he had picked up a BAR by this time for the added fire power. He was amazed that Barney charged the North Koreans, firing his carbine at anything that moved. The sergeant directed the troops over the hill in the morning and they set up machineguns and a defensive line where, as mentioned, they fought off ten attacks. during which Barney was wounded in the wrist.

Summing up the battle to this point: On the morning of 12 September, 3/7 had been relieved by 3/1 and 1/7 was in the process of being relieved by 1/1. LT Anthony and Sergeant McGarity of D/2/1 moved out toward Hill 749 to relieve 2/7.

Our 2nd Platoon's attempt lasted most of the day. The company had moved up along the north-south ridge onto the east-west ridge and were pinned down by mortars and artillery. I was the last in line, still on the steep north-south trail.

We had been strung out in bunkers along a lower east-west ridgeline during the night, but on the morning of the 12th, "Dog" Company moved up the next north-south ridge to another higher east-west ridge, populated by hordes of North Koreans. Progress was snail-like. For most of the morning, I remained in the bunker that I had slept in the night before. Finally, as other members of Company HQ were called forward, I found myself last in the single file line headed up the trail. Apprehensive, I found no marines crowded behind me. But we were surrounded on all sides by splinter cadres of gooks. With mortars and 76 artillery coming in, I ducked for cover, while keeping a watchful eye to the rear.

In the afternoon the Executive Officer, 2nd Lieutenant Stanley Olson, came back down the trail to my "last-in-line" position. He told me that we were in very bad shape. We had heavy casualties and the CO didn't know if we could hang on. He said that he had understood that "Fox" Company was to follow right behind us and tie in with us—to be our reserve if we got in trouble. We might need "Fox" to take over our positions before we were wiped out or overrun. He ended his observations with, "Go find Fox. They can't be far back there."

I dropped everything that wasn't essential. As I took off my pack, I thought I'm supposed to have an easy job. This is absolutely the scariest thing I've ever had to do. I now carried only my carbine and .45 pistol in a holster. Quickly I threw the carbine on my shoulder, turned and started down the steep trail thinking, "This is terrible. The gooks think that we are still down on that ridge below and are firing barrages of 76s onto it. As far as I can see there are no marines back there, anyplace." From where I was as the last man of "Dog," the trail ran well over a 1/2 mile to Battalion Headquarters, the CP, where "Fox" might be. And half of that could be ridgeline occupied by gooks attacking from the higher hills to the front or gooks infiltrating from the rear. The immediate problem were the 76s and mortars dropping dangerously close.

I slipped down the trail back to the bunker where I had been the night before. There was Santiago from my bootcamp platoon! He had been wounded in the butt. His company from the 7th Marines had pulled out the preceding night when we moved in. In the confusion of the night before, he was left alone in no mans land.

I threw his carbine sling over my shoulder next to my carbine, picked him up to a standing position by his belt and we moved forward. With his arm around my neck, we ran like mad across the ridgeline with 76s dropping on every side. One hit so close it knocked us to the ground but we finally made it to the relative safety of an out-cropping of rock. Poor Santiago was in pain, but I made him run as he had never run before. Then the trail, shielded by the rock, turned down toward Battalion HQ.

I knew he really was hurting from the run down the steep path, but I got him back to the battalion aid station where I left him. I searched for someone to tell of our need for rescue and finally was taken to the battalion executive officer. He said we would have to hang on, and that we wouldn't be relieved by "Fox" until the next day. In fact, "Fox" Company had never started up the hill. They remained there at Battalion HQ.

The Battalion Exec told me to get some hot chow and take the order back to my company. I was amazed. They had a camp stove set up at HQ. But, more than that, I had not thought about a return. This great job as runner had some drawbacks.

Just as scared as I had been at the start of this search for "Fox," I now began the run back up the trail. By this time I was tired and going up hill was much harder than coming down.

By the time that I made it back to the company it was getting dark. I found the Company Exec, LT Olson, and related the orders from Battalion. Thoroughly disgusted with Battalion's apparent lack of concern, he told me to find a hole for the night. And that I did. I found a deep one on the reverse slope down by our mortar squad.

Because of so many casualties, there were weapons of all sorts lying about. I picked up a BAR and an M1 rifle and pointed them to the rear as well as my carbine. My .45 was still holstered. We had had numerous attacks from infiltrators. The entire area in all directions hid numerous fragmented North Korean troops.

I slept deeply all night. Only once did I awake as there was a gook attack on the front slope, but as that subsided I groggily went back to sleep.

The next morning when I got out of my deep hole and mingled with the HQ group, our machinegun platoon leader, LT Brydon, asked me where I had been the night before because the HQ guys could not find me for my watch. I told him I had been right there within ten feet of him. We were all grouped fairly near each other.

From the crest of the ridgeline down the reverse slope, the other side of the slope facing the enemy, at the terminal end of the company was the Headquarters section. We were all in previously dug old gook holes. At least five deep holes had been previously occupied, surrounded by newly dug Marine holes. The company phone was nearest to the crestline. Officers (CO, Exec, machinegun platoon leader, rocket/mortar leader) and others (HQ personnel) fanned out and down the slope. Although only ten feet from the company phone, the hole I had found was off to the side and close to the mortar section which had set up further down the slope below HQ.

But missing phone watch seemed to be OK. Certainly, I had missed it, but my search for "Fox" the previous day may have excused me. Strangely, I was so close by the phone hole that apparently someone had not looked very intently to find me. At any rate, Brydon didn't chew me out and I wondered if one or more of the officers could not sleep and stayed on the phone through the night intentionally. These were precarious times.

I went back to my hole after talking to Brydon and settled in for some C-ration fruit for breakfast. Some time after 0800, the Doc, one of our corpsman, came over to brag about his son. He stood beside my hole, telling me about his new baby boy that he had never seen and reading from a recent letter from his wife. He was a very proud papa; he knelt down to show me pictures. Then he straightened up. Doc was above average height and I had to stretch my neck to look up at him. Sitting in my hole, I was able just to peer out with only my helmet above ground.

Since the hills were alive with gooks, it is not surprising that spotters, gook observers, were behind our positions. This would have to be an explanation for a salvo right on target, particularly on the reverse slope. And yet the gooks would zero in their own positions by mortars and artillery before a heavy attack. Of course, we were in holes the gooks had occupied the day before. In any case, without warning, a gook mortar barrage salvoed into our positions.

I heard the "swoosh" an instant before it hit and I fell to the bottom of the hole. But it wasn't fast enough. After the explosion, I felt stinging in my back. With one hand, I reached around and could feel pieces of metal. When I looked my hand was bloody.

Then I realized that the corpsman was lying there outside my hole, face down. The same mortar that landed beside my hole, landed at his feet. The front part of his body had been gutted; he was killed instantly. I looked down hill at the mortar section. Most of them had been blown out of their holes. The barrage was a direct hit. In an instant, most of the mortar section were killed or wounded.

I got up out of my hole and went up to Brydon's hole, near the crest. Another corpsman, new to the company, tended the wounded then put ponchos over Doc and the others. Later he came up to Brydon's hole and bandaged my back.

I did not go back to my hole. I stayed there with the new "Doc" and the lieutenant. Already, old Doc looked smaller in death than in life—as all newly dead look.* The new "Doc" spoke with tears of the old Doc's son and family. And his tears were catching.

Our Marine planes began rocketing the hill in front of us in close air support and I jumped every time a rocket hit. My lieutenant, Brydon, told me to go down the hill. I said I didn't want to. But I could not say why. Probably the reason centered in something emotionally deeper than words could convey.

With compassion, Brydon calmly, softly said, "If it makes you feel better, I order you off the hill." I said OK.

I don't remember much about coming off the hill. I do remember meeting "Fox" Company coming up the trail and waving a "Hi" to Bill McCartney, squad leader from our

---

*HM1 Billie Gene "Doc" Cooper from Council Bluffs, Iowa, was born on 1 October 1928. He died a few weeks before his 23rd birthday.

bootcamp platoon, moving through "Dog" at approximately 1100 hours. I remember getting back to Battalion HQ shortly after.

Of these facts, I am positive: we moved up to relieve 2/7 on the night of my 21st birthday and the next day, 12 September, I took Andrew Santiago of my bootcamp platoon back to Battalion Aid as I searched for "Fox" Company.

The next day I was wounded (13 September per DD 214). I remember late in the afternoon around 1600 getting aboard the first helicopter with four other wounded and looking out at two litters on the runners where badly wounded marines were strapped. (Operation WINDMILL I) I remember it was September 13, two days after my 21st birthday, and I finally knew the outcome of how I earned the Purple Heart.

My parents must have felt mixed emotions of deep concern as well as relief after receiving the following letter, written a week after the letter announcing our move back to the line.

September 18, 1951

Dear Folks,

I don't know if you received a telegram or not. Anyway I'm in a field hospital, but I'm OK. I just got several small pieces of shrapnel in my shoulder. But, they have been taken out, now. The holes are about as long as the length of your finger nail and not very deep. I've seen them in a mirror. They went in across my back rather than straight in.

There isn't much left of the 1st Marine Division. It's taken almost the whole division to take just a few ridges. My 2nd Battalion was company size the last I heard with 2/3rds casualties. There's hardly any 1st

Marines or 7th Marines left. And, now, the 5th are getting wiped out.

You remember the last battle that I wrote you about. Well, this was three times worse. We had more killed in 3 days than in the whole year. Every place we went, the gooks had mortars on us. One mortar hit right by my hole, and I got shrapnel in my shoulder.

Now, I'm about 20 miles back of the lines and I'm resting. I'll write you when I feel better.

Love,

Burton

Sergeant George McGarity, squad leader of LT Anthony's 2nd Platoon, "Dog" Company, remembers the 13th and 14th of September:

Another unit, I'm not sure which, moved through us the next day. [This was "Fox" Company relieving "Dog" on the 13th.] The following evening, the first squad was sent forward to reenforce their ["Fox's"] overrun positions. They had been badly mauled and were set up on a north-south position with no reverse slope. My information at the time was that all of the officers had been killed or wounded. I know when we arrived, an NCO told me where to place my men. The first squad spent the night expending as much of our ammunition as we could against the North Koreans attempting to take the position. At the same time, we had to listen to bugles, whistles and gooks telling us that, "Harry Truman eats shit!"

With the eventual coming of daylight, we were sent back to our own company. The memory of having to remove two dead ["Fox" Company]

Marines from the foxhole that PVT Valentine and I
took over that night remains with me to this day.
Again the first squad was fortunate, no casualties.
The NCO who positioned us on that night was one
squared away Marine, cool and competent.

Of the seven "Dog" Company officers, only two
remained after the battle—Machinegun Platoon Leader, LT
Brydon, as acting company commander, and 3rd Platoon
Leader, LT Gearhart.

From the following excerpts from *U.S. Marine
Operations in Korea*, Vol. IV., the official version continues:

> The attack of the 1st Marines, originally sched-
> uled for 0500 on 13 September, had been changed to
> 0900 by Division orders. [Nevertheless, "Fox" had
> moved the approximate 1/2 mile from 2d Battalion
> CP and through "Dog" at approximately 1100.] One
> reason for the postponement was the serious shortage
> of ammunition and other supplies after the urgent
> demands of the last two days. Another reason was
> the inability of VMO-6 helicopters, lifting two
> wounded men at most, to cope with mounting casu-
> alty lists. Enemy interdiction of roads added to the
> complications of a major logistical problem, partic-
> ularly in the zone of Lieutenant Colonel Franklin
> B. Nihart's 2d Battalion, 1st Marines.
>
> The hour had struck for HMR-161, and the
> world's first large-scale helicopter operation in a
> combat zone would soon be under way.
>
> Marine Transport Helicopter Squadron 161
> arrived in Korea on the last day of August, and by the
> 10th of September it had moved up to the front,

sharing Airfield X-83 with VMO-6. [See bottom right hand corner, Map 8 and south of Sohwa-ri, Map 9]

At 1600 on 13 September 1951—a date that would have historical significance—Operation WINDMILL I was set in motion.

Only two days had been available for training and rehearsals, but not a minute was wasted. All morning on the 13th the embarkation point section separated the supplies into balanced loads of about 800 pounds per helicopter. Loading commenced at 1520. Half an hour later, seven aircraft were ready to depart while four others went ahead to carry the landing point section to the previously reconnoitered site.

The route followed the valleys as much as possible, so that the helicopters were in defilade most of the way. Smoke was laid down by the 11th Marines for concealment.

The landing point section managed in 20 minutes to clear an area of 20 x 40 feet (later enlarged to 100 x 100 feet) and mark it with fluorescent panels. At 1610 the first HRS-1 hovered with cargo nets suspended from a hook released by manual control. A few minutes later it took off with five walking wounded and two litter cases. [See No. 4, Map 8]

[I was one of the five walking wounded inside that first helicopter.]

Each helicopter carried out as many casualties as possible, depending on the amount of gasoline in the fuel tanks. Only 30 minutes passed from the time one Marine was wounded and the time of his arrival at a hospital clearing station 17 miles behind the firing line.

Radio provided communications between helicopters in flight, HMR-161 headquarters, 2/1 CP, and the Shore Party team at the landing site.

Fifteen aircraft were employed for one hour, three for two hours, and one for two hours and 45 minutes—a total of 28 flights in over-all time of 2 1/2 hours. The helicopters landed at intervals of two minutes and took off as soon as the landing point section could put the casualties aboard. And though an altitude of 2,100 feet restricted loads, 18,848 pounds of cargo had been lifted into the area and 74 casualties evacuated when the last "chopper" returned to X-83 at 1840.

To even the most pessimistic observer Operation WINDMILL I was a complete success, so successful that a similar operation, WINDMILL II was conducted on the 19th. Two days later the first helicopter lift of combat troops was completed. A new era of military transport had dawned.

Although 2/1 alone had 240 Korean cargodors attached, the 7 1/2 tons of helicopter-borne supplies, largely ammunition, were vitally needed by the two assault battalions of the 1st Marines. After relieving Fox Company of 2/7 south of Hill 749 at 1100 on the 13th, Lieutenant Colonel Nihart's 2/1 jumped off to the attack an hour later. Stiff opposition was encountered from the beginning. The relief of the remaining two companies of 2/7 was complicated by the fact that they were some 400 yards from the position reported, on the reverse slope of Hill 749. Throughout the day these Marines were heavily engaged with the enemy.

On the left of 2/1, the 3d Battalion (Lieutenant Colonel Foster C. La Hue) could not make much progress toward its regimental objective, Hill 751, while the enemy was active on hill 749. A second attack of 2/1 at 1500 drove to the summit of that height after fierce fighting with small arms, automatic weapons, and hand grenades. There was still much fighting to be done before the entire objective would be secured since many enemy bunkers hidden among the trees remained to be neutralized. [See No. 6, Map 8]

At 1600 a gap of about 300 yards separated 2/1 from the two 2/7 companies. So fierce was enemy resistance in this area that it took until 2025 for Nihart's men to complete the relief after fighting for every foot of ground.

Air and artillery support had been excellent on the 13th despite the fact that neither could be called by 2/1 in some instances because of the danger of hitting elements of 2/7. Even so, 2/11 (Lieutenant Colonel Dale H. Heely) and other artillery units fired 2,133 rounds and Company C of the 1st Tank Battalion (Lieutenant Colonel Holly H. Evans) contributed 720 rounds of 90mm fire which knocked out six enemy bunkers. The 4.2" mortars had a busy day firing 261 HE and 28 WP rounds, and Company C of the 1st Engineering Battalion (Lieutenant Colonel John V. Kelsey) supported the attack by clearing mine fields.

An I-65 bootcamp platoon member, CPL Ross Norris was awarded the Purple Heart for wounds received on 13

September. His Silver Star Medal Citation reads:

> For conspicuous gallantry and intrepidity while serving as a Platoon Sergeant of Company C, First Engineering Battalion, First Marine Division (Reinforced), in action against enemy aggressor forces in Korea on 13 September 1951. Volunteering to lead a party of men in clearing a path through a mine field during an attempt to expedite the delivery of supplies for an infantry battalion, Corporal Norris bravely persevered with his task despite persistent enemy sniper and mortar fire covering the area of operation. Hearing a call for help from an area adjacent to the mine field, he immediately made his way to a position occupied by two seriously wounded men and, in the face of hostile fire, assisted in their evacuation before returning to his primary task. Although painfully wounded by a mine explosion while directing a group of native stretcher bearers in the removal of a deceased Marine, Corporal Norris calmly supervised the evacuation of another casualty and the body of his comrade before accepting aid himself. By his outstanding courage, marked fortitude and selfless efforts in behalf of others, Corporal Norris served to inspire all who observed him and contributed materially to the safety of many of his fellow Marines, thereby upholding the highest traditions of the United States Naval Service.

U.S. Marine Operations in Korea, Vol. IV continues with the official version:

> Mortar fire was received by the 1st Marines throughout the night, and 3/1 repulsed a series of

counterattacks by an estimated 300 enemy. Colonel
Wornham's regiment continued the attack at 0800 on
14 September.

Both the 2d and 3d Battalions inched their way
forward against a heavy volume of well-aimed enemy
mortar, artillery, and automatic weapons fire.

NKPA resistance persisted on the wooded northern slope of Hill 749, where hidden bunkers had to
be knocked out, one by one. It took constant slug-
ging for 2/1 to advance 300 meters before dusk,
enabling 3/1 to fight its way to the summit of Hill 751
[See No. 1, upper left, Map 10].

Again the flat trajectory fire of Company C tanks
had been helpful as 400 rounds were directed
again[st] NKPA bunkers, while the 11th Marines
fired 3,029 rounds.

The 15th was a relatively quiet day as compared
to the previous 48 hours. In preparation for an
expected passage of lines, the action took a slower
tempo as units consolidated positions. The principal
fight of the day was a continuation of the attack by
2/1 north of Hill 749. Although the battalion commander had arranged for a heavy artillery preparation,
the attack, which jumped off at 1710, was stopped at
1800 by a terrific pounding from NKPA mortars and
artillery coupled with crossfire of machine guns
from concealed bunkers. The assault troops withdrew under effective covering fire by the 11th
Marines to positions occupied the previous night.
Objective BAKER [Hill 749] yet remained to be
secured.

NKPA fields of fire were laid out for the utmost
effect. Marines with recent memories of college foot-

ball referred to the enemy's effective use of terrain as the "North Korean T Formation." On Hill 749, for example, the main ridgeline leading to the summit was crossed by another wooded ridgeline at right angles. Attackers fighting their way up the leg of the "T" came under deadly crossfire from the head of the imaginary letter—a transverse ridgeline bristling with mortars and machine guns positioned in bunkers.

In accordance with Division OpnO 25-51, the 5th Marines (Colonel Richard C. Weede) moved up to assembly areas on 15 September in preparation for passing through 3/1 on the 16th to continue the attack. The 3d Battalion, 1st Marines in turn would relieve 1/1 (Major Edgar F. Carney, Jr.), so that it could pass through 2/1 and carry on the assault to complete the securing of Hill 749.

The KMCs and Division Recon Company were to relieve the 5th Marines of responsibility for the HAYS Line, while the 7th Marines remained in reserve at Wontong-ni [See No. 2, Map 10 and Map 11].

The comparative quiet of the 15th was shattered a minute after midnight when the enemy launched a savage four-hour attack to drive 2/1 off Hill 749. The NKPA hurricane barrage that preceded the attempt, according to the Division report, "reached an intensity that was estimated to surpass that of any barrage yet encountered by the 1st Marine Division in Korea."

The thinned companies of 2/1 took a frightful pounding from 76mm, 105mm, and 122mm artillery supplemented by 82mm and 120mm mortars. Bugles and whistles were the signal for the onslaught. It was stopped by weary Marines who demonstrated at NKPA expense that they, too, could put up a resolute defensive fight.

Wave after wave of attackers dashed itself at the thinned Marine platoons, only to shatter against a resistance that could be bent but not broken. The fight was noteworthy for examples of individual valor. When one of the forward Marine platoons was compelled to give ground slowly, Corporal Joseph Vittori of Fox Company rushed through the withdrawing troops to lead a successful local counterattack. As the all-night fight continued, "he leaped from one foxhole to another, covering each foxhole in turn as casualties continued to mount, manning a machine gun when the gunner was struck down and making repeated trips through the heaviest shell fire to replenish ammunition."

Vittori was mortally wounded during the last few minutes of the fight, thus becoming the second Marine of 2/1 within a 48-hour period to win the Medal of Honor. His predecessor was Pfc. Edward Gomez of Easy Company. When an enemy grenade landed in the midst of his squad on 14 September, he "unhesitatingly chose to sacrifice himself and, diving into the ditch with the deadly missile, absorbed the shattering violence of the explosion in his own body."

In the battle for Hill 749, many members of bootcamp Platoon I-65 fought valiantly. In fact, one member exemplified the heroism of Medal of Honor machinegunners of Guadalcanal fame, John Basilone and Mitchell Paige. Although recommended for the Medal of Honor at the time, several years later, he received the Navy Cross. From the Office of The Secretary Of The Navy came the citation to this PFC who became an acting platoon sergeant:

The President of the United States takes pleasure in presenting the NAVY CROSS to

PRIVATE FIRST CLASS RICHARD N. BLASONGAME UNITED STATES MARINE CORPS RESERVE

for services set forth as the following

CITATION:

"For extraordinary heroism on the night of 15-16 September 1951 while serving with Weapons Company, Second Battalion, First Marines, First Marine Division (reinforced), in action against enemy aggressor forces in the Hwanggi area, East-Central Korea. Acting as platoon sergeant of the heavy machine-gun platoon, Private First Class Blasongame was put in direct command of the first section of heavy machine guns which were emplaced along a ridgeline on the point of the battalion perimeter, exposed to attack from three sides, and in close proximity to fortified enemy positions. With his gun section bearing the brunt of a series of determined attacks carried out by the enemy during the night, Private First Class Blasongame exhibited unusual courage, leadership, and initiative. Despite the fierceness and intensity of the enemy attacks, he maintained perfect fire control, manned a gun when one of the gunners was wounded, hurled grenades, rendered first aid, supervised the evacuation of the

wounded, and rallied his men to repulse each ensuing attack. When ammunition and grenades became
critically short, he left his foxhole and exposed himself to a hail of hostile fire to notify the company
commander of the situation and to supervise resupply. On one occasion, upon discovering that the
supporting troops on his flank positions had been
either killed or wounded, he refused to withdraw
his section and continued to hold the position, later
going to adjacent positions, bringing up reinforcements, and placing them in positions on his flanks.
When a grenade exploded under his last remaining
gun, inflicting wounds on his face and hands, and
jamming the traversing mechanism, Private First
Class Blasongame continued to fire by moving the
tripod from side to side. By the next morning, four
survivors remained out of his original sixteen-man
section, with three of the casualties having been
killed. Two hundred and eighty-seven enemy dead
were counted in front of the point position, representing only a small portion of the total casualties
inflicted during the night. Through his valiant and
inspiring actions in holding his position in the face of
an apparently hopeless situation, Private First Class
Blasongame upheld the highest traditions of the
United States Naval Service."

> For the President,
> /s/ W.B. Franke
> Secretary of the Navy

Probably exemplifying the courage as well as being representative of the 2nd Battalion, First Marines' battle for
Hill 749 is a story about "Fox" Company written for the

December 1951 issue of the "Pacific Stars & Stripes" by
CPL Murray Fromson. The date line is "WITH 1ST
MARINE DIV"(Pac, S&S):

Hill 749 is just another Korean ridge to Marine
replacements who have arrived here during the last
few weeks.

As you drive up the bumpy roads leading to the
frontline, the frozen snow capping 749 is deceiv-
ing. Its white, clean looking blanket has covered
pockmarks which tell the real story of what took
place only four short months ago.

It started on the evening of Sept. 15 and ended in
the early dawn of the 16th, but to members of F
Company, 1st Marine Regiment who have survived,
it seemed like a lifetime.

This is the story of one company of Marines
who fought off and annihilated an entire North
Korean regiment.

More, it is the story of the second platoon of F
which started out with a reinforced unit of 68 men.
When the battle finally ended all were either killed or
wounded in action.

Few of its surviving members are still in Korea
to retell the story of the heroic effort turned in by
these marines, who in the face of the most adverse
conditions imaginable, refused to yield ground and
withstood a fanatical banzai attack by the 91st
Regiment of the 45th North Korean Army.

Second Lt. Birney Adams, Tacoma, Wash., win-
ner of the Silver Star and three Purple Hearts for
his actions in this fight and the preceding day's
encounter, is one who lived to tell about it. And

although he was carried from the hill before the actual banzai started, he can unfold the story in its most minute detail.

Designated to replace the first platoon in the assault, Adams aided personally in coordinating the supporting weapons fire, artillery, mortars and air strike preparatory to the jumpoff.

The attack was delayed all afternoon of the 15th. But finally at 5:10 in the evening, the second platoon moved out. The objective, however, was changed at the last minute and the leathernecks had to advance without support. It was effected with the aid of one machinegun and an air strike which went after the original target.

The new objective was a knob, situated around a bend on the ridgeline spine which commanded the way to hill 812.

"We got to the bend without resistance," Adams said, "and when two of our men were shot all hell broke loose—and I mean all hell."

This was Adams' first opportunity to lead a platoon in the assault and he admitted later, "You're so damn scared you don't want to move, but you know the men are counting on you so you move."

The Reds had high ground, excellent cover and concealment, field of fire, fortified bunkers "at least six feet thick" and connecting trenches from the forward to reverse slope.

Two machineguns pinned down the platoon, in addition to a bevy of burp guns. Adams went after one himself (for which he received the Silver Star) and Pvt. Tom Ricardi, Brooklyn, got the other.

Ricardi, a young reservist, passed Adams on the

hill, threw him his carbine and said, "I'm goin' after the other gun." Armed with one grenade he crawled up the forward slope and lobbed the "pineapple" into the Communist position. But nothing happened. It was a dud.

With bullets whizzing overhead he rushed to the rear, grabbed a machinegun and set it up on open ground fronting the Red gun mount. A tremendous stream of fire followed to KO the Communists.

Adams describes Ricardi as, "the only man I ever saw who was unafraid at all times.' Originally attached to the first platoon, he volunteered to go along on the assault. Now in the States, Ricardi has been recommended for the Navy Cross.

A few minutes after knocking out the two Red machineguns, the Marines assaulted the hill. As the small force got to within 5 yards of the top, the Reds started rolling grenades down the slope. Within ten seconds more than 25 exploded in the midst of the assaulting element. Adams was hit in the left leg, but didn't realize the seriousness of his wounds until he tried to walk. His leg buckled from under him and he was carried from the scene.

Cpl. Bob Morgan (then a PFC), Oklahoma City, was appointed platoon leader as Adams left on a litter. Morgan and Cpl. Joe Vittori, Beverly, Mass., another volunteer, covered the withdrawal of the platoon which fell back to the point of its original jumpoff.

Morgan has been recommended for the Silver Star, while Vittori, an automatic rifleman later killed in the banzai attack, has been recommended for the Medal of Honor.*

When the withdrawal had been completed, Morgan, acting with all the cool efficiency of an experienced platoon leader, reorganized the men, aided in the evacuation of wounded and helped run up a supply of ammunition.

Shortly after midnight Morgan was relieved of his extra burden and Lt. Edward B. Boyd, Pierce, Nebr., stepped in.

It was comparatively quiet at midnight with only a few probing attacks breaking the still air.

Then at 1 a.m., they came.

The first wave of fanatical Reds, yelling, "Marines die, we die, all die!" hit the entire company line, with the second platoon bearing the frontal assault. Short on ammo—artillery and mortar fire from "Four Deuces" was called in and the enemy retired to his position. ["Four Deuces" referred to the large 4.2" mortars]

They came again about 2:30 and were repulsed only after almost all ammunition and grenades had been expended.

The final banzai hit F at 3:55, preceded by a heavy artillery barrage. The attack lasted one hour, but the Reds were whipped. As daylight broke on 749, 187 North Korean dead were counted in front of the company lines and an additional 400 to 500 were estimated killed.

---

*Vittori received the Medal of Honor, posthumously, which cited him for leading a counterattack, leaping from foxhole to foxhole covering casualties, manning a machinegun when the gunner was wounded and making repeated trips through heavy shell fire to replenish ammunition. This account doesn't mention this detail.

Only 11 marines were still in their holes when Company A marched through to secure Hill 812 ahead as well as 749—and they were all wounded. Those wounded could probably thank Navy Hospitalman Tony La Monica, Chicago, whose "selfless devotion to fellow men" gained him recommendation for the Navy Cross. La Monica himself was killed during the banzai.

The survivors have either been rotated or dispersed to other units, but it is doubtful that any will ever forget the nightmarish night on hill 749.

U.S. Marine Operations in Korea, Vol. IV officially continues the saga:

Not until 0400 on the 16th did the enemy waves of attack subside on Hill 749. NKPA strength was estimated at a regiment. A combined assault by an estimated 150 enemy on 3/1 positions to the west in the vicinity of Hill 751 was repulsed shortly after midnight, as were three lesser efforts during the early morning hours of the 16th.

When the 1st Battalion, 1st Marines moved out at 0830 to pass 2/1 and continue the fight, it was the first day of command for Lieutenant Colonel John E. Gorman. The passage of lines was slowed by enemy mortar fire, and NKPA resistance stiffened as 1/1 attacked along the ridgeline leading toward Hill 749. At 1800, after a hard day's fighting, Objective BAKER was occupied and defensive positions were organized for the night.'

Thus was the attack of the 1st Marines terminated. Around Hill 751, 3/1 remained in control. The regiment's other two battalions, 1/1 and 2/1, held a defensive line about 1,500 yards long on both sides of Hill 749.

Hill 749 had finally been secured. A number of mutually supporting hidden enemy bunkers had been knocked out in a ruthless battle of extermination, and veterans of the World War II Pacific conflict were reminded of occasions when Japanese resistance flared up in similar fashion after ground was thought to be secure.

From the information gathered about members of our 1950 bootcamp Platoon I-65, at least seven of the platoon were wounded during the fighting to take Hill 749:

	7th Marines	1st Marines	C Co. Eng.
12 Sept.	Nolen Sullivan		
	Andrew Santiago		
13 Sept.	Jim Swartzwelder	Burton Anderson	Ross Norris
	(Forrest)		
14 Sept.		Steve Kerr	
16 Sept.		Richard Blasongame	

With Hill 749 secured finally the 5th Marines came on line. Their mission was to pass through 3/1 in the vicinity of Hill 751 and attack to secure Objective DOG, a bare brown hill mass that loomed a 1,000 yards ahead. The last few hundred yards were certain to be rough ones, for the main east-west ridgeline leading to Hill 812 was crossed by a north-south ridgeline—the leg and head of another "T" formation. Just like Hill 749, a vicious crossfire awaited the 5th Marines. (See No. 3, Map 10)

Objective DOG was seized ahead of schedule by 2/5 and after two days of hard fighting, absorbing several enemy counterattacks, Hill 812 was tenaciously occupied. Next, Hills 980 and 1052 loomed ahead. For the 5th Marines the most unforgettable landmark, however, was known as "the Rock," a huge granite knob across the ridgeline approximately 700 yards west of hill 812. Rising only 12 feet high, "The Rock's" location made it visible from a great distance.

On 19 September, the 2nd Battalion (2/5) battled the enemy for the knob. The Marines held the top and eastern side, the North Koreans held the western side. At 0315 the following morning, the enemy tried to retake Hill 812. They pushed back "Easy" Company's left flank, but the company counterattacked and the 2nd Platoon of "Fox" struck the enemy flank decisively sending the enemy back to their side of "the Rock."

U.S. Marine Operations in Korea, Vol. IV. sums up this renewal of battle after the truce talks:

> This was the last action of a battle that had occupied all three Marine regiments from 11 to 20 September inclusively while the KMC Regiment patrolled aggressively on the Division left flank. Three of the four Division objectives had been secured after savage fights, but Objective CHARLIE (the ridgeline northwest of Hill 1052 in the KMC zone) had yet to be attacked when Division OpnO 26-51 put an abrupt stop to offensive movement.

> During these last days of summer (27 August-20 September), four valorous men of the 1st Marine Division were awarded the Medal of Honor, posthumously; 254 Marines were Killed In Action (KIA); and 1,688 Marines were Wounded In Action (WIA) with one missing (MIA). The enemy body count was 1,722 killed. Since the North Koreans diligently removed their dead, it has been estimated,

therefore, that twice that number were killed. Prisoners taken amounted to 256.

Finally, *U.S. Marine Operations in Korea,* Vol. IV closes this chapter of the 1st Marine Division on the East-Central front with the following:

> Not only was the fight west of Hill 812 the last action of the 1st Marine Division's nine-day battle; it was the last action of mobility for Marines in Korea. As time went on, it would become more and more apparent that 20 September 1951 dated a turning point in the Korean conflict. On that day the warfare of movement came to an end, and the warfare of position began.

With the end of the September battle, the Korean War came to a stalemate and the long war of the trenches began. The 1951 battles on the east-central front, however, were the bitterest and earned a Presidential Unit Citation for the First Marine Division, Reinforced, for halting the April Chinese Spring Offensive near the Hwachon Reservoir; for attacking northward in June, causing disastrous enemy losses around the 38th parallel; and, finally in September, for advancing the front against desperate enemy defenses in the "Punch Bowl" area.

On Hill 749, the 1st Marine Division maintained its renown.

The president of the United States takes pleasure in presenting the PRESIDENTIAL UNIT CITATION to the

FIRST MARINE DIVISION, REINFORCED

for service as set forth in the following

CITATION:

"For extraordinary heroism in action against enemy aggressor forces in Korea during the periods 21 to 26 April, 16 May to 30 June, and 11 to 25 September 1951. Spearheading the first counteroffensive in the spring of 1951, the FIRST Marine Division, Reinforce, engaged the enemy in the mountainous center of Korea in a brilliant series of actions unparalleled in the history of the Marine Corps, destroying and routing hostile forces with an unrelenting drive of seventy miles north from Wonju. During the period 21 to 26 April, the full force of the enemy counteroffensive was met by the Division, north of the Hwachon Reservoir. Although major units flanking the Marine Division were destroyed or driven back by the force of this attack, the Division held firm against the attackers, repelling the onslaught from three directions and preventing the encirclement of the key center of the lines. Following a rapid regrouping of friendly forces in close contact with the enemy, the FIRST Marine Division, Reinforced, was committed into the flanks of the massive enemy penetration and, from 16 May to 30 June, was locked in a violent and crucial battle which resulted in the enemy being driven back to the north with disastrous losses to his forces in the number of killed, wounded and captured. Carrying out a series of devastating assaults, the Division succeeded in reducing the enemy's main fortified complex dominating the 38th Parallel. In the final significant offensive of the action in Korea, from 11 to 25 September 1951, the FIRST Marine Division, Reinforced, completed the destruction of the enemy forces in Eastern Korea by advancing the front against a final desperate enemy defense in the 'Punch Bowl' area in heavy action which completed the liberation of South Korea in this locality. With the enemy's major defenses reduced, his forces on the central front decimated, and the advantage of terrain and the tactical initiative passing to friendly forces, he never again recovered sufficiently to resume the offensive in Korea. The outstanding courage, resourcefulness and aggressive fighting spirit of the officers and men of the FIRST Marine Division, Reinforced, reflect the highest credit upon themselves and the United States Naval Service."

For the President,

Charles S. Thomas

Secretary of the Navy

Figure 11 PLATOON I–65, FIRST REUNION
Back Row Burt Anderson, Jim (Swartzy) Forrest, S/SGT Barragan, Henry "Ham" Hamilton, Dick Blasongame
Middle Row Weldon Rosser, Loren Dickerson, Don Skains, Bill Oxford
Front Row Gene Burnett, John Camacho, Al Weideman, Bill Diffee, Otis Goldsmith
9/3/92

CHAPTER TWELVE

REUNION

Most of us who had begun our enlistment in the Corps as members of bootcamp Platoon I-65 received our discharge from the Marine Corps on September 4, 1953, at San Diego. Some few were discharged at their duty stations, and still others remained in the Corps. The majority, however, were "civilian" Marines—those who came for the fight and then went home. We were not the Thomas Jefferson "sunshine patriots;" we had stronger convictions. But a career in the military was just not the path taken by most of us.

Moreover, some of us were promised many incentives to "ship over"—to re-enlist. My decision was an intense one: to ship over and spend my life in the Corps or take a discharge and continue my education. To make the matter more difficult, a review board had chosen me from a selection of ten staff NCO's (Staff, Technical and Master Sergeants) to be commissioned within the organization, then immediately embark to Platoon Leaders School at Quantico, VA. This was not Officers Candidate School. I was to be commissioned before entering school. In fact, I was not scheduled for commission and school until October. Consequently I must "ship-over" before my discharge date in September. As an incentive, however, I would receive a re-enlistment bonus.

Call it Kismet or perhaps situations overcome by events. Nevertheless, before the time to reenlist approached, I met a girl on the beach in Oceanside, CA and that made all the difference. A difference, obviously, which resulted in not choosing the Corps as my career, but in choosing a wife, education, children and a lifetime career in aerospace.

In one way or another all the old members of Platoon I-65 must have faced the future in similar ways.

Although in the intervening years, I moved to California and he remained in Oklahoma, Ross continued to be my closest buddy. For more than 40 years, through good times and not so good times, we always kept in contact. Fortunately, he never lost his chuckle and good humor.

Of course, on occasion Ross and I wondered and laughed about our old buddies. We pondered at length, "What could have happened to so-and-so?" "Where have they all gone?" We had lost track of them all. But our lives continued. We made plans for tomorrow and did not attempt to look back to search for yesterday.

Alone, I wondered about "Harby" Harbison and "Little Jake" as well as others from "Dog" Company, whose names began to fade. I wondered what ever happened to all the old members of Platoon I-65.

Vaguely as in a barely remembered dream, fragmented scenes from Marine Corps days of girls, cars and trips to Gene Burnett's home floated through the fog of things past, but I pulled the curtain and turned to face new scenes of the future. Reality and the pressure of "now" took charge.

Not so with Gene Burnett. He had a quest and pursued it.

In April 1990, Gene's "traveling salesman" selling days came to an end when his doctor placed him on disability for a variety of medical problems. This gave him an opportunity to search out his long lost bootcamp buddies and he could not think of a better place to start than Oklahoma to search for Anderson, Rosser, Yellowhead and Meek. He felt his first target would be me.

During one of his "traveling salesman" trips to Oklahoma, he had found Bailey. Now, off he headed for Enid to find me.

Obviously, I no longer lived there and had not since 1957. In his search, however, he found my mother's house—but she was in a convalescent home. Fortunately a neighbor offered to help and he left his business card to send to me in California.

Not at all sure what Gene's motives might be, the neighbor called me and gave me his address and phone number. After 40 years, we spent about an hour on the telephone, rehashing old times. Then, we made arrangements to meet.

Before we hung up, I asked, "You know, I've thought about having a Bootcamp reunion. What do you think?"

Gene was unsure,"I wouldn't even know where to begin, Burt. It's been 40 years. Where do we start?"

"I have no idea, Gene, but I'm game if you are!"

So now the big search began for 65 other bootcamp buddies. The reward for a diligent search would be a successful reunion!

***

Reunions are fun. To renew old acquaintances from a past replete with stressful times and trauma in far away places, to renew the camaraderie of an era long past, to renew our esprit d'corps—all marvelous endeavors—meld in this nostalgic togetherness.

"Do you remember when...?" "Do you know what ever happened to...?" "Well, what have you been doing for the last 40 years?" The search commenced, the reunion was set, and old bootcamp buddies finally assembled eager to ask these questions.

My wife and I arrived in San Diego early to meet a mid-afternoon plane from Tulsa via Dallas. Ross was aboard. Maurine, unfortunately, was not well enough to attend. We checked in at the hotel and rushed off to the airport with plenty of time. But, of course, the plane was a little late.

At the arrival gate, we jostled with the expectant greeters as the passengers filed through our midst. No Rosser. In fact, the file had dwindled to a precious few, when we observed an old cowboy jauntily striding up the ramp boasting boots, jeans and Stetson. My wife, Joanne, called out, "Ross."

He did not seem to hear as he flashed past, making a spectacle, repeatedly yelling down the corridor for all to hear, "Anderson! Anderson! Where are you!"

Exiting travelers, startled, jumped out of the crazy man's way.

I felt a compelling desire to be someplace else. Ross had done it again.

He was exhibiting the same theatrics he had displayed when deplaning in San Francisco just a few years before. Unknown to his wife, he had secreted a tam and purse in a plastic bag which he carried aboard the plane. Upon arrival, he assumed the personna of San Francisco's Castro district, a tam on his head, a purse in his limp-wristed hand and a swing to his hips.

Stifling the urge to run the other way, my wife and I ran up and grabbed him on each side to quiet a Ross who had "run amuck." To our surprise, he began to laugh so hard it brought tears to his eyes. Ross was still hilarious as always.

Preparation was the key for this reunion in San Diego, where we became Marines. The head and stomach kind. And the first requirement that most of us quite unintentionally accomplished was to eat an adequate lunch. In fact, during the next few days, it was necessary to eat both breakfast and lunch. The second was to bring plenty of Maalox and aspirin. These would hold us in good stead for three days of indulgence.

Of the 30 members of Platoon I-65 who had been found at that time, 13 participated in the reunion. Ten brought their wives. Weldon Rosser was the only bootcamp squad leader to attend. Our DI, McFarland, could not attend. Right Guide Harold Heidt and squad leader William McCartney had not been found; squad leaders Richard Paddock and Johnny Pitts were deceased.

Jim (Swartzwelder) Forrest had been farsighted in choosing the Embassy Suites for our gathering because each evening from 5:30 to 7:00 was the complimentary cocktail hour as well as the free breakfast buffet each morning.

On our initial reunion afternoon, we gathered in the spacious, open 12-story central atrium for drinks and personal updates until the bar closed. Then we adjourned to Jim Forrest's hospitality suite where we ordered up pizza. Jim supplied more "adult beverages" as well as videos of his recent visit to Korea. Ross stuck a rendering of his Korean War Memorial to a mirrored wall for our admiration, and Dick Blasongame displayed his Korean War pictures. For my contribution, I called our DI, Ernest McFarland. Twelve of us talked to him.

Interestingly not only Jim Forrest had returned to Korea but also John Camacho and Bill Diffee. In fact, John and Bill were on the same Korean excursion when they suddenly recognized each other after a separation of 40 years.

Because the Marine Corps doesn't train on weekends, our reunion was scheduled on Wednesday, Thursday, and Friday. We would leave San Diego for home on Saturday.

On Thursday morning, however, we recuperated from the night before, prepared ourselves for the day, ate breakfast, and finally assembled in the hotel lobby. On this day, we journeyed to Camp Pendleton, up the California coast some 35 miles, for the days festivities. The 23 of us traveled in five or six vehicles.

Meeting at the Main Side Officer's Club, we stood for a group picture, then entered our reserved dining room for a sandwich lunch.

When finished, a Marine Corps bus and CPL Nazworth, our guide from Public Affairs, awaited us to continue our tour. Basilone Road, the Ranch House complex of the base commanding general, and the 31 Area, which was a "tent camp" in our time, brought back waves of old memories.

The loudest argument on the bus pitted those on one side or the other who adamantly knew which area was "Tent Camp 1 or 2 or 3."

Indeed, Weapons and Field Training Battalion (MCRD) Edson Range is located at one of the old Tent Camp sites. The bickering, however, revolved around which one. Of course, our contacts and guides were too young to know. Therefore, nothing was resolved and no one changed his mind.

Despite this quibbling, we arrived at the rifle range and were ushered into a simulation area to fire M16 simulators, which even produced a "kick' when fired. After the admonition of the DI to "Hold your breath!" I shot bull's-eyes.

Later we bused to the obstacle course with our host, S/SGT Barragan, to watch "boots" learn the fundamentals of surviving on the battlefield along with a brief lecture by a major with a "bird" colonel looking on. We witnessed hand grenade training while protected in a bunker, then, highly impressed with the difference in training between now and 40 years ago, we were taken to the Edson Range front gate for pictures. (See Figure 11)

Here we found a message. Featured at the entrance of the camp was a large informational signboard proclaiming: "WELCOME ABOARD PLATOON I-65 SEPTEMBER 1950"

By special request from Ross, we toured the Del Mar Boat Basin because in the early 1950's, he had been the sergeant-in-charge of the Special Services boat pool, which provided a lunch, tackle, bait, and fishing boat for the pleasure of off-duty Marines. Imagine going to work each morning and checking out the latest fishing reports. Can anyone conceive of having a softer job in the Corps?

After returning to San Diego that evening, groups of us went to dinner.

Friday morning required an early departure to the Marine Corps Recruit Depot. Our arrival time there was scheduled for 9:00 a.m. Piling into the cars and van, we left the hotel shortly after 8:30 a.m.

Strikingly, the barracks, stucco with red-tiled roofs, and the grinder appeared the same after 40 years. Although the barracks sported a fresh coat of beige paint—the 1950's barracks wore camouflage paint of two or three colors—the arched walkways adjoining the grinder behind which the barracks stood brought back images of ancient times.

Directed to parking on the grinder, we met our special guide and host, SGT Moss, who led us to view the rapelling tower, confidence course and obstacle courses, all designed as rigorous training to develop recruits into Marines.

Probably the most impressive of these physical conditioning and confidence building areas was the boxing matches, which pitted one platoon against another. The Marine Corps has taken a chapter from the maturation of inner city youth by incorporating the fundamentals of street fighting into the training. In a small padded area two recruits, provided with head protection and boxing gloves, box. With the fundamentals previously taught, the participants attack their opponent and protect themselves. A referee manages the proceedings. The DI's of each urge them on from outside the enclosure. Trailing back behind each DI is the rest of his platoon awaiting their battle. Those who have competed are allowed to assemble in a designated area to await completion of the competition.

How strange but exciting to us was this new regimen. At this place of so much activity across the grinder from the barracks, we had marched on our knees in the sand 40 years before. At that time no building obstructed the view of the fledgling airport of San Diego. There was nothing but sand between the grinder and the airport fence. Unbelievably, the training had changed and improved here on this once barren sand.

Before the graduation ceremony we visited the Command Museum with its plethora of dioramas depicting the history of the Corps.

Near 10:30, SGT Moss led us to the bleachers adjoining the grinder where we, members of Platoon I-65, were to be honored along with retired Women Marines of World War II as VIPs on this recruit graduation day. Somewhat surprised, we entered these VIP bleachers and acknowledged our welcoming sign.

The festivities lasted about an hour and started around 11:00 with a serenade from the band as we observed the recruit platoons in "Dress Blues," assembled across the grinder. As the ceremony began we were honored in the opening remarks. Then began the presentation of Colors, pass in review, graduates front and center, recognition of high shooters, most physically fit and honormen, and at last, dismissal and graduation for the new Marines.

Although the pomp and pageantry of the ceremony was very emotional, probably the most touching incident occurred during the Battalion Commander's welcome to the honored guests. A grandmother, a World War II Woman Marine, came forward from the VIP stands to greet her graduating grandson. A dry eye was hard to find.

The event over, SGT Moss herded us aboard a bus that took us to a luncheon buffet at the Officers Club; later we enjoyed a bus tour of MCRD.

Before leaving the base, I encountered a young, new Marine with his parents. His "Dress Blues" looked comfortable on this warm day. This made me curious. So I stopped and asked if I could feel the material of his tunic. Apparently, the fabric was a cool synthetic blend not the warm wool of yesteryear. I mentioned the difference to him and thanked him for stopping.

He said, "No problem, Sir."

With much more meaning than just a passing phrase, I replied, "Thanks again. I know you will do just fine."

That sentiment, affirming that these new Marines would do just fine, seemed to permeate our group. The training and making of boys into Marines was the subject for the rest of our stay.

After the banquet at the hotel that evening, John Camacho offered a prayer and a moment of silence for our deceased comrades. Gene Burnett told the story of how he found me. I, in turn, revealed the problems we overcame in bringing the group together for a reunion. Then, Gene became the Master-of-Ceremony and directed the presentation as each of us told the best and the worst of our bootcamp experience.

The ladies, however, had the best and last review of our

reunion. One wife, Joyce Dickerson, summed it up:

> I do appreciate the Marine Corps more. He's
> [Loren Dickerson] never told me much about his
> experiences of bootcamp or during the war—nothing
> like that. He's always kept it to himself. So now, I
> really appreciate having gone to the bases and seen
> the training that these recruits go through.
>
> I really appreciate what all of you men have
> proven during your bootcamp time; and, during the
> time, you defended your country. I think this is great
> training for young men. You can really see the pride.
> I mean I appreciate these soft little kids going in
> there and coming out men and Marines. You can
> really see that this training does a lot for them; and,
> I think that training and self discipline follows
> throughout life.

***

A manifest pride is what we Korean War Marines felt after our reunion almost a half century following our enlistment. A great feeling of elation and joy overcame us as we acknowledged the Corps' new warriors, and the expert training that honed them into Marines. Like us they will honor the motto, "Once a Marine, always a Marine!"

Indeed, we found the words to describe our gusto from those of Lieutenant General Lewis B. "Chesty" Puller, the Marines' marine, who observed, bluntly, "Old breed? New breed? There's not a damn bit of difference so long as it's THE MARINE BREED." For, "WE ARE PROUD TO CLAIM THE TITLE OF UNITED STATES MARINE."

SEMPER FI

THE END

A BAND OF BROTHERS

For many years after the war, I had toyed with this thought: at the instant I believed that I had been killed by mortar fire, my concern was not that I might die but that my death might bring sorrow to those who loved me. I felt no sorrow for me and my death; I felt great relief. Ultimately I would have no more worry. I was deeply concerned, however, with the ache I would cause in the hearts of loved ones.

Obviously, I did not die and that inner feeling of having found a hidden truth—human beings worry; spirit beings do not—seemed to open a philosophical door for me. Bluntly stated, my epiphany was that death is a change in being, not to be feared.

A British pilot and author, Richard Hillary, who survived being shot-down in the North Sea during World War II, wrote, "A man who has been rejected by death is easily tempted to take up the pen." A succinct summation of my thoughts.

My bootcamp Platoon I-65 was the perfect inspiration. For the most part, the members of the platoon were young men who experienced war and then came home to lead successful business and personal lives. I believe this was true because of the paramount importance of family values, ethics and morals in their life-styles. From their collective memories came much of the information incorporated here.

These are the "few good men"—Marines:

Floyd (Gene) (Smiley) Burnett is retired and lives in southern California with his wife, Betty. From his stories, two things are obvious: he has an amazing memory and he drove a DUKW, amphibian truck, for the 1st Amphibious Truck Company in Korea. His life career was in sales, primarily industrial equipment. Gene both encouraged me and contributed to this narrative.

James (Jim) Forrest (Swartzwelder) is retired and lives in central California with his wife, Virginia. In Korea, he was a BARman, scout, fire team leader, and Squad leader as a member of Fox Company, 7th Marines. He was awarded the Purple Heart medal for wounds. Dr. Jim's field is education. He is a retired district superintendent of schools. His stories have added another dimension.

John Camacho lives in northern California with his wife, Arleen. He was a machinegun squad ammo carrier and then radioman for Charlie Company, 1st Marines. His career path follows civil engineering. John not only supplied stories but also maps. He voices some compelling thoughts on war:

> I never have liked to describe the picture of war as I experienced it—the total absolute picture of death. It has no meaning to me. Korea was a chapter in my life that I have stored away because no one will ever understand nor will I try to explain it....
>
> Memory of it is like dropping a plate on the floor. Some broken pieces are big enough to see and others are so small you never see them again. Memories are like that, just bits and pieces....

Weldon (Ross) Rosser is retired and, with his wife

Maurine, divides his time between Mazatlan, Mexico and Tulsa, Oklahoma. Ross was a machinegunner with Item Company, 1st Marines. In civilian life he owned bars in Oklahoma City for 20 years, then switched to the heating and air conditioning business. Ross was a necessary part of my story. Of course, he has been for 50 years.

Phillip Meek has retired twice, once from the Marine Corps and again as County Deputy Treasurer and Tax Collector in central California, where he lives. Although he was a BARman and rifleman in Easy Company, 7th Marines in Korea, he became an officer and served in Vietnam. He retired as a Marine captain. Phil supplied ancient stories of liberty in Japan as well as details of the boot-camp rifle range.

John Ontiveros lives in southern Texas with wife, Mary. In Korea, he joined Able Company, 7th Marines. He was awarded the Bronze Star and Purple Heart. His stories about the actions which won the Bronze Star were fascinating. Several years later, John was discharged from the Marine Corps with a war related physical disability. More recently, he has retired from the U.S. Postal Service.

Richard (Dick) Blasongame is semi-retired and lives with his wife, Opal, in southern California. In Korea he rose to Platoon Sergeant of Heavy Machineguns, Weapons Company, 2nd Battalion, 1st Marines. He was awarded the Navy Cross and Purple Heart with Gold Star for a second wound. Dick is still somewhat involved in his plumbing contractor business. His several contributions to this volume are appreciated.

William (Gene) Burleson is a building contractor/land developer, living with his wife, Lois, in the Seattle area. He was in the 1st Medical Battalion in Korea. His stories about bootcamp, however, were priceless and I recorded his memories on tape during a visit to the northwest.

Steve Kerr is a Presbyterian minister in western Texas, where he lives with his wife, Bobbie. In Korea, he was a fire team leader in Item Company, 1st Marines and was awarded the Purple Heart. Steve provided much needed help with recounting the experiences of Hill 749.

Ross Norris lives in southern Texas with wife, Felicia. He was in Charley Company, 1st Engineers and was awarded the Silver Star and Purple Heart. His career involves oil field supply. He tells the following tragic story:

> On the morning of October 30, 1951, we were engaged in an operation called "Suicide Charlie," an endeavor involving all Charlie Company people: infantry, artillery, mortars, rockets, etc. My job as demolition man was clearing mines in the road and planting mines at strategic points. By the road where we were to jump off was a bunker from which peered the smiling face of Raymond Turner, whom I had not seen since our arrival in Korea. We had a long visit and, when the operation began, he would be a part of the overhead covering fire.
>
> The operation called for the hill to be taken, then we were to mine the area and withdraw, giving it back to the enemy—which is just what happened.
>
> It was late when we came back through the lines that night. But it also fell my duty to go back the next day and help get a couple of tanks that were left out in "no man's land." I was in a good mood thinking of another possible visit with Raymond, but was told that he was helping the people in the next bunker which had to be repaired when they caught a direct hit from mortar fire, killing all in the

bunker.

Raymond Turner was the only member of Bootcamp Platoon I-65 to be killed in Korea.

Nolen Sullivan, deceased in August 1993, lived in Louisiana with wife, Marilyn. In Korea, he was in Able Company, 7th Marines and was awarded the Purple Heart with Gold Star for second wound. He provided a story.

William (Bill) Oxford lives in southern Texas with wife, Ruth. In Korea he was with VMR-152, 1st Marine Air Wing. Bill is an independent consulting geologist, currently in environmental geology.

Henry (Ham) Hamilton is retired from the Marine Corps and lives in Alabama. He was not only in Korea, where he received the Purple Heart, but also in Vietnam. Ham has provided many stories for this narrative, and often was the subject of others.

William (Bill) Diffee lives in central California with his wife, Wanda. In Korea, he was assistant gunner, 4.2 Mortars, 5th Marines. Bill is with the U. S. Postal Service. Special gratitude is acknowledged for his research of old bootcamp files for names.

Two others provided special information:

Bob Johnson lives in central California with wife, Gerry. He was a "Sea-going" Marine aboard the USS Bon Homme Richard, CV/CVA 31. Bob retired from the dairy industry of the central California valley. And he just might be the poor boot who suffered the physical assault when we entered bootcamp. Something similar happened to him. We cannot determine, however, if we actually experienced our initial DI encounter together.

George Field is retired from AT&T after 36 years and lives in central Texas with wife, Iris. He was assigned to an

artillery forward observer team with 2nd Marine Division
scheduled for Germany in early 1950s. After all these years
we recently found that our families, Andersons and Fields,
were friends in the same little Texas town, Sutherland Springs,
during the first half of this century.

Special thanks go to the following bootcamp buddies:

Donald Skains and wife, Sallie, live in central Texas,
where he is an electrical contractor. In Korea he was in the
1st Shore Party Battalion.

Loren Dickerson and wife, Joyce, live in central
California. He is retired from Pacific Gas & Electric Co.
In Korea, he was in the 7th Marines Motor Transport.

Henry (Al) Weideman and wife, Patricia, live in southern California, where he is a retired high school teacher. He
became Sergeant of the Guard, 12th Naval District Brig, San
Francisco.

Otis Goldsmith is a retired teacher, also. He and wife,
June, live in southern California. Otis was a member of the
Marine Corps Eastern Division, Rifle and Pistol Team, even-
tually being selected to the All-Marine Corps Rifle and Pistol
Team.

Also, contributions are acknowledged from:

Cecil Gardiner and wife, Darleen, live in northern
California. He has retired after 30 years at Lawrence
Livermore National Laboratory, University of California.
In Korea, he was assigned to the 7th Marines Motor
Transport.

Charles Irwin and wife, Anna Lee, live in southern
Texas, where he has retired as an electrical engineer. He
was in 3rd Battalion, 6th Marines, 2nd Marine Division with
the U.S. Sixth Fleet.

Frank Leon and wife, Pat, live in Minnesota, where he
is semi-retired. He was awarded the Purple Heart for severe

wounds received only four months after we arrived. (June 1951) After a year of recovery, he was medically discharged in May 1952.

Milo Yellowhead and wife, Ollie, live in New Mexico, where he retired as a foreman for a uranium mining company. In Korea, he was in How Company, 1st Marines and was awarded the Bronze Star with V.

William (Bill) Hogue lives in southern California, where he was a machinist for 35 years but is now disabled due to a spinal injection for a milogram which paralyzed his left side. In Korea he was in 81-mm mortars, 3rd Battalion, 1st Marines. In bootcamp, he was our highest scorer at the rifle range.

Jim Heidt, our Platoon I-65 Right Guide and wife Jeannine live in southern California. Almost retired, he was a policeman, private investigator and since 1973 a manufacturer's representative and construction consultant. In Korea, Jim was a BARman in the Reconnaissance Company, Headquarters Battalion, 1stMarDiv.

Joseph Tim and his wife Gloria Lee live in the San Francisco Bay Area, where his career involves glass manufacturing. Awarded the Purple Heart, Joe was a radio/telephone/lineman for the Headquarters and Service Company, 7th Marines in Korea.

And thus are honored these significant veterans who have helped with the reunion of U.S.Marine Corps Bootcamp Platoon I-65, September 1950, as well as those who have aided with the preservation of our thoughts and feelings for posterity.

As always, SEMPER FI

COMMAND AND STAFF LIST DECEMBER 1950-MARCH 1952 1ST MARINE DIVISION

Commanding General

Asst. Division Commander

Chief of Staff

G-1 Administration

G-2 Intelligence

G-3 Training

G-4 Logistics

Special Staff

Adjutant

Air Officer

Amphibian Tractor Officer

Anti-Tank Officer

Armored Amphibian Officer

Artillery Officer

Chaplain

Chemical Warfare/Radiological Defense Officer

Dental Officer

Embarkation Officer

Engineer Officer

Exchange Officer

Food Director

Historical Officer

Inspector
Legal Officer
Motor Transport Officer
Naval Gunfire Officer
Ordnance Officer
Postal Officer
Provost Marshall
Public Information Officer
Shore Party Officer
Signal officer
Special Services Officer
Supply Officer
Surgeon
Tank Officer
Commanding Officer, Division Rear Echelon Headquarters

Headquarters Battalion

Headquarters Company
Military Police Company
Reconnaissance Company

1st Marines (Regiment)

Commanding Officer
Executive Officer
S-1 Administrative
S-2 Intelligence
S-3 Training
S-4 Logistics

Headquarters and Service Company
Anti-Tank Company
4.2 Inch Mortar Company

1st Battalion, 1st Marines (1/1)

Headquarters and Service Company

Company A (Able or A/1/1)

(All companies consisted of 3 rifle platoons, a
light machinegun platoon and a 60 mm mortar section)

Company B (Baker or B/1/1)

Company C (Charlie or C/1/1)

Weapons Company (Wpns/1/1)

(Heavy machineguns, 81 mm mortars, flamethrowers,
anti-tank rocket launchers)

2nd Battalion, 1st Marines (2/1)

Headquarters and Service Company

Company D (Dog or D/2/1)

(All companies consisted of 3 rifle platoons, a
light machinegun platoon and a 60 mm mortar section)

Company E (Easy or E/2/1)

Company F (Fox or F/2/1)

Weapons Company (Wpns/2/1)

(Heavy machineguns, 81 mm mortars, flamethrowers,
anti-tank
rocket launchers)

3rd Battalion, 1st Marines (3/1)

Headquarters and Service Company

Company G (George or G/3/1)

(All companies consisted of 3 rifle platoons, a
light machinegun platoon and a 60 mm mortar section)

Company H (How or H/3/1)

Company I (Item or I/3/1)

Weapons Company (Wpns/3/1)

(Heavy machineguns, 81 mm mortars, flamethrowers,
anti-tank rocket launchers)

5th Marines (Regiment)

Commanding Officer
Executive Officer
S-1 Administrative
S-2 Intelligence
S-3 Training
S-4 Logistics

Headquarters and Service Company
Anti-Tank Company
4.2 Inch Mortar Company

1st Battalion, 5th Marines (1/5)

Headquarters and Service Company
Company A (Able or A/1/5)
(All companies consisted of 3 rifle platoons, a
light machinegun platoon and a 60 mm mortar section)
Company B (Baker or B/1/5)
Company C (Charlie or C/1/5)
Weapons Company (Wpns/1/5)
(Heavy machineguns, 81 mm mortars, flamethrowers,
anti-tank rocket launchers)

2nd Battalion, 5th Marines (2/5)

Headquarters and Service Company
Company D (Dog or D/2/5)
(All companies consisted of 3 rifle platoons, a
light machinegun platoon and a 60 mm mortar section)
Company E (Easy or E/2/5)
Company F (Fox or F/2/5)
Weapons Company (Wpns/2/5)
(Heavy machineguns, 81 mm mortars, flamethrowers,

anti-tank rocket launchers)

3rd Battalion, 5th Marines (3/5)

Headquarters and Service Company
Company G (George or G/3/5)
(All companies consisted of 3 rifle platoons, a
light machinegun platoon and a 60 mm mortar section)
Company H (How or H/3/5)
Company I (Item or I/3/5)
Weapons Company (Wpns/3/5)
(Heavy machineguns, 81 mm mortars, flamethrowers,
anti-tank rocket launchers)

7th Marines (Regiment)

Commanding Officer
Executive Officer
S-1 Administrative
S-2 Intelligence
S-3 Training
S-4 Logistics

Headquarters and Service Company
Anti-Tank Company
4.2 Inch Mortar Company

1st Battalion, 7th Marines (1/7)

Headquarters and Service Company
Company A (Able or A/1/7
(All companies consisted of 3 rifle platoons, a
light machinegun platoon and a 60 mm mortar section)
Company B (Baker or B/1/7)
Company C (Charlie or C/1/7)
Weapons Company (Wpns/1/7)

(Heavy machineguns, 81 mm mortars, flamethrowers, anti-tank rocket launchers)

2nd Battalion, 7th Marines (2/7)

Headquarters and Service Company
Company D (Dog or D/2/7)
(All companies consisted of 3 rifle platoons, a light machinegun platoon and a 60 mm mortar section)
Company E (Easy or E/2/7)
Company F (Fox or F/2/7)
Weapons Company (Wpns/2/7)
(Heavy machineguns, 81 mm mortars, flamethrowers, anti-tank rocket launchers)

3rd Battalion, 7th Marines (3/7)

Headquarters and Service Company
Company G (George or G/3/7)
(All companies consisted of 3 rifle platoons, a light machinegun platoon and a 60 mm mortar section)
Company H (How or H/3/7)
Company I (Item or I/3/7)
Weapons Company (Wpns/3/7)
(Heavy machineguns, 81 mm mortars, flamethrowers, anti-tank rocket launchers)

11th Marines (Artillery)(4.5 Rockets, 105 and 155 howitzers)

Commanding Officer
Executive Officer
S-1 Administrative
S-2 Intelligence
S-3 Training
S-4 Logistics

Headquarters Battery
Service Battery
Battery C, 1st 4.5 Inch Rocket Battalion

1st Battalion, 11th Marines (1/11)
Headquarters Battery
Service Battery
Battery A (A/1/11)
Battery B (B/1/11)
Battery C (C/1/11)

2nd Battalion, 11th Marines (2/11)
Headquarters Battery
Service Battery
Battery D (D/2/11)
Battery E (E/2/11)
Battery F (F/2/11)

3rd Battalion, 11th Marines (3/11)
Headquarters Battery
Service Battery
Battery G (G/3/11)
Battery H (H/3/11)
Battery I (I/3/11)

4th Battalion, 11th Marines (4/11)
Headquarters Battery
Service Battery
Battery K (K/4/11)
Battery L (L/4/11)
Battery M (M/4/11)

1st Amphibian Tractor Battalion

Headquarters Company
Company A
Company B
Company C

1st Armored Amphibian Battalion

Headquarters Company
Company A
Company B
Service Company

1st Combat Service Group

Headquarters Company
Maintenance Company
Supply Company
Support Company
Truck Company
1st Fumigation and Bath Platoon
1st Air Delivery Platoon

1st Engineer Battalion

Headquarters Company
Service Company
Company A
Company B
Company C
Company D

1st Medical Battalion (USN Personnel)

Headquarters and Service Company
Company A

Company B
Company C
Company D
Company E

1st Motor Transport Battalion
Headquarters and Service Company
Company A
Company B
Company C
Company D
Automotive Support Company
Automotive Maintenance Company

7th Motor Transport Battalion
(The 1st Amphibian Truck Co., DUKWs,
subsequently assigned here.)
Headquarters and Service Company
Company A
Company B
Company C
Company D

1st Ordnance Battalion
Headquarters Company
Ordnance Supply Company
Ammunition Company
Ordnance Maintenance Company
1st Service Battalion
Headquarters Company
Supply Company

Support Company

1st Shore Party Battalion
Headquarters and Service Company
Company A
Company B
Company C

1st Signal Battalion
Headquarters Company
Signal Company
ANGLICO

1st Tank Battalion (M-26, Pershing and bulldozer-fitted Shermans)
Headquarters Company
Service Company
Company A
Company B
Company C
Company D

Marine Observation Squadron 6

Marine Helicopter Transport Squadron 161

FIRST MARINE AIRCRAFT WING (1ST MAW)
Commanding General
Asst. Commanding General

Chief of Staff
Asst. Chief of Staff, G-1 Administrative
Asst. Chief of Staff, G-2 Intelligence
Asst. Chief of Staff, G-3 Training
Asst. Chief of Staff, G-4 Logistics

Marine Aircraft Group 33 (MAG-33)

Marine Air Base Squadron 33 (MABS-33)

Marine Aircraft Maintenance Squadron 33 (MAMS-33)

Headquarters Squadron 33 (HQSQ, MAG-33)

Marine Service Squadron 33 (SMS-33)

Marine Aircraft Group 12 (MAG-12)

Headquarters Squadron 12 (HQSQ, MAG-12)

Marine Service Squadron 12 (SMS-12)

Marine Air Base Squadron 12 (MABS-12)
(Commissioned 1 Dec 1951)

Marine Aircraft Maintenance Squadron 12 (MAMS-12)
(Commissioned 1 Dec 1951)

Marine Wing Service Squadron 1
(MWSS-1)
Marine Ground Control Intercept Squadron 1
(MGCIS-1)

Marine Transport Squadron 152
(VMR-152)

Marine Fighter Squadron 212 (VMF-212)

1st 90 mm AAA Gun Battalion
(Arrived 29 Aug 1951)

Marine Fighter Squadron 311 (VMF-311)

Marine Night-Fighter Squadron 513
(VMF(N)-513)

Marine Night-Fighter Squadron 542
(VMF(N)-542)

Marine Fighter Squadron 323 (VMF-323)

Marine Air Control Group 2 (MACG-2)
(Arrived 11 Apr 1951)

Marine Tactical Air Control Squadron 2
(MTACS-2)

Marine Ground Control Intercept   Squadron 3
(MGCIS-3)

Marine Attack Squadron 121 (VMA-121)
(CO arrived Pohang, K-3, 22 Oct 1951)

Marine Fighter Squadron 214 (VMF-214)

Marine Fighter Squadron 115 (VMF-115)
(Arrived Pohang, K-3, 25 Feb 1952)

Marine Fighter Squadron 312 (VMF-312)
redesignated on 1 Mar 1952
Marine Attack Squadron 312 (VMA-312)

Marine Photographic Squadron 1
(VMJ-1)
(Commissioned 25 Feb 1952)

Headquarters Squadron-HQSQ, 1st MAW

EFFECTIVE STRENGTH OF THE
1ST MARINE DIVISION

Listed below are selected dates and figures which represent the effective strength of the 1st Marine Division throughout the period 1951-1952.

DATE	ORGANIC USMC and USN	ATTACHED U.S. Army	ATTACHED KMC	TOTAL
30 Mar 51	25,831	236	3,128	29,195
30 May 51	25,820	302	3,266	29,388
30 Sep 51	24,160	54	3,035	27,249
30 Mar 52	26,140	59	4,378	30,577

All foregoing organizational and effective strength data from—
U.S. Marine Operations in Korea, 1950-1953, Vol. IV,
The East-Central Front, Headquarters, U.S. Marine Corps,
1962

THE KOREAN WAR
CHRONOLOGY OF EVENTS

1945   Japanese defeated in World War II
       Above 38th Parallel-Japanese occupation troops sur-
       render to Soviet troops
       Below 38th Parallel-Japanese occupation troops sur-
       render to American troops

1948   Above 38th Parallel-Soviets proclaim the
       "Democratic People's Republic of Korea" ruled by
       puppet Premier Kim Il-sung
       Below 38th Parallel-under UN patronage, Syngman
       Rhee is inaugurated as president

1949   The Communist regime of Mao Zedong dominates
       mainland China after defeating the Nationalists led by
       Chiang Kai-shek, whose forces retreat to Taiwan

1950   June 25   North Korean invaders cross the 38th
                 Parallel at nine points, attacking numerous
                 South Korean (ROK) positions; UN
                 Security Council demands withdrawal

       June 27   President Truman announces US air and
                 naval assistance; UN Security Council calls
                 for UN members to provide aid

June 29   Seoul, the South Korean capital, falls to the
          North Koreans; Great Britain orders Far
          Eastern Fleet to aid ROK

June 30   US ground troops committed by Truman

July 5   First contact by US ground troops with North
          Koreans at Osan, south of Seoul

July 7   General Douglas MacArthur named comman-
          der of all UN forces

Aug 1-   Pusan Perimeter, a desperate UN stand against
Sept 16   surrounding North Korean forces, established;
          General WaltonWalker orders "Stand or die."

Sept 4-   Most members of US Marine Corps Training
Sept 8   Platoon I-65 enlist and are sent to the Marine
          Corps Recruit Depot, San Diego

Sept 15   1st Marine Division makes successful amphibi-
          ous assault on Inchon; attacks toward Seoul;
          UN forces break out of Pusan perimeter, head
          north

Sept 26   Seoul falls to Marines (X Corps)

Oct 9   UN forces cross 38th Parallel

Oct 14   First contingent of "Chinese Peoples'
          Volunteers" cross the Yalu River into North
          Korea

Oct 19   Pyongyang, North Korea, falls to advancing
          Eighth Army in west

Oct 26   In east, Marines land at Wonsan; move to Hungnam and advance to the Chosin Reservoir; ROK troops reach Yalu River at Chosan; X Corps advances up east coast

Oct 27-   First Chinese offensive halts UN advance;
Oct 31   ROK 6th Division decimated

Nov 17   Honor Platoon I-65 graduates from Marine Corps Recruit Depot, San Diego

Nov 24   MacArthur launches final offensive toward Yalu River

Nov 25   Second Chinese offensive launched

Nov 26   Chinese attack Eighth Army in west; general UN withdrawal follows

Nov 28-   In east, Marines and 7th Division break
Dec 11   out of Chinese encirclement at Chosin Reservoir; fight back to Hungnam; Navy evacuates all X Corps troops
             Majority of graduates from Training Platoon I-65 ordered to Camp Pendleton for Advanced Infantry Training

Dec 23   General Walker, Eighth Army commander, killed in accident

Dec 25   General Matthew Ridgway appointed UN ground forces commander; General Van Fleet appointed Eighth Army commander; Chinese cross 38th Parallel

Jan 1   Third Chinese offensive launched

Jan 4   UN forces evacuate Seoul; Communists cap-
             ture capital for second time

Jan 8-   US 2nd Division halts Chinese offensive
Jan 15   at Wonju

Jan-   Recent bootcamp graduates of Platoon I-65
Feb   continue Advanced Infantry Training at
             Camp Pendleton

Feb 14   Navy Transport General G.M. Randall
             embarks for Korea with the marines from
             Camp Pendleton's Advanced Infantry
             Training

Mar 1   The Randall makes port at Kobe, Japan;
             shore liberty is granted

Mar 5   The Randall docks at Pusan, Korea

Mar 7   Operation Ripper begins; the author enters
             combat

Mar 15   UN forces retake Seoul

April 10   Truman sacks MacArthur; appoints Ridgway
             to succeed him as UN commander

April 22-   Chinese Spring Offensive neutralized by
April 25   Marines

June- July	Chinese and North Koreans neutralized at Iron Triangle, Bloody Ridge, Heartbreak Ridge in central Korea; Marines battle for the Punchbowl in the eastern sector
July 10- Aug 2	Cease-fire conferences at Kaesong
July 15	1st Marine Division relieved; move into X Corps reserve
Aug 27	1st Marine Division returns to action; attack past the Punchbowl to Hills 749, 812 and the "Rock"
Sept 20	Warfare of movement ended; warfare of position began
Sept 21	Operation Summit is, historically, the first Marine helicopter assault, precursor of Vietnam tactics
Oct 25	Cease-fire conferences resume at Panmunjom

1952

mid-Mar	Survivors of 6th Replacement Draft depart Korea via east coast village, Sokcho-ri
Mar 17	1st Marine Division shifts from eastern Korea to the extreme western side
Mar 30	Remnants of 6th Draft arrive San Francisco aboard USNS W. H. Gordon

Spring	Large scale rioting at UN Prisoner of War camp on Koje Island
May 12	General Mark Clark relieves General Ridgway
July 4	Largest aerial victory - 13 MIG 15s shot down, one probable, seven damaged
Aug 29	Biggest air strike of war - 1,193 sorties

1952-1953

	War of Outposts, Patrols and Bunkers
Feb	General Maxwell D. Taylor assumes command of Eighth Army
July 27	Armistice agreement signed at Panmunjom

***

The Korean War lasted three years, one month, and two days. The Marines lost 4,262 killed in battle and 20,038 wounded. The Medal of Honor was awarded to 42 Marines—26, posthumously.

INDEX

BIBLIOGRAPHY

BOOKS

Guidebook for Marines, Leatherneck Association, 1950

Hoyt, Edwin P., The Bloody Road to Panmunjom, Stein
    and Day, 1985

Moskin, J. Robert, The U.S. Marine Corps Story, 3rd Ed.,
    Little, Brown, 1992

Ridgeway, Matthew B., The Korean War, Doubleday,
    1967

Spurr, Russell, Enter The Dragon: China's undeclared war
    against the U. S. in Korea, 1950-1951,
    Newmarket Press, 1988

U.S. Marine Operations in Korea, 1950-1953, Vol. IV,
    The East-Central Front, Headquarters, U.S.
    Marine Corps, 1962

MAGAZINES

Keene, R. R. "Operation Ripper," Leatherneck, April
    1991

Keene, R. R., "Marine Pilots Get into the Fight,
    <u>Leatherneck,</u> May 1991

Keene, R. R., "Fix Bayonets: On to the Punchbowl,"
    <u>Leatherneck,</u> June 1991

Keene, R. R., "Truce Talks, The Stalling Begins,"
    <u>Leatherneck,</u> August 1991

Keene, R. R., "The Hill Battles," <u>Leatherneck,</u> September
    1991

Mundy, C. E., "The Spirit Of The Corps," <u>Leatherneck,</u>
    November 1992

BIOGRAPHY

In June 1950, the North Koreans thrust over the 38th parallel into South Korea to launch the "Forgotten War." It was a call to arms for young men like Burton F. Anderson who sought the heroics of World War II soldiers in far-away places and thought that these experiences had passed them by. With fervor he joined the United States Marine Corps. Six months later, he was in Korea and a combat Marine.

The Korean War became his rite-of-passage, his metamorphosis to manhood, his maturation—an ancient story lived by so many young Marines.

As a young man in his twenties, his war experiences etched in his memory, he sought writing as a profession as well as a catharsis. Although he graduated with majors in English and Education for both Bachelor's and Master's degrees, Mr. Anderson faced reality and began his career, not as a writer, but as a teacher before spending thirty years in the aerospace industry. Now in retirement, he has returned to his quest of forty years ago.

KOREA–THE FORGOTTEN WAR

YOU'VE READ THE BOOK. . .

Now purchase a copy for your friends and relatives so they may also understand and honor those "few good men" of the "Forgotten War".

---✂--

WE CLAIM THE TITLE

Name_____

Street Address_____

City_____

State_____Zip_____

Make Checks payable to: **Tracy Publishing**
Mail to: 7960 B Soquel Dr.
Suite 118
Aptos, CA 95003

Allow 3 to 4 weeks for delivery. Offer expires 12/95.
Prices and availability subject to change.

	Quantity*	Total
US $14.95 x	_____	= $_____
$1.08 x	_____	= $_____
Sales Tax (7.25%) on orders shipped to California addresses		
$2.50 x	_____	= $_____
Shipping & Handling		
My Check total		$_____

ORDER FORM

*Quantity discount rate of $14.00 per book on orders of 5 or more.